WHY WE FIGHT

T0386790

MIKE MARTIN

Why We Fight

HURST & COMPANY, LONDON

First published in hardback in the United Kingdom in 2018 by
C. Hurst & Co. (Publishers) Ltd.,
41 Great Russell Street, London, WC1B 3PL
© Mike Martin, 2021
This updated paperback edition, 2021
All rights reserved.
Printed in the United Kingdom by Bell & Bain Ltd, Glasgow

A Cataloguing-in-Publication data record for this book
is available from the British Library.

ISBN: 9781787384897

This book is printed using paper from registered sustainable
and managed sources.

www.hurstpublishers.com

To the wars we are about to fight

CONTENTS

FOREWORD TO THE PAPERBACK EDITION
(2021)

When soldiering in Afghanistan it was clear to me, and it is even clearer now, that the reasons we ascribe to motivation in war—or politics, for that matter—are wide of the mark. Partly it is because the commentariat has never experienced war; partly it is because there are social taboos in how we describe wars; but mostly it is because of the way human cognition has evolved.

I think humans are driven to fight in wars because they have evolved to pursue status and belonging to coherent social groups. These drives or urges evolved for very good evolutionary reasons and—usually—result in massively increased survival and reproduction. However, these (mostly) unconscious mechanisms also interact with each other in ways that create interpersonal, and intergroup, conflict. Individual humans may or may not be aware of these drives but they show up clearly in psychological experimentation, and species-wide data on, say, homicides.

What fascinates me is how our conscious brains interpret those unconscious urges, primarily by thinking and talking about the social architecture that we use to build societies—namely, moral codes, religious doctrine, and ideological frameworks such as capitalism or communism. This allows us to explain away urges towards violence in ways that are socially acceptable. Even more intriguingly, it appears that we not only deceive others as to our true motives, but also ourselves.

So, we are driven to war to seek status and belonging, which we justify by articulating the frameworks that help us build groups and negotiate status: moral codes, religions and ideologies. In other words, we are driven by our subconscious emotions to do things which we later rationalise. Importantly, we are not driven by morals, religion or ideology to fight or kill.

This idea comes as no surprise to psychologists, but to 'traditional' social and political scientists who hold the rational actor model as an unstated assumption in their scholarship, it is close to heresy. To these scholars my argument is simple: that humans make social and political decisions (of which the use of violence is probably the most extreme) based on emotions and not reason, hence we need new sociological and political models that take this into account when seeking to understand the world. This has already been done in economics with the massive growth of behavioural economics—factoring in how people behave based on their biases—so why can it not play a role in the study of war and politics?

In the face of this traditional consensus, it has been heartening to hear several prominent scholars in conflict studies calling the ideas in *Why We Fight* 'ingenious', 'intriguing' and 'insightful'. Perhaps more importantly, these senior voices recognise the implications of *Why We Fight* for the discipline as 'radical', 'pivotal' and 'devastating'. As a result, the book seems to have caught the attention of many, and I have been lucky enough to present my ideas in a number of keynote speeches and annual lectures. Even better, it has inspired a number of PhDs, and the ideas form the basis for the conflict analysis training that I deliver to a couple of serious, global militaries.

More broadly, the ideas presented in this book—the oxytocin ratchet between in-groups and out-groups; the interaction between status-seeking and belonging-seeking; and the role of social ideas in helping us express our unstated emotions—give us new ways to understand social phenomena like identity politics, terrorism, authoritarianism, culture wars (particularly on social media), mass murders like school shootings, and the effects of inequality on polities. At a larger scale, it gives us new ways to understand phenomena like Russian revanchism, the rise of China, and the potential for civil war within the United States of America.

Understanding these ideas helped me greatly in catharising myself of the anger that I felt at the utter futility of fighting in Afghanistan, while at the same time being exhilarated by my brief experiences of combat. Understanding better how our brains have evolved—and how this has affected our cognition—helped me disentangle my thoughts and feelings from that turbulent period. Other veterans of that conflict have also confirmed and endorsed much of what I wrote after reading *Why We Fight*. This is the nicest thing that can happen to an author: knowing that your writing meant something to someone.

The title of *Why We Fight* stems from the genesis of the project in trying to explain violence and war. But it could have just as easily been called *Why We Don't Fight* or perhaps even *How Societies are Built*. This is not because I became confused when writing; rather, it reflects how society and war are not discrete. Society is the context for war. They are both results of the same processes. Most importantly: society and war are both reflections of our evolved cognitions.

This fundamental truth makes it hard to describe or categorise this book. Is it Popular Science? Is it War Studies?

'Big Ideas'? Politics? History? Psychology? Even Philosophy? The book has been placed in all these categories in book-shops and online, and more. But whilst it draws on all of these areas, I would rather it be seen as a way to understand and improve the world in which we live.

In seeking to understand how the brain has shaped war and society, and society and war, *Why We Fight* demon-strates three things that are critical for humans to bear in mind as we navigate the 2020s.

Firstly, living in bigger social groups is better for the aver-age individual therein (hence why humans have evolved the desire to belong to them). A group is better than no group; and a bigger group, all other things being equal, is better than a smaller group. Generally speaking, bigger groups enjoy lower levels of internal and external violence, stronger/bigger economies (lower prices), higher levels of technology, and are able to navigate the world's other groupings more successfully. We are about to see a perfect natural experiment that may demonstrate some or all of these points: the jour-ney that the United Kingdom, my own country, makes as it leaves the European Union. There are other examples that may play out too: the Catalan region, Scotland, the United States, etc.

Secondly, at every scale, it takes a huge amount of con-scious work to solve five inherent problems that groups throw up (discussed in chapter 6, these are: identity, hierar-chy, trade, disease and punishment). These problems are caused by unconscious urges, but we can consciously over-come them—much like humans have been doing since prob-ably before they learned to speak. That we live in an age in which we have never known more about how the mind works should make this easier, but this appears not to be the case. Drawing upon such knowledge should be mandatory when we devise our political systems and approaches to problems. Needless to say, all of these group problems have been on display during 2020, as governments around the world have responded, or not, to the Covid-19 pandemic.

And, finally, if you don't solve these problems, and are not able to live in bigger groups, the inevitable result will be more violence and war. Worryingly, the world in 2020 is not solving its problems: climate change, data sharing, fair corporate taxation, plastic and overfishing in the oceans, transnational migration, Covid-19, etc. These are all challenges that sit between the national and the global and require global solutions. Yet (actually: because of these global problems), we are stuck with, or even retreating to, the nation state, many of which are under pressure from separatism.

So, for the 2020s, the key question is whether we can attain the level of global governance required to solve these problems without a major intercontinental war. This seems like a bold or even brash claim. But I base it on historical analogy: humans have traditionally not been very good at moving from one level (or type) of political organisation to another without mass violence.

Examples abound: the wars of religion leading to the Westphalian principle of state sovereignty, and the two great wars of the twentieth century putting paid to monarchy and nationalism, and launching the quasi-global system of the United Nations, Bretton Woods, and GATT that is currently unravelling. We are unwilling to relinquish old paradigms of how we organise our groups without going through a war that enables us to consider new ideas without preconditions.

But what would this new set of global governing ideas look like? What are the frameworks that enable us to manage, or even reverse, the global imbalances that have built up within the system?

And how do we make these ideas and frameworks sufficiently robust—or flexible—that they are able to withstand the blistering pace of technological change which over the last thirty years has largely hollowed out the wages of the working classes in rich countries, with the inverse effect in developing countries, particularly China? Technological change in the next thirty years is likely to eviscerate the salaries of the managerial and knowledge classes all over the world. Remember, revolutions are started when the middle classes are sufficiently disenfranchised to harness the discontent of the working class. How do we cope with these rapid shifts when national, let alone supra-national, policy-making is often conducted at a glacial pace?

Surveying the landscape, I fear now, more than I did in 2016–17 when writing *Why We Fight*, that men and women will fail to come up with the ideas and frameworks required to enable us to organise globally. I also fear that there is a high degree of probability that humanity will become entangled in major wars, and fairly soon.

I wish that this were not so. But if conflict is coming, we will be better placed to resolve it if we can think clearly about where it has come from—and that includes understanding and speaking to our deepest, oldest instincts and needs.

Mike Martin   *Queensland, Australia*
January 2021

PREFACE AND ACKNOWLEDGEMENTS

I wrote *Why We Fight* because I found that my experiences as a British soldier in Afghanistan, and as a conflict scholar thereafter, were unsatisfyingly discordant. The lived experience is, by definition, an individual experience—whereas conflict scholarship, and the wider social sciences, seek to understand phenomena on larger scales. *Why We Fight* attempts to integrate these two views using the incredible advances that have been made in the cognitive sciences over the last thirty years.

This discordance between the experienced versus the studied extends to the media and to politicians when they talk about conflict and other forms of violence. Thus, terrorism is 'caused' by an ideology that radicalises young people and 'causes' them to blow themselves up. Consequently, the British government's approach to stopping people from becoming terrorists or supporting terrorism, known as *Prevent*, contends that 'confronting the extremist ideology' is the strategy's centrepiece.[1] But how can an idea *cause* someone to blow themselves up? This is puzzling from a biological and cognitive point of view, because killing yourself, especially before you have children, is the ultimate anti-evolutionary act—the ultimate reduction in fitness.

This had been the case in Afghanistan, where actual firefights were explained, and written about, in ideological terms: the battle was to 'save' a village from the Taliban's religious extremism, for example. But I knew full well that these particular clashes were about a decades-old feud that had been touched off by personal slander or disrespect—in some cases, I fought in the firefights and then later interviewed combatants on both sides.[2] It left me with a feeling that historians in half a millennium's time were not going to understand what caused the conflict in Afghanistan, or what drove people to fight in it. Are we guilty today of misreading Europe's sixteenth-century Wars of 'Religion'?

Why We Fight began to germinate shortly after the Islamic State attacked the Bataclan theatre and other targets in Paris in November 2015. In an email chain with my publisher Michael Dwyer we lamented the victims, and discussed how the French government and European politicians had responded to this terrorist atrocity and others. Themes appeared and reappeared: in-group solidarity in the face of the attacks, a desire for revenge even when it was unclear upon whom it should be visited, and a strong focus on ideology as the main explanatory factor behind such actions.[3]

Debating these themes left me unsatisfied. How could ideology *cause* violence? How could an idea *cause* someone to deprive themselves of their own life? What was the link between the two? Inevitably, the broader questions around what precipitated violence and war also surfaced: why *do* we fight? Each question I 'answered' seemed only to lead to another series of questions, all of which began with 'why'.

Eventually, passing through ideology, religion, morals, tribalism, and emotions, I ended up where it all began: with human beings. More specifically, the human brain and how it evolved. After all, 'nothing in biology makes sense except in the light of evolution';[4] and war, as a universal human activity, must have strong biological underpinnings. And if conflict can be described inconclusively in so many ways (religious war, tribal war, etc.), perhaps the universal essence of war, as advanced by Carl von Clausewitz and other prominent strategists, is shaped by one main common feature: human psychology.[5]

Writing this book has brought together several themes and phases in my life: wanting to soldier since childhood, and then soldiering; studying biology, and then scrutinising conflict at a doctoral level; and a later career working and travelling in different cultures, always exploring politics and conflict. Even the immediate context to my writing of the book—as chief operating officer of Common Purpose, a global leadership development organisation that aims to help people become leaders across, rather than of, groups—has played a role in the book's evolution.

* * *

My first thanks go to Michael Dwyer at Hurst for nurturing the ideas behind *Why We Fight*, and for taking a risk in commissioning the book before my ideas were fully formed. I would also like to thank Lara Weisweiller-Wu and Alison Alexanian, for brilliant editing and publicity, respectively, and to Daisy Leitch for pulling it all together..

Furthermore, this book could not have been written without support from King's College London and Professor Theo Farrell, a long-term mentor and former head of the world-class War Studies Department where I am a visiting fellow. Beyond this, *Why We Fight* is a timely and welcome return to biology, my first intellectual home. Thus, for my early intellectual development (and for not giving up on me when others would have), I am incredibly grateful to my tutors at the University of Oxford: Mark Fricker and Alex

PREFACE AND ACKNOWLEDGEMENTS

Kacelnik. My unceasing amazement at the elegance of science is due to you.

I wish also to thank dearly a procession of long-suffering friends and family who have offered shrewd comments on earlier drafts: Chris Ankersen, Alex Barnes, Jamie Bryan, Josh Bryan, Eddy Canfor-Dumas, Hassan Damluji, Tom Dougherty, Theo Farrell, David Fisher, Phil Hyett, James Ivory, Frank Ledwidge, Mark Linder, Peter Martin, Mike Niconchuk, Dale Pearson, and Tom Rodwell. This book would not be what it is without all of your kind, patient, yet well-honed advice. My thanks also to the anonymous peer reviewers. Naturally, any omissions are mine. Finally, the arguments in *Why We Fight* are my own personal views and do not represent any of the organisations with which I am affiliated.

INTRODUCTION

'There is no instance of a nation benefitting from prolonged warfare'

Sun Tzu[1]

Humans fight to achieve status and belonging. They do so because, in evolutionary terms, these are the surest routes to survival and increased reproduction. Status—which denotes our hierarchical position compared to others—helps humans to find sexual partners of a higher quality, to attain resources, and to control others. And so we fight over it. As for belonging, in order to protect ourselves against violence inflicted by others, humans build bigger and bigger social groups, which, on the whole, are more secure and less prone to internal aggression.[2] The evolutionary benefits of group living are such that we all seek to belong to these in-groups. Lastly, men and women improve social cohesion and solve the problems thrown up by group living by using moral codes, religions and ideologies.

Both of these motivating desires—towards status and belonging—are subconscious, heuristic drives. Heuristics are rough rules of thumb that, more often than not, give the right evolutionary answer.[3] Thus, on average, humans with a higher status, and who belong to a solid in-group, will have more surviving children and grandchildren. Biologists call this increased 'fitness'. Averages, of course, hide the fact that on many occasions, for individual human beings, the pursuit of status and belonging reduces fitness. It might not work out for you, but it will work out for most that try it—hence these drives, and the genes that underpin them, remain in the gene pool. Finally, there is an interaction between the behaviours of leaders and followers that enables them to help fulfil each other's drives for status and belonging respectively.

The conscious brain has enabled us to take our subconscious drives (towards status, belonging, and other goals) and channel them into some of mankind's highest achievements—think of the complexity of science, the art in a fine gallery, or of the size of the societies that we have managed to build using moral codes, religions and ideologies like liberal democracy, or communism. Such frameworks enable ever larger groups of people to work together in (mostly) non-violence by determining how they define who is in the group, or who leads the group and makes decisions, among other questions. We have used our conscious brains to create a more evolutionarily favourable environment for ourselves: belonging to a group of people is an evolutionary prize *par excellence*.[4]

This brings us to the relationships between the drives—status and belonging—and the frameworks—moral codes, religions and ideologies. To understand this, we turn to one of the most profound insights in cognitive science: that the slower, conscious brain most often post facto 'rationalises' the faster decisions that the subconscious brain has already taken.[5] It does this in order to justify our subconscious desires to other people by making them more socially palatable, and in the process we usually self-justify as well. Reasoning thus confers a fitness advantage in our socially competitive milieu, by making our selfish human drives more acceptable to others.[6]

Thus, when it comes to war, humans are driven to fight because of their subconscious motivations to seek status and to belong. And the large groups that we have built using conscious frameworks endow the evolutionary prizes of status and belonging with even greater significance. When we are subconsciously driven to fight for status and belonging, we consciously interpret this, and justify it, as fighting for moral reasons, religious reasons, or ideological reasons. And because we are fighting for our own group, and our position within it, we also interpret the causes of conflict as being the very things that bind such groups together—morals, religions and ideologies.

This idea, and the wealth of supporting evidence presented in this book, lay the foundations for different approaches to conflict analysis, conflict resolution, and especially, counter-terrorism—currently a subject of much debate in European societies. Ideology, no matter how 'twisted', does not cause people to kill themselves and others. Religious differences do not cause wars. These are merely the conscious frameworks that we use to justify our intuitive desires for status and belonging, to others and to ourselves.

On terrorism, I will argue that suicide bombers are desperately seeking to belong.[7] Often to not very much: a group of five friends, enmeshed in a wider societal framework. As for civil wars, religious differences in Northern Ireland or Israel/Palestine, for instance, do correlate with different sides in the conflict—but don't cause it. In these conflicts, as has been repeatedly shown, the various protagonists respond to symbolic concessions, indicating a recalibration of status between groups, rather than a reasoned argument about whose interpretation of a religious text is more accurate.[8]

More obliquely, the desire to fight wars against other groups may be determined by the coherence of our own groups, and whether we feel that we belong to them—in other words, the chaos wrought by destruction and inequality within, rather than between, groups may actually be what leads to war. I will also argue that leaders who start wars are pursuing status, just the same as people who kill in gangs, or in bar fights—and that these different forms of violence share the same, evolutionarily-shaped drives.

This is a book about the evolution of the human mind, and about how its cognition first drives and then justifies violent human behaviour in the pursuit of evolutionary goals. It will, I hope, explain why we fight.

The study of war

Conflict has been studied for a long time. Thucydides, who began writing his *History of the Peloponnesian War* in 431 BCE, wrote that war was caused by the three motives of 'fear' (of others), 'honour' (pride in your group) and 'interest' (possible resource gain).[9] That I was able in 2011 successfully to use that very framework in a study of the war in Afghanistan[10] shows that there are some immutable principles underlying human society in general, and why we fight in particular.

In another modern example, major strands of research into the causes of civil war around the turn of the millennium sought to determine whether these conflicts were caused by greed (~resources) or grievance (~group identity).[11] The parallels with Thucydides are clear: as has been recognised by many through the ages, war has an essence that remains the same irrespective of time period or technology levels. It follows, then, that this essence stems from individual human psychology.

Yet, in the twentieth century, conflict as a phenomenon has been studied through two broad lenses:[12] anthropology, which tends to focus on non-state societies, and international relations (including myriad sub-disciplines, such as conflict studies), which examines war between nation states. Historians also study war, but tend to focus on particular conflicts, rather than analysing the broader phenomenon.

Historically, anthropology—admittedly a vast discipline of which I will only give the briefest of précis here—was mostly, or at least often, the study of people who live outside the strictures of modern nation states. In the twentieth century its practitioners spent much time arguing that different peoples and their behaviours were entirely determined by their unique cultural and social experience or learning. In this view, the mind was a blank slate at birth, a *tabula rasa*, ready for cultural imprinting.

This was a laudable reaction to the racist, eugenicist policies of many governments in the first half of the twentieth century. Extrapolating from this view, hunter-gatherers lived peaceful lives, and war only came with the advent of sedentarism and agriculture—approximately 12,000 years ago.[13] At the extreme, where warlike hunter-gathers were found, they were said to have been corrupted and to have learnt warlike behaviour through contact with European, settled societies.[14]

Within these assumptions, anthropologists debated the causes of war. War was a cultural expression; it was a ritual; an urge; even in some cases a mental illness. Rarely was the next question asked: why? Why did it exist as a ritual? Why was it an urge?[15] Later, others within the discipline—led by Marvin Harris—began to argue that people fought over the resources needed to live. In this telling, war became about meat protein, or hunting grounds.[16] Again, however, very few asked why groups would aim to maximise their access to meat protein.

Finally, in the 1970s, this 'resource competition' view was extended by scholars like Napoleon Chagnon, who began to incorporate some evolutionary theory: to them, the resources that were fought over—overwhelmingly by men— were women, for reproduction.[17] Although this was a narrow view of the resources needed to survive and reproduce (clearly men need mating partners, but also food, water and so on), it marked the point at which anthropologists began to situate their analyses within the human motivational framework provided by evolution. It gives us the beginning of a strand that leads into this book.

International relations—also a massive discipline, also with multiple sub-disciplines—seeks to understand and categorise the relations between states. It divides into two main schools: realism and idealism. On the one hand, realists argue that conflict between states is part of the state of man. Due to the anarchic nature of the international arena, states pursue self-interest in competition with each other. Different scholars argue either that states primarily pursue power because it is a universal means of achieving the other things that states need, like resources (classical realism), or that states seek security above all else (structural realism). On the other hand, idealists argue that international relations are governed by norms, and that ultimately the good intentions of other states can be relied upon. War, to idealists, is outdated—the product of misunderstandings, evil leaders or flawed political systems.[18]

Conflict, or War, Studies is another major sub-discipline within international relations, and particularly focuses on intrastate, rather than interstate, warfare. Using a combination of huge quantitative datasets, and/or interviews with commanders and combatants, scholars debate a broad range of causes of conflict, from resources[19] or religion[20] to ideology[21] or ethnic strife.[22] Others highlight poverty,[23] or perceptions of inequality.[24] More recently, so-called multivariate analyses of war argue that conflicts occur only when multiple circumstances come together. The simultaneous presence of factors such as political instability, rough terrain, and even large populations increases the chances of war.[25] Here too there are some strands that lead into this book.

As we can see, all of these disciplinary approaches share similarities. Without coming down on any particular side in each discipline's debate, power, resources, security and identity feature prominently as causes of war. This echoes my central thesis—power is analogous to status, belonging is analogous to identity, and, as I will argue later on, biologically speaking, status and belonging are resources.

However, both anthropology and international relations analyse the phenomenon of war at a group level. Tribes, or states, are treated as unitary actors, and are often bestowed with the drives of individual humans—namely, that they seek power, or mating partners, or other resources. The unspoken assumption is that the group acts as an organism and that if some people lose their lives in combat, it is for the 'good of the group'. In biology this is called a group selection argument; that is, natural selection acts on the level of the group, rather than on the level of the individual.[26]

I go into this is more detail in Chapter 5, but suffice it to say, arguments among biologists over group selection have raged for more than sixty years, and have now been settled conclusively in favour of an individual level of selection.[27]

Group selectionists have not demonstrated how a biological trait would spread through the population when it does not benefit an individual (even when it does benefit the group). War is a very clear case of this: in some wars up to 25 per cent of men are killed, many of them before they reproduce.[28] This is otherwise known as a strong negative selection pressure. And in biological terms, we have to explain why such individuals fight for their groups, in evolutionary terms that aid the individual, when it might be better for them to avoid fighting (and dying).

With a view to this, one traditional argument as to why individuals fight is that they benefit from the spoils.[29] Or, at least, that they would be willing to risk fighting in order to gain some share of the pickings. In times of scarcity, where individuals can either fight, or starve to death, this argument has merits. It is credible also where there is an extreme risk / reward trade-off, such that the possible risks are outweighed by the potential rewards. One example is where soldiers are allowed to rape—as has been common throughout history—or given land in return for service—as in the Roman Empire and elsewhere.[30] Certain men who survive war will also enjoy a fitness increase on their return due to their increased status after having fought, or due to male casualties leading to male scarcity in the reproductive pool. However, it has been shown that war does not increase the *average* reproductive issue of those who take part. This is because all those who participate, survive and increase their reproductive fitness are counterbalanced by a greater number who die or are injured (and therefore do not reproduce). On average, going to war reduces your individual reproductive fitness.[31]

In evolutionary terms, group selectionists must demonstrate that going to war increases an individual's chances of producing surviving offspring rather than staying at home, enjoying the security provided by your tribesmen/compatriots/co-religionists, and finding a mate. The problem is that the spoils of war do not always accrue to those who are fighting and dying. Often, they fight and die so that *other* people in their groups can reproduce.[32] Humans live in hierarchical groups, and those with a higher status tend to control the spoils and receive more than their fair (equal) share of them. As the scale of human organisation increases, this becomes truer and truer: big groups have well-developed hierarchies that soak up lots of resources. In an army of 100,000 men, the commander and his retinue will do very well; rank-and-file fighters very poorly.

For completeness, we should also consider examples of conscription or other means of compelling people to fight, like feudal levies or their (assumed) prehistoric forebears. Undoubtedly, in specific wars this has worked as a mechanism to raise armies.[33] However, spread over thousands of generations of evolution, it is hard to argue how it works. That is, if people were consistently forced to fight against their will, why haven't they evolved behaviours that enable them to escape the selection pressure of war? Humans have evolved all sorts of mechanisms to respond to and evade social control, and to regulate hierarchy—think of lying, or how satire exposes the weaknesses of those who wield power. A leadership with limited rather than extreme power will generally lead to a more equitable share of resources, which will increase the fitness of individuals. So, why haven't we evolved something to escape forced conscription, in order to balance the strongly negative selection pressure for those who take part?

In fact, conscription is far from ubiquitous, and there are countless instances of huge armies being raised without forcing people to fight—think of the young men rushing to enlist at the onset of the First World War. Where used, conscription is actually used to reinforce an already existing social norm which, as we will see in more detail, must rely upon some kind of biological propensity that has been shaped by evolution (social norms generally rely on biological propensities).[34] That is, the conscription actually mirrors the biological system, and reinforces the costs of not fighting for your group: ostracism and death (pre-historic ostracism meant certain death). Social norms that have outsized effects on survival and reproduction are not cultural 'imprints'— this is effectively the *tabula rasa* view of the human mind that I will argue strongly against in Chapter 1.

There is one final possible explanation, furnished by biology. Perhaps war is a genetic relic from the human prehistoric past. In this line of argument, we are driven to do something today that made evolutionary sense in prehistory. Another such relic is the fact that humans love sugar and fatty foods, even though they are bad for us in large quantities, because in the prehistoric environment sugars and fats represented highly calorific, and relatively rare, resources.[35] There are plenty of these relics in our body plans as well—our present-day tailbone is not nearly as useful, with our current bipedal gait, as when we lived in trees, using all four limbs.

But sugar and tailbones are not like war. Although they are undoubtedly harmful, backache, diabetes and obesity tend not to kill us before we have children, whereas war often does, in large numbers. This is the harsh logic of evolution. It is not clear why evolution has not removed warlike traits—particularly an excitement about, and an instinctive motivation towards, fighting—from the gene pool. Evolutionary logic says that motivational systems creating positive emotions around particular behaviours or experiences can only have developed because our ancestors who were driven to do those things had more surviving children than those who did not.[36] The positive emotions associated with war suggest that, despite loss of life, it must have paid off evolutionarily in the past (and probably continues to do so). Had the increased reproductive benefits attached to going to war diminished to below the existing loss of reproduction from its roughly 25 per cent death rate,[37] then warring would have been selected out of the population as a behaviour. It is not enough to say that people fight in wars because they are exciting. War is exciting because our ancestors received an evolutionary benefit from it, and hence we are motivated to prosecute it.

My own journey to war was one of strongly wanting to fight, and when I saw action my experiences of combat were such that it was the most exhilarating thing that I have ever done in my life. In talking to soldiers and veterans, this is the most common response to the act of going to war, or putting yourself in harm's way for your group. This book will explain why we have evolved to fight in wars.

Caveats

Why We Fight draws upon scientific enquiry that aims to amass evidence in order to support various theories, some of which have more evidence supporting them than others. For example, whilst it is possible that we may discover evidence that contradicts the theory of evolution by natural selection—for example, a complex organism is discovered that has not come about via that process—the chances are so imperceptibly small that I would bet all of my worldly possessions on natural selection being correct.

However, not everything in this book is as well supported as the theory of evolution. It is possible—in fact, in the fast-moving cognitive sciences, very likely—that new scientific evidence will emerge that overturns the assertions presented in this book. This is the nature of science. And all scientists accept—or even delight in the fact—that their research and understanding may one day be superseded by different interpretations supported by newer evidence. So, while some of the arguments in this book will still be current many years hence, some may not last the decade. Some may not even make the printing deadline. I welcome this. *Why We Fight* exemplifies only our current understanding of the cognitive basis for conflict.

In Chapter 1, for instance, the multi-modular structure of the brain that I describe is well established. On the other hand, some of the ideas about how consciousness works are newer and are the subject of vigorous current debate. Somewhere in the middle, the arguments around group selection have raged through biology for decades, and there is a significant minority of scientists, including some well-respected ones,[38] who support group selection (or some of its newer variants like multilevel selection).[39] But, on balance, group selection arguments are not well supported, except in highly specialised cases (see Chapter 1).[40]

For readability, I have at times simplified the science (or not mentioned all the specific caveats), whilst remaining true to the essence of the findings I present. However, I am confident that the main argument of the book—that we are driven to fight because of the subconscious desires towards status and belonging, and that these are post-facto rationalised through conscious frameworks—is well supported by the evidence. Similarly, I argue that status and belonging are the two main drivers of human conflict; this does not mean that other cognitive drivers—like fear—have no role to play, but that they are subordinated to the main evolutionary drives of status and belonging. Furthermore, fear is the preserve of those who are forced to fight, while—as established above—this book is concerned primarily with those who want to fight.

I would also like to venture briefly into evolutionary psychology, a field of biology upon which this book draws extensively and which seeks to explain psychological traits (like a desire to go to war) using the past selective environment of humans (including in pre-*Homo* eras). That is, it contends that our current psychology has evolved as a result of adaptations to recurrent problems in our ancestral environments. One of the standard assumptions of evolutionary psychology is that the environment that most shaped modern humans—known as the Environment of Evolutionary Adaptedness—was the Pleistocene, approximately 2 million to 12,000 years ago.[41]

Whilst this assumption still largely holds, there is also evidence that humans have continued to evolve the genetic basis for their psychology after that era (we will discuss this further in Chapter 6).[42] Examples of traits that have further evolved in just a few thousand years include cow's milk (lactose) tolerance and intelligence.[43] There is also evidence that one of the areas in which we have evolved the most in the last 12,000 years is the degree to which we are sociable—as a direct result of the larger and more complex societies that we now live in, necessitating ever greater degrees of cooperation.[44]

The brain is a highly complex system, with multiple factors all interacting with each other to deliver outcomes.[45] These include the genetic basis, the childhood environment, learning, the current environment, and so on. I would like to stress that *Why We Fight* categorically does not argue for biological determinism. The expression of all traits—from backbones to courting—are a complex blend of the abovementioned factors. In many cases, we have a good idea of the (genetic) heritability factor—the degree to which either genetics or the environment contribute to the variation in a particular trait.[46] In others, we do not—it is exceedingly complex.

It is important to remember that, while evolution—in combination with the environment—has shaped a current individual's body plan and cognitive systems, an individual, once born, will also learn and, later, respond to stimuli. Because of these layers of influence, it is impossible to determine the degree to which evolution has shaped an individual's response to a particular stimulus in a particular moment. However, the degree of influence is much more obvious when studying not a specific individual, but an average individual within a population. This is reflected in the subject of this book—why humanity fights, rather than why a specific human fights.

Because of this average-centred perspective, *Why We Fight* is an exploration primarily concerned with those who fight most, on average: men more than women, and young men more than old men. However, for the same reason, it is relevant to everybody. The species-wide averages charted in this book have profoundly shaped our societies and their activities. This is clear, for instance, when looking at the sexuality spectrum. Though the male status-seeking I argue to be a driver of war originally evolved to maximise individuals' reproduction, all modern-day men have inherited the same averaged predispositions to seek status, regardless of whether their sexuality enables them to have biological offspring with their chosen partner.

Furthermore, in seeking to understand why we fight, I am not seeking to dismiss anthropology or international relations, both of which have generated huge amounts of revealing data about conflict. But I am seeking to move the focus of the analysis to the individual. As a human behaviour, war is illuminated by looking at it through evolutionary theory, and particularly the cognitive sciences. Later on in the book, when I analyse group-level dynamics, I do so abstracting from the individual level. My assumption here is that group-level dynamics are complex interlinked collections of individuals' motivations.

Finally, *Why We Fight* may come across as slightly abstract. This is because evolution works in terms of averages across the entire population and across time: what evolves is the result of genes that increase the reproductive fitness of individuals when summed over thousands of generations. Hence, this book deals with the largest of scales: millions of years, and billions of people. This, in turn, means that one can readily cite particular historical examples, or contemporaneous sociological trends, that contradict my broader argument. I anticipate this, and indeed I have no wish to diminish the importance of history or sociology in understanding human affairs. But I am trying to answer a separate set of questions: about why the individual brain has evolved the way it has, and how, on average, that has created a set of characteristic human behaviours that result in violence and war.

Definitions

There are many definitions available to the scholar wishing to understand violence, war and conflict. Is an argument conflict? Is a fist fight violence? When does the term 'war'

15

come into play—at what scale? Is it determined by the number of participants or of casualties, or by something else?

In *Why We Fight*, I define these terms as simply as possible. Thus, violence is defined as fighting by individuals that results in death—a homicide, in other words (I will usually preface the term 'violence' with the word 'individual' or 'intragroup'). Conflict or war—I use the terms interchangeably—is simply intergroup conflict: this can be at street gang level, or involve multi-national coalitions. It is collective violence, against other collectives.[47] Importantly, this includes terrorism, because, as we shall see, even individual perpetrators of terrorism (so-called 'lone wolves') operate from within small groups. They are individual representatives of groups at war with other groups.

In my discussion of conscious ideological frameworks, particularly in Chapters 7 and 10, 'god' remains uncapitalised where it refers to the general concept of a deity. This is because even seemingly non-specific phrases such as 'a God' tend to suggest or favour the conception of a monotheistic, Abrahamic deity. *Why We Fight* is concerned with the universal human phenomenon of belief in the supernatural.

Finally, because a death is an easily determined binary data point, violence and fighting that do not result in deaths are absent from my analyses.[48]

* * *

Why We Fight will begin by describing how the human mind has evolved. It will explain how our ancestral environment has shaped current motivations and behaviours. Chapter 1 will argue that the mind is not a blank slate ready to be imprinted upon by culture and environment at birth, but that it has evolved the way it has in order to maximise the survival and reproduction of individual humans. This means that there is a difference between the brains of individual humans that is, at least in part, down to their differing genetics—as with other human traits, like height.

The next chapter will look at the evolution of the brain mechanisms that motivate subconscious desires and emotions, starting with a look at how the social emotions—like anger and jealousy—actually regulate violence. Then, Chapter 4 will explore the desire for status. The story of how status-seeking leads to violence begins well before the human lineage—in the primordial environment of single-cellular organisms—and finishes with multinational coalitions fighting it out. Looking into the human brain, we will understand how it, and the hormone testosterone, motivate us to try and climb the hierarchy, and how this can result in violence.

Chapter 5 shows how humans and their ancestors sought to escape the violence wrought by status-seeking individuals through building social groups. The advantages of group living selected those humans who had evolved a 'groupishness' instinct—a desire and a motivation to belong—regulated by the oxytocin hormone. Exploring the neurological basis of oxytocin, and how it evolved, paints a timeless picture of human in-group/out-group dynamics that every reader will recognise. This chapter will show why people fight to retain membership of their groups.

Chapter 6 picks up the theme of human groups. Group living brings a number of advantages—not least in reducing human violence—but these advantages can only be realised if five basic problems are solved to the satisfaction of most of a group's members. The five problems are: identity (who is in and who is out), hierarchy (who is in charge), trade (what are the terms of exchange or sharing), disease (how to control it when so many genetically similar individuals live in close contact), and group-mandated punishment (who is it acceptable to punish, for what, and how hard). These problems are the sources of individual human violence in groups.

Chapters 8, 9, 10 and 11 will then describe how humans have consciously built frameworks—moral codes, religions and shared ideologies—to solve these group problems at progressively larger scales. Firstly, in Chapter 8, we will look at the evolution of consciousness and reasoning, and how these brain attributes interact with other aspects of our brains and our behaviour that we are less aware of consciously. This chapter will also show that our brains consciously reason in order to explain our subconscious to others in our social groups, rather than to produce logical outcomes.

The next three chapters—9, 10 and 11—will look at how our brains have evolved morality, a belief in the supernatural, and the ability to structure our social groups using shared ideologies. In each, we will explore the set of underlying mechanisms (many of which overlap across the chapters), and in so doing will demonstrate that these frameworks cannot 'cause' conflict. Rather, they are the product of millions of human brains, consciously reasoning over thousands of generations, attempting to explain the underlying motivations to seek status and belonging among their peers.

The conclusions of *Why We Fight* outline further research that would extend and enhance (or replace) the arguments in this book. I conclude by arguing for a reassessment of how we approach conflict scholarship, resolution, and activities like counter-terrorism. Cognitive science has opened up an entire new world of knowledge over the last thirty years—it would be remiss of us not to apply it to some of the most pressing behavioural problems that confront us.

1

EVOLUTION AND THE HUMAN MIND

'Nothing in Biology Makes Sense Except in the Light of Evolution'

Theodosius Dobzhansky[1]

There are two central ideas to this chapter: firstly, that natural selection (and hence evolution) occurs at the level of the individual rather than at the level of the group; and secondly, that evolution has shaped our brains so that on average certain behaviours and ways of processing information predominate (and our brains are not blank slates 'filled up' with culture and learning). If readers are already comfortable with these two ideas, they may wish to pass to the next chapter, which looks at how our brains motivate our subconscious drives; otherwise, you may wish to read on, as this chapter provides an essential foundation to the ideas that follow in the rest of the book, beginning with a very brief précis of the evolution process itself.

The process of evolution by natural selection has created and shaped all human adaptations—there is no aspect of individual human biology that has not been shaped by evolution, including our behaviour.[2] The central actor in evolution is the gene. Genes code for the proteins that make up an organism. The genes of an organism, and there are about

20,000 genes in the human genome, are like the organism's blueprint. Each cell in the organism carries this blueprint, and so when cells divide and replicate, the genetic material also replicates. This is also true of the sex cells—eggs and sperm—that combine to form offspring. But this replication of genetic material is not a perfect process. Every time the genetic material copies itself to make another cell, there is a minuscule chance of a random error.

It is this random error—known as mutation—that is key to the whole of evolution. This is because randomly mutated genetic material produces randomly different forms of the proteins for which it codes. Slightly different forms of the proteins mean that the organisms will differ slightly. And these slight differences—known as variation—fare either slightly better or slightly worse in the environment. In evolutionary terms, faring slightly better or worse means having more or fewer children who survive and reproduce.

Those organisms that produce more offspring are able to get more copies of their genes into the next generation; those organisms that die before they have offspring get no copies of their genes into the next generation. This means that the well-adapted human body, as judged by the huge number of individual humans on the planet, is made up of a vast number of adaptations that have helped our ancestors survive and reproduce. This chain of ancestors goes all the way back to pre-cellular life forms over 4 billion years ago. This explains how stunningly complex traits—like, for example, dolphins' sonar communication system—can arise out of a series of random mutations: evolution by natural selection occurs over vast timescales in tiny increments.[3]

How do these tiny increments work? Well, there are two main types of selection: positive and negative. A trait is positively selected when it confers a survival and reproduction benefit on its host, such that over generations this trait, and its underlying genes, will spread throughout the population. Sometimes the selective environment will change (as with an Ice Age) and this makes a previously beneficial trait (such as an adaption for hot climate) no longer beneficial. If this reduces the survival and reproduction rates of the host, then the trait will be under negative selection, and there will be fewer examples of it in the descendent generations.

If a trait is negative, but not so negative as to affect the rates of survival and reproduction, then it may hang around in the body plans of an organism. A good example of this is the already-mentioned pleasure hormones that are released when we eat sugar: in a resource-scarce environment, this motivated us to eat as much sweet food as possible. In the modern day, in an age of plenty, it is not so useful and leads to diseases like diabetes. But the desire for sweetness is not so negative that it drastically affects our survival and reproduction, and things that are slightly negative often do not get selected out.[4]

Sometimes, different variants of a trait persist concurrently in the population over evolutionary time, as with the ratio between left-handers and right-handers. Left-handers have remained as 10–13 per cent of the population since the Stone Age, possibly because of the advantages in fighting other (right-handed) humans as a left-hander—the angles and approach strategies are different. These advantages disappear when there is too high a percentage of left-handers.[5]

There is also a distinction between the social and physical environments and the different types of selection pressures that they represent; this is because the physical environment changes a lot less over evolutionary time than the social. For example, the qualities of gravity feel no different to you and me than they did to the first land-dwelling vertebrates. This stability means that there are certain properties of tetrapod bone structure, including in we four-limbed humans, that are set and have not changed. Tetrapods have a good solution to the problem of bearing weight under gravity, and any mutations are likely to result in a lower survival and reproductive outcome (a lower fitness).[6]

The social environment—made up primarily of other humans, but also more broadly other animals—is a completely different matter. In this environment, humans have to react to situations as they occur. Here, doing the same thing every time a situation occurs—say, always dodging left when being charged by bull, or always sharing your meat when asked to—would be a distinct disadvantage, because the other animals or humans would evolve a response to outwit you. It is much better if behavioural responses are flexible. As we will see more clearly later on, many human brain adaptations have evolved in response to aspects of the social environment, including cheating, deception, and cooperation.[7]

There remains a key question within this very elegant process: to what degree do our genes determine the variation of a trait? This is the age-old 'nature versus nurture' debate. Take height as an example: there are several genes that contribute to this trait in humans. But the degree to which they are able to determine the height of an individual depends on factors in the environment, not least humans' diet during the critical phase when they are growing to adult height: South Koreans are 3–8 centimetres taller than their North Korean neighbours, despite sharing almost completely homogenous genetic codes.[8]

Technically, genes are expressed in their own genetic and environmental context. This means that the same piece of genetic code may produce wildly different outcomes, depending upon the other genes contained within the organism, and the vagaries of the environment. A major part of the human selective environment is the social environment in which we live, and so the same version of an imaginary gene that contributes to, for example, timidity, may express itself in completely different ways depending on the genes with which it shares its host organism, and the behaviours of other humans in the environment. We cannot say what a gene 'does', only what it does in a particular environment.[9]

It is these multiple influences on expression that make it fiendishly difficult to pick apart the different influences on any particular behaviour (or indeed any trait). Gene expression is a highly complex area of biological science, because it explores the interactions between the gene and the environment. For example, some traits are expressed directly by genes—whether or not you have cystic fibrosis—while some are entirely environmental—whether you feel disgusted at eating horse meat as opposed to cow meat—and most are somewhere in between.[10] That said, different brain regions develop at different stages—for instance, the parts of the brain that reason, or assess and analyse social norms, develop late into adolescence. The later a brain region develops in an individual human, the more its development will be shaped by the (social) environment rather than by genes.[11] And luckily, in this book, we are looking at broad averages of behaviour (why humans fight, rather than why you specifically fight), so the environmental effects on variation are somewhat masked.

Finally, what is evolution not? Despite its obvious power as a narrative framework for how and why life exists in the way it does, there are several limits to this explanatory value.

Nowhere is this more evident than when it comes to human behaviour. It is very important to stress that evolution is not deterministic. By this I mean that one cannot say, 'Humans have evolved to fall in love, therefore we all fall in love'. Humans *have* evolved to fall in love, but clearly not all humans do fall in love. The theory of evolution does not claim that having evolved in a certain manner leaves us biologically trapped into behaving in that way and no other.[12]

This is because evolution has prepared our bodies as a statistical bet on the future, based on the lives and deaths of our ancestors. For example, on average, over evolutionary timescales, it has been more advantageous than not to have a fear response. This does not mean that a fear response is always the right thing to do: imagine if it causes you to run away fast and you end up tripping up and falling over a cliff-edge. Clearly in this instance you have been killed by your fear response, but that does not negate the fact that in most cases it may help to save you.

Thus, the further into this book one goes, the easier it becomes to cite counter-examples to the general trends that I present, but to repeat: genes are selected that—on average, over evolutionary time, with all the multiplicity of different environmental and genetic interactions possible—deliver an *average* increased reproductive payoff. This is why individual humans do things that are contrary to their survival and reproductive maximisation, yet on average the individuals in the species are incredibly successful at surviving and reproducing.[13]

Group selection

Group selection is a proposed mechanism of evolution whereby natural selection occurs at the level of the group, rather than at the level of the individual (or, more technically, the gene).[14] Group selection states that groups compete in evolutionary terms, adapting to the environment as units. Traditional studies of war in the social sciences—for example, in anthropology and in international relations—have held this argument as an unstated assumption: these disciplines see war as a competition occurring between two groups. The 'best' one wins, and proliferates. In this view, the planet today is full of the descendants of groups that won wars in the past. And this is precisely why it is such an alluring perspective for scholars attempting to understand war from an evolutionary point of view.[15]

Group selection can be more formally defined as the differential extinction or proliferation of groups. Thus, groups compete in the environment and against each other, and those groups with better-adapted characteristics—say, a better mechanism for coordinating, or a more efficient way of making war—will survive to become bigger and more successful groups. Group selection leads to the evolution of group cooperative or altruistic traits—like religion, morality and tribalism—that benefit the group, often or sometimes at the expense of the individual.[16] But today's groups are not necessarily full of descendants of those individuals who fought the wars that were won, because of the very high death rate of combatants in conflict. Hence—at least in part—the puzzle whereby soldiers risk their own reproductive success for that of others in their group.

The original evidence for group selection came in the 1960s from social insects like ants. However, ants have a specific reproductive system—called haplodiploid—which means that relatives share a higher proportion of genes than in other species, encouraging them to sacrifice themselves for the relatives (as this won't prevent their genes from making it to the next generation).[17] As for the evolution of reciprocal altruism—namely, organisms doing good for others in the group in the expectation (or experience) that others will do the same for them[18]—it is unclear how this would work in non-haplodiploid species. Evolution occurs when initially randomly occurring variations in individuals prove beneficial and are selected for,[19] but, by definition, altruism (on average) reduces the fitness of altruistic individuals (who deprive themselves of food, for instance). It is the non-altruistic group members who survive and reproduce more. So how do altruistic traits spread?

More technically, group selection fails to satisfy the criteria upon which natural selection is based.[20] Firstly, natural selection relies on units that replicate, or make copies of themselves. Groups do not do this—they grow and splinter and merge, but they do not create copies of themselves (for example, the USA is a very successful country—it is large and rich—but there are not many mini-USAs). Linked to this are the group selection criteria of selective success. Success in natural selection is judged on the number of copies of the replicating unit. Humans are successful because there are lots of them; bacteria and viruses, even more so. But this is not how a group's success is measured. Those groups deemed more successful ('better-adapted') are bigger, or stronger, or have greater longevity—the success applies to the entity itself.

Secondly, natural selection relies on random copying errors (random DNA mutations) in the replicating units. Even assuming that groups could replicate, and that size was analogous to selective success, the changes that happen in groups—for example, adopting or adapting this or that religion—are anything but random: human leaders arrive at conscious choices about how best to change their societies in order to increase their success vis-à-vis other societies. For these and other reasons, a 2011 letter to the highly prestigious scientific journal *Nature* clearly refuted the latest version of group selection theory. Its 137 signatories, prominent evolutionary biologists, argued that it was 'based upon a misunderstanding of evolutionary theory and a misrepresentation of the empirical literature'.[21]

All of this is not to say that groups don't compete—they clearly do. But it does tell us that groups don't compete through natural selection. It also tells us that pro-social behaviours, like sacrificing yourself in a war so that settlers from your group can come and populate the territory that your army has invaded, appear at first glance to make no sense in evolutionary terms. Group selection arguments still have to explain the evolutionary pay-off for the individual combatant (how it results in an on-average increase in individual reproductive success), in the face of the great risk of negative selection that being a combatant entails. Moreover, under group selection logic, for the entire group to become warlike, these traits would have to spread through the entire population in a process of normal 'individual' evolution— therefore demonstrating the reproductive advantages of combat, over and above the losses experienced, against the survival and reproductive advantages of staying at home.

Finally, I would like to touch upon gene-culture coevolution (also known as Cultural Group Selection and Dual Inheritance Theory).[22] This idea treats culture as another evolutionary system that acts in parallel with genetic evolution. Of course, elements of culture 'evolve' much faster than genes, meaning that a group of humans can adapt to local conditions, and this will affect that group's survival and reproduction.[23] So, in this line of thinking, one could argue that monotheism spread at the expense of polytheism in the Roman Empire and the Arabian Peninsula because monotheistic groups were more successful (grew bigger, were more cohesive, lasted longer) than polytheistic ones.[24]

But the same arguments still stand in refutation:[25] these are ideas that are consciously designed and do not replicate with random mutations; groups that are more successful are not more numerous—they are bigger, or longer-lasting; and these cultural norms, like sacrificing yourself in war for your group, run up against individual survival and reproduction. The group selection theory, therefore, fails to explain how, on average over evolutionary time, an individual is more likely to survive and have more offspring, even though they are taking a grave individual risk in going to war.

That said, elements of human culture—for example, the domestication of fire—have changed the selection environment for humans and led to genetic evolutionary change; in this example, to the structure of the human gut.[26] In Chapter 6, we will investigate how the development of human groups has progressively created a selection pressure for humans to evolve to become more pro-social.

Evolution of the human brain

The human brain has evolved to solve problems both persistent (like gravity) and variable (like human politics) in the environment.[27] Our cognition—the total sum of conscious and unconscious processes that occur in our brains—is the product of millions of years of our human and non-human ancestors being selected for a slightly better adapted ability to respond appropriately to their environments. They understood intuitively, for instance, that rocks fall when released; they fell in love, ran away from snakes, or formed coalitions with other individuals.

Brains are collections of neurones (nerves). In very basic animals, like jellyfish, neurones join into several 'ganglia' (which look like balls of tangled string), and these control the simple functions of the body: for example, muscle contractions to expel waste products.[28] More complicated animals—like reptiles—have single brains that are able to control more complicated bodily systems. These brains have simple response systems that receive stimuli and give a stereotyped response. A great example, as it is one that humans still use, is the fear response to predation: this evolved over hundreds of millions of years ago in the reptilian lineage.[29]

As animals have evolved increasing complexity, these structures have been modified by selection, and newer structures have evolved that solve more complicated evolutionary problems. They do this by generating more complicated motivational and emotional systems that motivate particular behaviours. So, for instance, the emotion of love 'feels' good, because our brain has structures in it that reward long-term pair bonds in humans: this is because, on average over evolutionary time, long-term pair bonds have meant the survival of more offspring. That is, on average a human child has a higher chance of surviving and reproducing itself if both parents are present and cooperate over its infancy and development.[30]

Overall, different parts of our brains have evolved to solve different evolutionary problems: a good analogy is that the brain is like a Swiss Army Knife.[31] This model of the brain is known as the multi-modular structure.[32] Each module is a neurological structure, or collection of structures, that deals with specific evolutionary challenges, like finding a mate, recognising faces, or acting appropriately when faced with wild animals.[33] Some modules—like the fear response—are localised to specific parts of the brain, but in most cases behavioural responses are governed by spatially distributed neural networks; they are spread throughout the brain.[34] So, rather than referring to a specific cerebral area, a brain module is a concept of a structure that solves a specific evolutionary problem; it is a useful shorthand, as it enables us to talk about how and why the brain has evolved.[35] Modules evolve and adapt to the environment in the same way as, for example, a knee joint does. And, like physical structures, modules come about because genes interact with one another, in a manner dependent on the environment, and code for proteins.

This idea of the brain draws on exactly the same thinking as in the evolution of the rest of our bodies. It stands in opposition to the brain posited as a general computational device, a blank slate at birth that is then 'filled up' with cultural norms from our environments. Such an understanding of personal development goes back to Aristotle, was strongly advanced by Locke and Rousseau in the seventeenth and eighteenth centuries, and is well ensconced in modern Western liberal culture,[36] but the problem is that it ignores how our brains have evolved and how they respond to the environment. Rather, the strong scholarly consensus is currently that the brain has an evolved modular structure.[37] This topic could (and does) fill several volumes, and what follows is a simple outline that will be sufficient for our purposes.

Until recently, it was thought that brain modules only tended to operate in the lower or automatic functions of the brain; for example, recognising suitable mates—we just 'know' whether someone is attractive or not.[38] The subjective, positive feeling of being attracted to them is how you experience your brain motivating and preparing your body to mate with them. Here, your brain modules are enabling you to respond economically (in terms of time and energy spent) to a high-frequency problem that has an obvious impact on survival and reproduction.[39] To do this, modules have proprietary access to certain physiological systems. Thus, in the case of finding a mate, your brain module automatically processes sights and smells, and in response increases your heart rate, improves your muscle tone, dilates your pupils and causes you to blush.

The human brain has all these different structures of cognition from sequential evolutionary ages, and all the different parts of the brain are to a huge extent interlinked, greatly influencing each other.[40] Thus, the self-aware, higher-order brain functions can control these lower-order impulses to a degree, provided we recognise that we are, for example, fearful.[41]

Everyone has experienced feeling scared when walking into a dark house at night. We have also experienced that feeling disappearing or abating once the conscious brain has processed that there are no physical threats nearby. Conversely, the lower-order, non-conscious parts of the brain can influence our conscious thoughts: if you meet someone for the first time with a cold drink in your hand, you are more likely to come away thinking that they are a cold person.[42] This is a clear example of the significant interlinking between different bits of the brain (a reaction to a tactile experience triggering a related emotional response).

It is important to note that the human brain is not perfect for every situation. Brain modules work on average rules of thumb, hence they sometimes 'misfire' and act on the wrong stimuli. In other words, in order for modules to evolve and be selected, they only have to give the appropriate response on average, when summed across evolutionary time.[43] This is particularly true with modules that have evolved to deal with evolutionary problems presented by other humans: these more complex problems require broad responses.

So, for example, let us say that a brain module evolves that enables humans to spot infidelity in their long-term sexual partners. This enables them to spot infidelity 90 per cent of the time, which enables them to ensure that their own off-spring are being resourced maximally by the couple (and hence will survive to reproduce themselves). However, 10 per cent of the time, this module misfires and over-inter-prets the situation. On these occasions, the resulting violence might precipitate the rupture of the couple, and the loss of the offspring. Although this is a simplified example, it demonstrates on average how this brain module offers a fitness advantage. It also explains why evolved brain modules can motivate individual humans to carry out actions that are a detriment to their own fitness, despite increased fitness being the purpose of evolution: if having the module and behaving in this way generates a fitness advantage for the majority, it will not be selected out. Brains, and evolution more generally, operate on such statistical rules of thumb.[44]

These simple rules of thumb are used to cut through the mass of data in front of us, and to simplify our decision-making.[45] They are simple categories that mask great detail, and they operate subconsciously: the conscious brain is slower and more energy-intensive. In other words, our brains have evolved this way because otherwise we would be para-lysed with indecision. For instance, humans have a series of rules about how to treat family members—in the main, for example, we do not use lethal violence against them. This is because they are likely to share our genes, and because they represent our closest support circle. Our ancestors who followed this rule managed to get more copies of their genes into the next generations. In another example, we tend to echo the thoughts and opinions of those around us, displaying groupthink, because those ancestors that did this were less likely to be ostracised from their social groups (and hence were more likely to survive).[46]

From an evolutionary point of view, this all makes perfect sense. If modules were so tightly defined that they only acted upon very precise stimuli, any slight change in those stimuli—for instance, an adaptation in another species—would render the module non-functional, with potentially catastrophic effects on reproduction and survival. By contrast, modules that act on a broader range of similar stimuli are better able to offer the appropriate response on average, even though sometimes it would be an overreaction.[47]

Thus, in most circumstances, it is better to suffer from some false positives when modules fire, than even one false negative. Consider not having a fear response when one is needed: this is why your heart beats slightly faster when you enter a dark room, even though you are very sure that there are no snakes or attackers in there. This overreaction is also why pornography stimulates people when there is no actual opportunity to mate.[48] These overreactions are particularly prevalent in the social environment, where the modules governing an individual's responses need to be broad and flexible enough to respond to another individual's actions (which are themselves broad and flexible).

The brain, however, has an extra level of complexity built into it. Once the brain is created through gene expression, the individual neurones interconnect in a stupendously large number of ways, dependent on how the environment stimulates them. That is, depending on the stimuli in your environment, the brain makes new connections, reinforces repetitively used pathways, and degrades others that are less useful—in other words, it learns.[49]

But because the modules underlying this activity are neurological structures that have evolved to solve particular evolutionary problems, we find that very common evolutionary challenges—finding a mate, escaping predation, learning to communicate—are all genetically predisposed to a relatively high degree, and have the same basic properties irrespective of how individual cultures or human beings display loving, fighting, or speaking.[50] This is not to say, for example, that languages are not vastly different from one another. But all human languages have the same basic grammatical properties that reflect underlying neural structures.[51] Similarly, whilst the expression of romantic love varies across cultures, the experience of 'love' (butterflies in your stomach, deep attachment, thinking about someone all the time, and so on) is present in all humans. There are a large number of these human behaviour attributes that are universal across individuals and cultures—all of which stem from brain modules that have evolved to solve problems common to the entire species.[52]

In summary, the brain has a basic modular structure that is laid down by genetic code. These modules evolved to address particular problems in the environment. In addition to this, from birth (or even before) the neurones in the brain make interconnections based upon the stimuli that the brain receives (that is, based upon the environment), which enables the brain to learn. This, and the impact of the conscious and reasoning brain (which we will discuss in Chapter 8), is what leads to the complexity of human behaviour.

Information processing

Finally, human brains process information through what are called cognitive domains.[53] Whereas modules solve specific computational problems—like recognising putrid meat—domains enable us to process information on particular unchanging realms of our environment. They act on areas of understanding, which means that every human on the planet understands certain things in the same way—like categories of knowledge. In other words, our brains have evolved certain standard ways of processing certain types of information. The most researched and best understood cognitive domains are folk-biology, folk-psychology and folk-physics; there are other proposed candidates like numbers (maths) and music.[54] Thanks to these, all cultures create very similar taxonomies of plants and animals;[55] all individuals understand that dropped objects will move downwards until they hit something; and we all have an intuitive grasp of how, more or less, other human beings will act in certain situations.[56]

Such enhanced understanding of the unchanging environment conferred an evolutionary advantage. For example, your life may be saved by knowing that water flows downhill; by remembering a specific plant species is 'nutritious', 'medicinal' or 'poisonous'; or by recognising certain behaviours in non-family members as a possible sign of imminent attack. These intuitions and natural categories of knowledge are successful because they have closely evolved to reflect phenomena in the environment.[57] These are beneficial not only for individuals but also for cooperation; the large body of intuitive (folk, or naïve) knowledge possessed by all humans creates stability in our thoughts and belief systems, allowing cultures to develop (see Chapters 9–11).[58]

That said, there is variability in the ways that individual brains interpret other forms of data, particularly social information. This is because, unlike the physical properties of the environment (like gravity), the social environment—how to deal with deception, for instance—is highly dynamic.[59] The key question is how much, if any, of this variability in brain output (that is, variations in behaviour) can be put down to genetics, and how much to the environment shaping the brain through learning. For instance, for each trait (such as height), there will be genetic variation in its expression (tall or short) among individuals of a population. The relative importance of the genetic factor in this variation is known as heritability. This applies not only to 'physical' traits like height: if we follow the argument that the human brain has evolved by natural selection, then there must be variation in its properties that are partly down to its genetic pre-determinants—variation being necessary for evolution.

In biology, the standard way to determine the relative contributions of environment and genes to a trait is a 'twin study'. Although there are several, the main kind of twin study makes a comparison between identical (same genome) and non-identical twins (with a 50 per cent similar genome on average).[60] Twin studies, when conducted across thousands of twins, are one of the great natural experiments. Technically, the results tell us the level of heritability: how much of the variation in a trait's expression between individuals is down to genetics and how much is down to the environment.[61]

Twin studies looking at the differences in what people think—that is, 'ideological' differences—paint a fascinating picture. For example, intelligence (IQ) is around 50% heritable (depending on age).[62] These findings extend to other ideological 'leanings': the degree of your religiosity (as opposed to your choice of specific religion) is about 30% heritable.[63] A person's political views as judged on an equality-inequality spectrum,[64] and the degree to which they turn out to vote,[65] have heritability factors of 28% and 53% respectively. There is even heritability of 20% in how trusting someone is.[66] The degree to which someone has ethnocentric attitudes are deemed to be around 20–40% heritable.[67] In summary, genetics has a key role to play in how people think.

This is even more true in the case of political standpoints, in terms of the standard left-right, liberal-conservative, 'change'-'status quo' spectrum: the degree to which people are open to new things versus holding status quo views is 43% heritable.[68] This relatively high level of heritability tells us that one's conservative-liberal politics is not simply an individual, non-inherited product of our environment— there is also a strong genetic component. At the same time, there is significant variation in political standpoints among individuals within a population. In the United States, for example, polling over recent years tells us that approximately 38% of the population self-declare as 'conservatives'; approximately 20% as 'liberals'; and around 40% as 'moderates'.[69]

This leads us to an interesting question: why have human populations retained (two) different genotypes of the same trait, such that some individuals are more predisposed to be liberal and others more conservative? Just as the vertebrate/ invertebrate trait in our ancestors eventually came down firmly on the side of backbones, surely there must be one set of political views that is more evolutionarily successful, and should therefore predominate among the population. It is highly unlikely, for example, that the variation arises afresh in each generation through mutation, as in the case of cystic fibrosis. Furthermore, we don't know why the conservative types—broadly speaking, those who prefer the status quo and are more neophobic—appear to be more numerous than liberals—who naturally prefer change and are more neophilic.

One possible answer is that different political leanings exist as an evolutionary stable ratio. That is, there are advantages to liberals in existing in a population with 'conservatives' in it, and vice versa. When it comes to being open or hostile to change, there is no evolutionary 'best' answer, like there might be with, say, hearing or vision. Indeed, there is value to an individual—a chance to get ahead—in doing things differently from many others in the group. In fact, then, society's different political leanings may all need one another.[70] Note that the evolutionarily stable ratio does not exist for the benefit of the group—which would be a group selection argument—but for the individuals therein.

Another argument to explain the maintenance of genetic political predispositions is that, in earlier human history, being conservative was a clearly advantageous trait expression: when life was much more dangerous and one was more likely to die a violent death, a 'conservative' cognition would, on average, have kept you alive. You would be more pro-in-group, would be more fearful of outsiders and threats, and so on.[71] In other words, in the Stone Age everyone was a conservative and 'conservatism' was therefore genetically dominant—but now that life has become much safer over the last 10,000 years, conservatism is no longer selected for as strongly. This has allowed other political genotypes to become more prominent in the population.[72] Under this theory, we are seeing evolution in process—in the absence of an evolutionary pressure (a close connection between conservatism and survival), the proportion of conservatives to liberals should shrink further.

In reality, we don't know the answer. The idea of human populations becoming more liberal due to removal of a past evolutionary pressure matches the idea that humans are evolving to become more sociable. In this formulation, we are building bigger groups, and becoming less violent, which is causing reduced selection for war-prone genotypes like conservatism or groupishness. Each feeds into the other; and, as we stand in 2018, we might be viewing this particular piece of evolution mid-process.[73] I am also very aware that, as a liberally-minded person, I am attracted to arguments like these because of confirmation bias.

This chapter has been the shortest of précis of human cognitive evolution. But it equips us well for the rest of the book. Although complicated, we understand that the mind is not a blank slate, and has evolved like any other facet of life on earth: it has been slowly modified over tens of thousands of generations. This evolution has been due to selection at the individual rather than the group level.

Whilst some brain modules are very old and solve physical problems like gravity and predation, and have come to us from our reptilian ancestors or before, others—like the social emotions—are more human in their uniqueness, and have evolved through social selection—essentially an arms race with other human beings. This evolutionary process, combined with the learning that every human starts in the womb, creates the complexity of human behaviour.

2

DRIVES

'*Why do you want to go?*' asked Jerry.

We were at a bowling alley with Jerry's young family, for a going-away party. After absenting ourselves from the group to buy some drinks, we plunged into an ancient conversation, generational in its frequency, yet surprisingly still a puzzle—to me, to him, and to wider society. I was about to go to war for the first time. Jerry, my older brother, was trying to work out why.

I wanted to go so much, and it was so obvious to me that going to Afghanistan was the right thing to do, that it hadn't even occurred to me that others, Jerry included, would be confused by my decision to take on a fair amount of risk, for some sort of gain that was difficult to define. Unlike some who have fought through the ages, my decision to fight was entirely voluntary.

*I pondered his question for a moment, and answered from the gut. '*I want to see how I do,*' I replied, pausing before adding, '*I want to prove myself*'. Saying it out loud made it sound ridiculous, like a throwback to some prehistoric behaviour totally out of place in the third millennium. But that didn't diminish the strong pull, the yearning that I felt towards going. In fact, I had always felt this pull. I had always wanted to be a soldier, since I was a child.*

41

Jerry shrugged and nodded, and seemed to understand. A psychiatrist, and wiser than his younger brother, it probably made more sense to him than it did to me at the time. But that was the end of our conversation. Entertaining my niece and nephew took over, and it was inappropriate to talk about war, and death, in front of them.

There was also another feeling that emerged in other conversations. I was proud, I think, of Britain, and perhaps of the 'British way of doing things'. I could not have described to you what that actually meant, but there was a faint feeling of oneness with my tribe—the British. I certainly had pride that the British Army knew what it was doing, and that this was a group that I wanted to be part of. This was also true of others I knew: having trained together, we didn't want to let our mates down in this great adventure.

By contrast, in the UK war is meant to be a burden and a duty for soldiers.[1] They are sacrificing themselves for their countries, so that their societies can thrive and survive. But the vast majority of the young men (and they were mostly young men, especially in the combat roles) absolutely couldn't wait to get into their first battle. When you looked at your comrades during a firefight, more often than not they would be wide-eyed and breathless with excitement. They looked like they belonged in that Afghan ditch, grinning with Taliban rockets exploding overhead, even though they were a shopkeeper's son from Milton Keynes. They didn't feel like they were sacrificing anything.

This dissonance was tackled head on by a Danish tank captain who stood up after a talk I gave in Copenhagen. He commented that talking about the rush and thrill of war for young men was almost a taboo. How could a liberal and mostly pacific society, such as Denmark's, acknowledge that its soldiers in fact sought combat? The Danish general with whom I was sharing the podium looked distinctly uncomfortable with the conversation as it developed; but then, he had never been in combat.

And how desperately these young men wanted to experience combat! Soldiers, and officers, would engineer their travels, volunteer for patrols and such, just to get to the hallowed position of being 'in contact' (the slang for being under fire, derived from the radio signals sent by the unit at the time). Out the other side—even better if they had fired their rifles—you could see the relief and joy on their faces. They had made it. They were men. At times it was so fun that it felt like a game, until it became crushingly serious, when a comrade was killed, or injured, or you ended up in a situation so terrifying that you felt like a trapped animal about to be killed.

Afghanistan was as exciting as I thought it would be. I saw just enough combat for the exhilaration to tarnish slightly and for me to wonder when my luck would run out. But experiencing combat was, hands down, the greatest rush of positive emotions that I have ever experienced in my not-unadventurous life, before or since. Fighting, when you and a small group of humans are trying to out-shoot and out-manoeuver another group of humans, and they you, is the ultimate team sport.[2]

3

THE SUBCONSCIOUS

*'Negative emotions like loneliness, envy, and guilt have an
important role to play in a happy life; they're big, flashing signs
that something needs to change'*

Gretchen Rubin[1]

The human brain has evolved to motivate behaviour that
increases the reproductive fitness of individuals, on average.
The next two chapters explore two such evolved behaviours:
status-seeking and the desire to belong. For each, we will
look through different lenses: first, understanding how the
selection pressures shaped the cognitive mechanisms motivating these behaviours; then looking at the behaviours
themselves; before finally exploring the mechanisms behind
them. We will focus on the intuitive, subconscious nature of
these behaviours: status and belonging are heuristic brain
mechanisms—automatic shortcuts. First, however, we will
explore how and why the brain produces emotional feelings.
Why do we feel good, or bad, or experience desire towards
something? How do we motivate ourselves?

The human desires that guide us—attraction to sexual
partners for reproduction, excitement about food, and so
on—are proximate mechanisms for what, over evolutionary

timescales, has delivered reproductive success.[2] Simply put, hormones that make you feel good (or bad) motivate you to carry out evolutionarily beneficial behaviours and avoid those that are evolutionarily negative; we do certain things because they feel good, and doing them increases our ability to produce surviving offspring. Hormones motivate you to respond to social clues in particular ways—technically, it's the social clues that provoke your behaviour, and your hormones that modulate or motivate it.[3]

The reason that these hormones feel good is because our ancestors—through selection of random traits caused by mutation—evolved brain mechanisms that produce hormones that worked to activate our subjective pleasure circuits.[4] These systems motivated them to carry out particular behaviours, and in so doing, have more surviving offspring than those who did not evolve the same motivational systems. Alternatively, activities that make us feeling unwell or even in pain—like not eating—do so because those negative feelings motivated our ancestors to improve their reproductive fitness—in this case, to find food and eat.

In short, when we encounter stimuli, we undergo brain processes that produce hormones motivating us to do particular things. This is because they have been selected over generations to favour that response. Many of these hormones also operate on feedback loops. For example, mothers and children who are close to one another release oxytocin to facilitate bonding. The resulting cuddling then causes more oxytocin to be produced, up to an optimum level. Thus the same hormone can be a trigger for a behaviour as well as its result.[5]

Social emotions

Emotions are contained in brain modules that offer a quick way for stimuli to be turned into a physiological response. Like all other brain modules, emotions evolved to solve particular evolutionary problems faced by our ancestors. This physiological response—for example, increased heart rate or pupil dilation—is often followed by a physical action. The completed circuit generates an appropriate response: the individual jumps up and moves away when they see a snake. These emotional responses to stimuli most likely evolved out of reflexes in simpler animals, which in turn evolved out of responses to chemical gradients in the environments of bacteria.[6] The emotions are quick, subconscious responses to persistent evolutionary challenges, like finding mates or avoiding parasites.

In other words, the actual subjective feeling of an emotion, whether pleasant or unpleasant, good or bad, is how you experience your brain motivating a particular response from you.[7] The 'feeling' in and of itself means absolutely nothing. For example, the subjective human 'feeling' of fear is your conscious brain's 'reading' of this primal, emotional response. And although many animals have the emotional response of fear, in the sense that they respond quickly to dangerous stimuli in particular ways (such as running away), it is highly unlikely that they 'feel' the texture, flavour or timbre of the emotion in the same way that humans do.

The social emotions were evolutionarily preceded by the basic emotions, originally categorised by Darwin: fear, anger, disgust, surprise, happiness and sadness.[8] Basic emotions evolved in response to stimuli in the non-social environment like predators or parasites. Fear and disgust represent some of the earliest emotional adaptations that evolved in recognisable form around 450 million years ago in our reptilian ancestors.[9] In fact, fear and disgust most probably have an even older genesis, in the predator- and waste-avoidance reflexes of the first animals with nervous systems. From these developed several social emotions: (social) anxiety is a development of fear, (moral) disgust a development of the original (parasite-avoidance) disgust, and anger (about other people) is a development of the original anger mechanism that prepares an animal for combat.[10]

The social emotions began developing well into our primate past. All of our primate ancestors lived in social groups, and simple social emotions are present in all extant primate species, from anxiety[11] to empathy and reconciliation.[12] Primates even use their vocalisations (a non-language form of communication) to express emotions and maintain their social relationships.[13] But these are generally examples of one individual trying directly to communicate to, or manipulate another. It is very hard to demonstrate in primates (without falling into the trap of anthropomorphism) more complex group-orientated social emotions, like shame or embarrassment.[14]

Social emotions solve persistent problems in the social environment, and evolved through social selection. They enable humans to recalibrate their social relationships, either though motivating themselves to process (and then respond to) social stimuli in particular ways that enhance their ability to live in groups, or through signalling to others what they feel. In most cases they do both.[15] They evolved to help individuals regulate their position in the wider group, and thus to stop themselves being ostracised. The total number of social emotions is huge, and there is little agreement on how to categorise them, or how they are related[16]—I could list a thousand different fine grains of emotion on a spectrum encompassing love and envy, guilt and jealousy. Some of the major ones are described below.

We begin with love. Whereas other animal young quickly become independent—deer, for example, wean at about ten weeks and can then obtain food for themselves—human infants remain helpless for a much longer period. Because of this, human male-female pairs that endure long beyond copulation are evolutionarily favoured. One of the main supportive adaptations for this long-term pair bond is the emotion of (romantic) love, which generates strong attachment to another human by creating highly pleasurable 'feelings' associated with spending time with them.[17] Like many other social emotions, love is both an individual response to another individual, as well as a signal of hard-to-fake commitment. In other words, it has evolved to evoke reciprocal emotions in others. The emotion of love is linked to the evolutionary basis for groupishness, discussed in Chapter 5.

Once primates and humans began to live in larger groups, the emotion of love was not enough to support pair bonds. The groupings of a greater number of unrelated individuals increased the opportunities for members of pair bonds to have sexual intercourse with other individuals (to 'cheat'). This represented a significant evolutionary problem. For men, the problem arose in that a pregnancy arising from their woman's infidelity could then force them to spend resources and time investing in someone else's offspring (and genes). For women, the problem simply arose when the father of their children started sleeping with someone else, with or without a pregnancy, as the time now devoted to a rival female put you at risk of losing your co-carer and resource / protection provider. This is reflected in the types of jealousy that men and women respond most strongly to, even today: men have been shown to exhibit more jealousy over sexual infidelity, and women over emotional infidelity (displaying commitment to someone else).[18]

Jealousy can be triggered by a wide range of stimuli, for example proximity of a human's mate to another potential mate, or subtle social clues, such as glances or other non-verbal gestures. In males, it can result in aggression or limited violence as a means of controlling one's partner, accompanied by strong feelings of possession. In females, the emotion of jealousy can motivate violence towards the rival or the cheating partner; it can also act as signalling behaviour to the group indicating who her partner is, thus making it more difficult for them to cheat.

Taken together, jealousy and love enable the stability and longevity of the pair bond. This has a dramatic effect on the evolutionary fitness of the pair in question. And whilst it is true that jealousy does cause violence, like the other social emotions it offers a broader range of responses to a situation. For example, violence can be threatened but not carried out, or controlled violence and coercion can be used. It can also act not as a tool of direct harm, but as a warning to others. These behaviours reduce the overall amount of violence that would otherwise result if the 'jealous reactions' did not exist—thus, social emotions help us regulate our behaviour.[19]

In slightly larger groups one of the main evolutionary challenges is that of making reciprocal altruism work. For each individual this means avoiding helping out another individual without them reciprocating. Enter vengeance. Vengeance's evolutionary function is to push up the costs of cheating to the cheater: if they cheat or steal from you, then they will pay a price. Vengeance also acts as a signal to the rest of the group: 'this is what happens when you cheat me'.[20] Vengeance makes transgressing group norms more expensive, and as such, it encourages pro-social behaviour. Like jealousy, in the actual instance of emotional expression, vengeance does cause violence (although it is often controlled), but overall vengeance reduces violence, in deterring cheating and acting as a signal to others that enforces group norms.[21]

Anger is a similar story. One of the basic emotions, it originally evolved to prepare animals for combat against predators by preparing their muscles and heightening their senses. It was also adapted by evolution into a social emotion, where it is used to signal to others that violence might be forthcoming. Individuals learn to recognise that others who display anger (with a sweaty face and dilated pupils, for instance) are more likely to use violence. This causes a recalibration of social relationships within the group (e.g. one of the individuals backs down): it deters future aggression.[22] Social anger, whether sincere or successfully faked, is a signal whose aim is to change the behaviour of another person.[23] As with jealousy and vengeance, anger does sometimes lead to conflict, but its broader effect of regulating social relationships means that violence levels across the group will be lower.

There are a number of other social emotions that calibrate social relations. These include embarrassment, guilt and shame. All demonstrate either to the self or to others that you have broken a social norm or contract, and seem to fulfil a social appeasement function after wrongdoing. Embarrassment and shame will help an individual avoid ejection from a group after cheating, if these emotions are perceived by others as being honestly expressed. Shame helps us maintain our reputations when we have committed a social faux pas. It helps rebuild trust. Guilt, on the other hand, is an internal emotion, only displayed if consciously desired, and seems to motivate individuals towards pro-social future behaviour, in anticipation of others' responses to their bad behaviour. All three evolved to enable humans and their ancestors to sustain group membership by discouraging them from acting against group norms.[24]

This has been the briefest look at the social emotions. They allow individuals within the group to maintain their own group membership by regulating their social position and signalling imbalances of resources, or information about who cooperates and who cheats. In some cases they will directly cause violence, but because the social emotions facilitate much finer-grained communication between individuals, the overall effect is a lessening of violence. They negate or reduce the problems of living in groups. Even the disgust emotion protects individuals from the greater likelihood of disease in groups (whether spread by other people or toxins).[25] It is clear, then, why individual social emotions benefit the individual, and hence why they evolved—they protect you in social interactions.[26]

These multiple individual-to-individual emotional interactions within a group are complimented by what are known as collective emotions. This is what occurs when a high number of individuals within a group mirror one another's social emotions, and it, too, is beneficial. In many instances, it is of high survival value to display the same emotional response as others in your group. Fear is the obvious example: other individuals may have noticed the snake that you have missed, or they may have spotted something about an out-group that you did not.

Status and belonging

Attaining power and status, a key theme in this book, feels good. This is because humans have evolved mechanisms that reward us for being powerful. Why? Because being powerful was, and remains, a proxy for an ability to attract sexual mates and then well resource the resulting offspring. Even though today's societies are very different from the Pleistocene environment in which most of our hominid evolution occurred, achieving status (as measured by your position in your society) still means you are more likely to have better health outcomes,[27] are more likely to be able to escape as a refugee if your country is devastated by war, and are more likely to be able to survive or manage life-threatening natural events like a drought.[28] In short, status still offers an evolutionary benefit, and so seeking it feels good.

The same is true of belonging to an in-group. Our motivational systems offer reward by making us feel good when we are securely attached to a group. This attachment is a proxy desire for being protected, having access to mating partners, and having access to resources. Both status-seeking and belonging are very broad heuristic mechanisms in our brains and lay the foundations for much of human behaviour.

Finally, there is a distinction to explore that frames the following two chapters: that between leaders and followers in war. Leaders wage wars because, cognitively speaking, they seek status over leaders of other groups, and/or seek to reinforce their status within their own groups. Status is a proxy for the (biological) good things in life—mating partners, food, and the other resources necessary for survival and reproduction—and it is achieved through successful competition. This does not mean that contemporary leaders of countries are consciously seeking to dominate other leaders in order to appropriate their resources, or to improve their status so that they can have more mating partners. It means that their motivational systems are primed by evolution to seek status because doing so has resulted in better survival and reproduction, on average over evolutionary time.

As for followers, it is possible that men who go to war are also seeking status, and that this translates into greater reproductive success. But if you take into account the overall chances of increasing reproduction (that is, those who die in combat as well as those who survive it), for the average participant there are no overall reproductive benefits to taking part in conflict.[29] I would argue that war, motivated by status-seeking, only pays off in fitness terms if you are at the top of the hierarchy (a leader)—as evidenced by leaders' greater access to resources, in terms of both direct war spoils and, for instance, the massive harems once kept by the most senior war leaders as a privilege of their status, increased by victory in battle. For all others, the risk-reward balance is unfavourable.

However, there is an even stronger selection pressure that motivates individuals to go to war—maintaining belonging to an in-group that protects us, helps us find mates, and helps us use resources more efficiently than we could if solitary. Refusing to fight—to participate in group activities—risks you being cast out. Losing membership of an in-group through ostracism has been akin to a death sentence for almost all of humanity's evolutionary history. Without a group to protect you, it would not be long before you died at the hands of a predator, or another group of humans. The desire to belong acts as a proxy for protection, a greater choice of mating partners and access to resources—all of which are intrinsic to evolutionary fitness.[30]

Finally, what of the interaction between leaders and their followers? This is clear cut: war is often framed by leaders as a defence of the homeland, or of values, religion or tribe. The so-called War on Terror is framed by the US and its allies as an attack on democracy and its associated values,[31] and by the other side—Islamist extremists—as an attack on the Muslim religion:[32] the conflict is framed by leaders around that which holds their respective groups together, generating a sense of belonging for followers. Followers, for their part, provide a group for leaders to lead, and so with the status that they seek.

4

COMPETITION AND STATUS

'a warre of every one against every one'
Thomas Hobbes[1]

Well before the human lineage, organisms fought for status as a means of increasing their reproductive fitness. This is no different when we look at our ancestral primates, or humans, as a study of primate body sizes and human homicide will demonstrate later. We will then look at the similarities in how our brains treat 'social objects'—ranging from individual others, to massive groups. This will show that the same cognitive processes drive both individual humans killing others, and the leaders of fighting coalitions of millions.

Competition

Our journey towards understanding warfare begins with individual organisms competing. Conflict—actual fighting—is simply the most extreme form of the intraspecific competition described here. Between species, the dynamics are often those of predator-prey: for example, one animal species wishes to eat the other. But intraspecific conflict occurs when animals of the same species compete over resources. In evolutionary terms, humans and other organisms compete with one another over resources in order to increase their individual ability to survive and reproduce.[2]

Those individuals that are better adapted to compete with their conspecifics (members of the same species) will secure more resources, which in turn helps them to have more surviving offspring. The drive and ability to compete evolved very early on and grew out of individual cells, or sub-cellular elements. The first cells, approximately 4 billion years ago, were in competition with neighbouring cells for access to nutrients: their ability to move evolved as part of that search for nutrients. Inevitably, if all cells were trying to maximise their own share of nutrients, there was a selective advantage to the first cell that managed to, say, expel a toxin poisonous to other members of its own species. This was the beginning of the arms race: once the toxin offered a selective advantage to those who could produce it, it would spread in the population. This would then create a further selection pressure in the population for adaptations that were able to defend against the toxin. Those individuals unable to compete then failed to reproduce, and their evolutionary lines stopped. The descendants of the winners of this intraspecific competition are all around us today.

At its most basic, each individual animal is trying to increase access to food, water and sexual partners. In biology, these are known as 'real' resources. That is, they directly impact on the ability to survive and reproduce; for example, access to food and water needs to be maintained at a near daily rate. Animals also compete over so-called 'surrogate' resources. These are things like territory, status, membership of groups, and alliances with other group members.[3] Considered on their own, surrogate resources are worthless, but obtaining them offers greater access to the real resources—they act as proxies for increasing reproductive fitness.[4] In evolutionary terms, therefore, competing for real resources or surrogate resources amounts to the same thing—they both enhance reproductive success. Accordingly, our brains treat them in the same way.[5] For example, more food (a real resource) and more status (a surrogate resource) both help individuals to find more sexual partners, which in turn allows them to have more children, giving them control over more descendants able to fight for them. Each leads to the other.

In any environment, the real resources are limited, and are the ultimate objects of competition between individuals. They are represented by specific objects in the environment, like a watering hole, or an animal's carcass. Surrogate resources, on the other hand, do not necessarily have to be limited, or at least are not usually limited to the same degree. Consider, for example, group membership—many individuals can be members of a group. Or consider status—several individuals may enjoy different degrees of status in a group. This is particularly true of humans, who have non-linear dominance arrangements in their complex social groups— effectively, there are many different ways for humans to achieve status—unlike chimpanzees, who have linear dominance hierarchies (with an alpha male). Furthermore, surrogate resources are longer lasting. If an individual competes for a carcass, they then have to compete again for the next one. But if they compete for and gain higher status, that may well help them win multiple future competitions over different carcasses. For these reasons, individuals more often compete over surrogate resources as a way to increase their ability to survive and reproduce. Achieving surrogate resources enables access to a greater number of real resources over a lifetime, and potentially over the lifetime of your children if you are a primate (as status can cascade down the generations).[6]

Lastly, there is a relationship between density and competition. As animals reproduce, their density in a given area increases (all other things being equal). This density leads to increased competition, because resources have to be shared across a larger number of individuals—this is true for bacteria on a sugar substrate, or buffalo grazing on grassland. This increased competition leads to a loss of reproductive output, because time and energy that could profitably have been spent consuming resources or finding mates must instead be wasted on competing with other individuals. In addition, increased competition can lead to a lower average rate of survival, because some individuals will die or become seriously injured through competing. So, in an evolutionary sense, competition is, on average, bad for individuals.[7]

Thus, the greater the level of competition facing an individual animal, the less likely they are to reproduce and survive, and the smaller their contribution will be to the future gene pool. Competition for resources, caused by population growth, then limits that population growth: this is known as the intraspecific competition trap, and is the process by which population levels stabilise, rather than inexorably increase.[8] Even though competition between individuals does not make evolutionary 'sense' when averaged across the individuals in the group, individual animals are forced to fight, because once an individual animal is prepared to compete and use violence to gain resources, it will immediately become more successful than those who are not willing to do so. It is the original security dilemma, or conflict trap; the state of 'warre of every one against every one'.[9]

But what about competition between individual humans? In relation to how other individual animals compete within a species, are the dynamics comparable, or even recognisable?

Human homicide and primate size

The simple answer is yes—human homicides, for males at least, appear mostly to be driven by status disputes. That is, men most often kill other men over questions of who is higher than whom in the hierarchy. For women who kill, it is a different story: female homicide is most often driven by issues surrounding reproduction like competition for mates, protection of their offspring, and conflicts over resources needed for offspring.[10]

In the following study of human homicide, I use death rates as a proxy for levels of individual, intraspecific competition in humans. There are several reasons for this. Death from violence is what one might call a binary data point. You are either dead or you are not; and if you have died a violent death it is usually possible to distinguish your corpse from someone who has died of natural causes. This is true of both recently killed corpses and those discovered during archaeological digs from the Neolithic period. And whilst there are complications with how one defines homicide (for example, different legal systems have different positions on the concept of intent), it is something on which all states collect data.[11] For example, England has compiled homicide statistics since the 1200s.[12]

I will also say something about those who commit violence. It will perhaps not surprise you that the overwhelming majority of violence is committed by young men in their twenties—up to 95 per cent of homicides are committed by men according to a UN study.[13] In fact, in almost all countries around the world, men constitute the overall majority of both killers and also victims. For example, in the US between 1980 and 2012, men outnumbered women as victims more than 3:1; worldwide the ratio is 4:1.[14] Women do, of course, commit violence (measured here by homicide), but this should be considered the statistical exception rather than the rule—and, as we have seen, it is statistically most often for reasons related to their offspring (e.g. protecting them from an abusive step-parent). To reinforce this point, when countries see an increase in homicide rates—killings per head—it is always the male homicide rate that increases, while the female homicide rate stays static.[15] So, for these reasons, I will here use male pronouns when talking about killers, whilst accepting that a small proportion of homicides are committed by women.

What are the similarities between homicides and intraspecific violence in animals? Are homicides really just about gaining or holding onto resources? A glance at the newspapers does not immediately lead us to this view. What about heinous, sick killings? What about stylistic violence, or homicides where men torture and eat their victims? For obvious reasons, these types of stories feature more prominently in the media, as do stories where violence and homicide are treated as a pathology or sickness. Most humans have a lurid fascination with killing, probably because it pays to understand the phenomenon as well as we can: being killed represents a strong selection pressure. And because most of us are not killers, it is psychologically comforting to paint the behaviour as an aberration. The press, however, relies on the sensational to pique human interest. In reality, homicide throughout history has been commonplace and ordinary, and although some killers do exhibit elements of psychopathology, most are in no way mentally abnormal.[16]

What do the social sciences say about homicide? Many scholars take the view that countries or regions within them—for instance, the southern United States—have higher homicide rates because of 'cultures of violence'. According to this view, local beliefs and value sets that legitimise, valorise and glorify violence will cause higher rates of homicide.[17] In my opinion, this is not quite right. Aside from the fact that it is very difficult to define culture in a way that stands up to statistical scrutiny, this view has the equation the wrong way around. Rather than culture determining human behaviour, I believe that a 'culture' is the sum of the behaviours (and interactions thereof) of human individuals in a group.[18] For clarity, I accept that aspects of 'culture' do correlate with, or even facilitate, human behaviour, in that higher homicide rates can be found where there are social narratives that in some way elevate violence as a virtue, such as in the southern United States.[19] However, in my opinion, to state that culture *causes* violence and homicide relegates humans to passive recipients of social forces and removes human agency (which is required by most definitions of homicide, in the concept of intent). It is a similar argument to the one stating that religion causes war, or ideology causes people to blow themselves up.

This approach also treats 'culture' as if it were a single, definable variable in a statistical analysis, whereas it is clearly a multi-faceted dynamic (set of) concept(s).[20] Cultures persist when reinforced by consciously created societal structures like laws, and by things like ecology—in modern terms, whether you live in an area full of mansions with swimming pools, or, in ancient terms, whether you hunt in an area that is plentiful in bison.[21] Also, cultures change. For example, culture is unstable on an intergenerational scale as a determinant of things like violence, because each generation will reject some of their forefathers' values and approach life in a different way. Similarly, laws change, and these affect the sums of patterns of behaviour in societies.[22] I will accept, however, that in groups or societies where violence is prevalent, this raises the cost of non-violence in the sense of a security dilemma. In that sense, culture provides a context to violence, but does not cause it. This is particularly true when it comes to crimes involving men jostling for status (of which more below).[23]

So, violence is not a pathology, nor is it 'caused' by culture; rather, violence as a strategy must be an evolutionary adaptation.[24] In fact, it would be extraordinary if the use of violence as a strategy by humans had *not* been shaped by evolution, when one considers that this has been the case for practically everything else that humans are and do. Please note that where the term 'strategy' is used, it does not mean that individuals sit down and consciously ponder whether to murder people; we are concerned with evolutionary strategies, based on our brains intuitively making decisions that, when summed across the population, and over evolutionary time, on average increase survival and reproduction. So, where does violence work as an evolutionary strategy? Why does it make sense to use violence?

We have already discussed one correlate of overwhelming importance: youthful maleness. What are the others? These men are also overwhelmingly likely to be unmarried, poorly educated and unemployed (both victims and killers).[25] Killers and victims are likely to know each other, but be unrelated. What about motives? In all societies except those with the lowest homicide rates, the most frequent reasons for people killing each other have been status-driven, the result of altercations over trivial disputes—bragging matches, insults, revenge for previous abuse, jealousy/infidelity, and gossip. A surprisingly high percentage of homicides occur over games of pool, darts or gambling. This is followed by acquisitory homicides (such as robberies that end in death) and other crime-related homicides (drug deals gone wrong, gang wars, and so on).[26] This seems to have changed little over the ages: Royal Courts in thirteenth-century England record status disputes that are indistinguishable from their modern counterparts.[27] For example, in London in 1278, a Geoffrey Bereman was killed by an acquaintance and the latter's servant after a quarrel involving a mistress. In other cases found in the same court documents, two people were killed over disputes that arose from games of chess—the medieval equivalent of glassing someone over a game of pool.[28]

As well as being the most common, homicides caused by status disputes are also the most statistically variable. That is, in different populations with different homicide rates, it is always the differing frequency of trivial altercations that accounts for most of the variance in the overall homicide rate. When the overall rate varies, the few homicides committed by the insane, blood relatives or women do not vary nearly as much.[29] In other words, when homicide goes up overall, what is really increasing is the rate of killings that arise from these 'trivial' altercations between young men. At this point, I would like to emphasise that the word 'trivial' comes from the literature on the subject. Clearly the men who entered into these disputes did not see them as such— on the contrary, it was a matter of life and death—and I am not using the word to patronise or demean these young men or their milieu. They were (and are) fighting and dying over something clearly very important to them.

We've seen that the vast majority of homicides are caused by perceived competitions over status, face or positioning within the social hierarchy.[30] In evolutionary terms, and to imagine this better, cast your mind to a small band of hunter-gatherers 20,000 years ago: remember that, for them, status is a surrogate resource. The second most common cause of homicide—acquisition and other crime—is also clearly about real resources. Jealousy, too, is about one's own 'resources' being utilised by you or taken away by another, both in an evolutionary sense, and in a literal sense—for most of the history of humanity, females have been treated as resources by males.[31]

In evolutionary terms, status—a surrogate resource—enables men to gain more real resources, including mating partners.[32] The reciprocal of this is that those partners seek higher-status men; experiments have observed women showing preference for men who are better dressed and have nicer watches. This is because they are resource-rich, which translates into more resources for one's future offspring.[33] In other words, men seek status because ancestral women have sought (and had more children with) higher-status men. This neatly matches the reasons animals compete as understood in intraspecific competition theory: a large majority of human violence—as measured by homicides—is ultimately driven by mechanisms that have evolved to help men maintain their status. But why is it so overwhelmingly committed by young men? Surely women need resources for reproduction as well?

To answer this question, we have to look at the differences between males and females right across the animal kingdom, but particularly across the mammalian class. The key difference between the sexes is that of parental investment: the relative amounts of time and energy (and thus opportunity cost) that each sex invests in the joint offspring. In stark biological terms, males can invest a fraction of the resources that females put into rearing offspring. The nine-month human gestation period is the most obvious example of this, but breastfeeding also keeps women temporarily less fertile, and represents a further time cost to rearing offspring. Because females themselves are the limiting factor, they choose their mates carefully: quality is much more important than quantity.[34]

This means that men have the potential to have many more children than do women. Thus, over a lifetime of attempting to maximise their reproductive rates, men and women face different limiting factors. For men, the rare resource is fertile women; for women, the rare resource is the total time when they are fertile. For example, let's say having a single child stops a woman from having other children for a year (pregnancy plus breastfeeding). If we assume fertility from the ages of 15–50, then the maximum number of offspring per woman would, in theory, be thirty-five. A man could impregnate thirty-five women in a month, or certainly in a year. This means that in humans, as in most other animal species, the male is the more competitive sex when it comes to acquiring a mate.[35]

This male–male competition has interesting effects. Firstly, it creates a selection pressure for men who are more successful in competition with other men. In non-primate animals, such as deer, this means a selection pressure for males that creates and sustains physical advantages in a fight, like antlers, strengthened craniums and a larger size. But this effect extends across the primates.[36] Thus, closely-related primate species with slightly different sexual characteristics allow us to see some striking relationships. For example, the size difference between the sexes—known as the degree of sexual dimorphism—varies between primate species with different mating systems. Species that practise higher degrees of polygyny have greater intramale competition because some males in the group monopolise large numbers of females, leaving fewer for the rest to compete over. This in turn means that these species have far greater degrees of dimorphism,[37] because male size is selected for ability to fight, which is part of competition.

Of course, as men have been saying since time immemorial, size is not everything. In the primates, intelligence—particularly social intelligence—enables men to dominate other men, achieving status. This is why intelligence is also selected for—because it is usually much more effective for gaining—and particularly maintaining[38]—status than violence. It carries less risk of accidental injury, and is a much easier way to dominate large groups, using words and building coalitions (although a combination of the two works particularly well).

Female primates are optimally sized for their ecological niches—that is, how much food is available.[39] The underlying ecology also dictates the distribution of females over space, which affects the degree to which males are able to dominate them. Closely-grouped females, due to dense resources, leads to a greater ability for males to keep harems. This is what leads to differing degrees of polygyny between species in the first place. In highly polygynous species, where high-status males monopolise large groups of females, the competition will be intense, because there are large numbers of males who do not get to mate, and the males will be (relatively speaking) huge.[40] Consider, for example, the harem-keeping gorillas, where males are almost double the size of females. In such set-ups, females, by contrast, almost all get to mate.[41] Species with a greater difference in reproductive outcomes between males and females also mostly tend to have greater intramale competition, and so greater sexual dimorphism. This relationship is most clearly underlined by the fact that, in some species of bird and lizard, it is the females who have a greater reproductive output, and are thus the bigger, more competitive sex.[42]

Monogamous species, by contrast, have lower levels of reproductive variance between males and females, and lower levels of size difference between the sexes.[43] Human males are on average about 15 per cent bigger than females, and humans are classified today as mostly monogamous: genetic evidence suggests that we have only recently (in evolutionary terms) stopped being polygynous.[44] Human polygyny reached its peak in the first city-states as late as around 5,000 years ago, when high-status men would have harems that numbered in the thousands (this was also when levels of material inequality between men first skyrocketed). Consider Rameses II, born around 1,300 BCE. He had over 200 wives, and around 100 children.[45] It is not clear how many mistresses he kept as well. Or, in perhaps the most famous example, 8 per cent of the men who currently live in the area of Asia between the Pacific Ocean and the Caspian Sea have been shown to be descended from one man who lived approximately 1,000 years ago: Genghis Khan.[46]

This evolutionary history of polygyny, with higher-status males dominating harems, and lower-status males losing out and not being able to mate, has shaped human male brains. Throughout human history, male status has meant a higher number of mating partners, thus creating a strong selection pressure towards those males who seek, and are able to attain, status.[47] Not finding a mate represents the ultimate negative selection pressure. In the terms of our argument, then, what are the differences between polygynous societies (more male competition) and monogamous societies (less male competition)?

On average, polygynous societies have higher levels of violence, crime and homicide.[48] This is because of the greater proportion of males without mating partners (defined here, for statistical reasons, as unmarried). The evidence for a correlation between these factors is unambiguous, but some stunningly original research also demonstrates a causal link. In China, the advent of the one-child policy resulted in a preference for sons, unfortunately leading to an increase in female infanticide. The result was a skewed sex ratio between males and females, which eventually (~20 years later) has fed into a marriage market where the relative absence of females makes it more difficult for men to get married. In other words, it mimics the effects of polygyny: a 0.01% change in the sex ratio towards males (i.e. more men) causes an unbelievable 3% increase in violent crime.[49]

Thus, in evolutionary terms, in a society where there are more men than women, inevitably this means that some men will not have the opportunity to get married and have children. This is reflected in the fact that young men, on average, take more risks—in a reproductive sense, what have they got to lose?—and exhibit more risky, status-elevating behaviour. It is important to emphasise that they are not all fighting directly over women. Rather, if you have almost no hope of reproducing because all the high-status men have monopolised the women, then it is worth taking risks to elevate or defend your status.[50] Consider: if the top 50 per cent of men (in status terms) have two women each, this leaves the bottom 50 per cent no chance to mate. Some scholars have even argued that rulers deliberately imposed monogamy on society in order to reduce rates of internal violence, leading to a more cohesive, more taxable society.[51]

(It is worth clarifying that this does not mean that brains are different in traditionally polygynous versus monogamous societies—mass monogamy is too new for that—but rather that the same brains are responding to the environment, the mating system, that surrounds them.)

Now think back to our archetypal killer: a young male, unemployed, uneducated and unmarried. In reproductive terms, he is at a critical stage of his life. This is the age at which men establish their reputations (status) in their communities—remember, too, that for much of evolutionary history humans only lived to 35 or 40. And over evolutionary time, men have, on average, been reproductively more successful where they have rigorously sought and defended status and 'face' between the ages of around 17 to 30. In evolutionary terms, chasing status—the proximate drive that has evolved to fulfil the ultimate reproductive goals—has proven the best way on average to find and keep a partner. This is particularly true when men are young. Improving one's status at the age at which one 'becomes a man' and 'enters society' has an outsized effect on one's reproductive chances.[52] In terms of evolution, this is the main goal.

Here we return to trivial altercations in bars amongst unemployed, uneducated and unmarried men.[53] In this context, status vis-à-vis other men is highly important. These are fights over status amongst people who have no other means of attaining status (for example, a job or education).[54] Evolution has shaped our cognition with something like the following rule of thumb: if a young man finds himself in a low-status position, he should take more risks when it comes to any challenges to his status. Over evolutionary time, and summed across the human gene pool, this strategy has resulted in more offspring than any other, because men with higher status have produced more offspring. In the evolutionary environment of widespread polygyny, a lack of status for a young male was the greatest possible threat to reproductive fitness.[55]

This chapter has so far shown direct parallels between why individual animals and individual humans fight. But does this have any relevance in war? It seems far-fetched to argue that foot soldiers in modern wars are fighting to receive resources that will benefit their survival and reproduction. At first glance, this might appear to have been true in groups of thirty when women were carried away by the victors: sex and rape have been a major part of war throughout history.[56] But, as discussed in the Introduction, more recent studies have shown that, overall, the average potential reproductive gain in the event of a fighting victory does not outweigh the average reproductive losses experienced by non-leading combatants (who are the majority of fighters).[57] We will have to leave a little longer the puzzle of why foot soldiers fight for their groups; now we turn to leadership in war.

Leadership in war

In evolutionary terms, leaders of groups at war—from leaders of gangs, to leaders of multinational coalitions—are fighting for the same reasons as individual animals and humans. Vis-à-vis leaders of other groups, they are motivated to dominate them (achieve status over them).[58] Leaders are driven to seek status in just the same way as other people—more so, in fact, because status-seekers are over-represented as a personality type in leaders.[59] There are two ways in which wars help human leaders achieve status: within group and without group.

Within your own group, fighting and winning a war is a sure-fire way of beating off any internal challengers to your leadership. As the Native American Shoshone used to say, 'How would we select our leaders if [they] did not prove themselves in such [battles]?'[60] Solidifying your internal leadership position helps you—in evolutionary terms—to accrue more than your per capita share of resources, especially mating partners. There are echoes of this even now—approval ratings for democratic leaders almost always improve when they launch wars.[61] Externally to the group, and thinking back to our Pleistocene warrior leading a band of thirty, there would have been a distinct real resource benefit to war, and the total resources accrued to a group after a conflict (territory, women, access to water, livestock or fishing spots) would disproportionately flow to the leaders.

When fighting other groups, therefore, there is a clear benefit for leaders in terms of both real and surrogate resources. But these benefits no longer flow in quite the way they did when evolution first shaped us. Previously, including quite recently in historical terms, status would have translated into more resources. Now, for instance, the rise of monogamy reduces the prospects of a correlation between higher status and more mating partners, while the emergence of non-hereditary and non-proprietary forms of rule like democracy reduces the number of leaders who personally profit from victory in war. This does not negate the fact that human leaders still work on cognitive rules of thumb that promote seeking status over other leaders, and thus are driven to use warfare as a way of solidifying their group underneath them, obtaining a higher status and so a greater share of resources. Leaders, like killers, still seek the proximate goal of status, but mostly, today, this does not translate into reproductive and survival success. (I make no moral equivalence between killers and leaders, and am merely pointing out that they are motivated by the same subconscious drives.)

So how can we test the idea that human war leaders are fighting for status, just as individual humans and animals are when they fight? Intriguingly, evidence for this comes from a curious statistical relationship that was discovered in the 1960s.[62] It appears that leaders—of any scale of group—use the same psychological rules of thumb when leading. In other words, when a human is competing (or fighting) with another human, the same calculations about relative positions, relative strengths, escalation, rapprochement, hierarchies, coalitions and truces are used as when that same human is leading a multi-national coalition of millions of people.[63] Cognitively, when it comes to fighting, leaders treat a group of one the same as they treat a group of millions. The dynamics of bluff, commit, back down, escalate and retreat are the same whether we are leading a street gang, or the North Atlantic Treaty Organization (NATO).[64] To the brain, all are social objects to be manipulated. If you think about it, this is more likely than not. Humans have gone from small groups to multimillion groups in a timescale that hasn't allowed for significant biological and cognitive evolution: human leaders must approach these different scales of groups in the same way. Evolution has simply tinkered with the cognitive system that we use for individuals and hijacked it for understanding groups (more on this in the next chapter). In other words, the very same status-seeking that drives interpersonal violence pushes leaders to clash as well.

Famously, the US/Iraq War of 2003 was framed by the fact that US President George W Bush's father, George HW Bush, had fought an earlier war in Iraq, and that Saddam Hussein, the Iraqi leader, had tried to assassinate him. When discussing his own Iraq War of 2003, George W Bush even said of Saddam Hussein that 'this is a guy that tried to kill my dad at one time'.[65] He also remarked that the First Gulf War was about 'routing Saddam Hussein [rather than the Iraqi forces in general] out of Kuwait',[66] exhibiting a trend common to modern leaders. Tony Blair, the UK prime minister, similarly framed the 2003 conflict as being about removing Saddam Hussein specifcially.[67] Though we cannot definitively attribute motive to politicians' word choice, the language used in these cases at least suggests some influence from underlying cognitive processes: namely the treatment of different-sized social groups as if they were a single person.

This facet of our psychology is reflective of the heuristic and categorising nature of human cognition: we use categories to simplify the mass of data that our senses produce for our brains.[68] If, for instance, we were to bring to our conscious attention all of the relevant social dynamics in an opposing group—even a small group of around ten—it would rapidly become overwhelming. Much easier that we simplify, and treat groups, no matter what their size, as if they were people, with their own personalities. We have even extended this to our legal systems in the modern age: corporations are treated as legal persons.

This curious relationship—where the same dynamics are in play whether we are looking at a one-on-one relationship, or 1-million-on-1-million—is known as a power law. Power laws are found all over nature and human society, and appear to reflect something deeper about the nature of humans' cognitive approach to the environment. Since first being discovered, they have been found to govern such things as the numbers of large cities versus small ones, income distribution, the number of high-status versus low-status individuals, the number of friends people have, and frequencies of words in a language.[69]

As it happens, this phenomenon also has effects on the distribution of war around the globe. It creates a precise mathematical relationship between the number of conflicts that occur at each size of conflict (measured by number of causalities). This is immediately obvious as soon as you think about it—there are lots of gang fights or border skirmishes all over the world, but (thankfully) there has only been one war on the scale of World War 2. Put more precisely, as the number of casualties in a conflict increases tenfold, the probability of that conflict occurring decreases by 2.6 times.[70] Extraordinarily, this relationship holds for all known interstate wars since 1400.[71]

In addition, power law distributions are non-scalable. This means that the difference in likelihood between a 1,000-casualty war and a 10,000-casualty war is the same as the difference in likelihood between a 10 million-casualty war (the same order of magnitude as World War 2) and a 100 million-casualty war (a war scale that has not yet occurred).[72] The same relationship also holds for the size of terrorist attacks.[73] Put simply, the percentage chances of a conflict being escalated by a factor of ten are the same, no matter the original size of the conflict.[74] Critically non-scalable relationships like this only exist when the same mechanisms and dynamics underlie them.[75] So, it is highly unlikely that some wars are caused by ideology, while others are caused by religion, or tribalism, or greed. It means that there is an underlying mechanism that links together all the different modes of warfare, across all the different eras of human history. This linking factor is the way that individuals and group leaders view other individuals and group leaders: through human social cognition and the pursuit of status.

This holds no matter the size of the group fighting, and also matches those dynamics that we explored earlier at the individual level. Consider such personifying statements as 'Google is trying to do X' or 'Spain wants to do Y'.[76] Our language use reflects our deeper psychological processes, and particularly our mechanisms for understanding the world, including cognitive shortcuts (heuristics).[77] None of these examples reflect conscious thought: they are simply rules of thumb that humans obey most of the time. But we are not trapped into always following them. Of course, it is possible to think consciously about problems, and avoid using such informal guidelines. For instance, we are able to analyse and break down enemy groups and attempt to understand their internal dynamics—indeed, this is what intelligence analysis is. But, in summary, humans treat other individuals, and out-groups of any size, as the same cognitive social objects to be processed, responded to, or dominated.

The neurological basis for status-seeking

We now know why humans, particularly males, seek status, which both causes interpersonal violence and guides the behaviour of human group leaders. This status-seeking behaviour is born of an incredibly quick reaction—it takes around

1/25th of a second for humans to detect differences in social rank.[78] The mechanism is also widespread across many animal species, reflecting the ancient evolutionary origins and advantages of moving up the hierarchy.[79] Impressively, humans are members of multiple and complex hierarchies—you can be simultaneously a team leader at work, the newest and worst member of your football team, and a yellow belt at judo— whereas animals tend to have more simple linear hierarchies.[80] But the actual mechanism involved in status-seeking—testosterone—is the same whether you are seeking to dominate single or multiple hierarchies.

Testosterone motivates us to attain a higher relative standing in the social hierarchy in terms of esteem, respect and influence.[81] Before going further, we need to address the myth that testosterone causes aggression. In actual fact, testosterone provokes status-seeking, and if the best way of achieving higher rank were lying supine and raising our legs in the air, then that is what we would do.[82] The thinking that aggression was a result of testosterone came about because, in reality, such behaviour is in many cases the best way to improve our social standing. But how does this mechanism actually work in humans?

The vast majority of testosterone is produced in the male testes, and in the female ovaries (small amounts are also produced elsewhere in the body). For males, testosterone production in the testes is ultimately controlled by the hypothalamus in the brain. In the terms of our earlier descriptions of the brain, a module has evolved that senses dominance hierarchies, and is linked to the hypothalamus. This controls the testes to release testosterone, which motivates us to behave in a way that helps us climb a hierarchy (we will see later how this mechanism has evolved into one of our moral senses around authority).

COMPETITION AND STATUS

Testosterone binds to androgen receptors that are scattered throughout the body and brain (its other main function being to develop the 'maleness' of a human body). Levels of testosterone are seven to eight times higher in males than in females, and higher consumption within the male body means that production can be twenty times higher than in females, thus fitting the evolved behaviour that we described earlier in the chapter—on average, males are greater status-seekers than females. Some, of course, would say that even a casual acquaintance with human behaviour would support this!

Human males produce testosterone when they come across a status challenge.[83] This could occur, for example, in an adolescent who is fairly low-status in the general scheme of things but intuitively perceives that there is a high payoff to achieving as much status as possible whilst still in the prime of reproductive age. This status-seeking behaviour is further exacerbated by the fact that the part of the brain responsible for understanding and responding to complex social norms—the pre-frontal cortex—is not fully developed until the end of adolescence, say, around the age of twenty-five.[84] In other words, such adolescents have the drive, but not necessarily the subtle skills, required to achieve high status—which may well be why young males trying to climb the ladder resort more often than other demographics to aggression, rather than Machiavellian manipulation—their brains are less capable of doing otherwise.

Of course, testosterone is also produced in high-status males, again particularly when they are facing a status challenge: levels of the hormone are highest when dominance hierarchies first form, or when they are undergoing a reorganisation.[85] Fascinatingly, testosterone also increases during sports competitions, which are, at their simplest, a status and dominance challenge. Levels even rise when people are watching sport and their own teams win, telling us that testosterone is related to the psychology, rather than the physicality, of dominance and aggression.[86]

Findings like this also tell us something about the overall relationship between testosterone and status. Testosterone causes individuals to seek status in response to a challenge, but levels also rise and remain high for some time after it has been won; if the challenge is lost, then levels diminish. This is true both in real contests, and in ones where lab participants were told to imagine winning a game of chess, for example.[87] Amazingly, in rats and mangrove rivulus fish, winning not only affects levels of testosterone, but also increases the expression of genes that create androgen receptors in the brain—so winning makes you more receptive to the status-seeking effects of testosterone.[88]

This, of course, is a positive feedback loop (up to a limit). A status challenge will cause you to release more testosterone, motivating you to use status-seeking behaviour; should you then win that challenge, you will produce more testosterone; which then motivates you to seek more status; and so on. This is what hubris is: testosterone increases confidence and optimism, and reduces fear and anxiety; it makes you less able to identify emotions; it boosts impulsivity; in short, it makes you cocky.[89] And finally, the link back to our evolutionary motivations: when we win it feels good; and when we achieve high status it feels good—because, on average, higher status results in greater reproductive fitness.[90]

Finally, status-seeking is a heuristic. It is a rule of thumb. Consider the earlier evidence about status challenges as the main cause leading to homicide: few people plan to kill others, it just happens. But this is also what happens when the (male[91]) leaders of two groups get together. Both have won the dominance challenge within their own groups. Both therefore have above-average levels of testosterone, making them arrogant, and less likely to be able to read other people. And both, when interacting with one another, are much more likely to enter into a further status confrontation, as a result of those higher levels of status-seeking.

In reality, the classic security dilemma is, at its heart, a dominance trap between two leaders driven to seek status.[92] This simple dynamic echoes across intraspecific competition in animals, through homicide committed by individual humans, and up to the leaders of a multi-national war coalitions.

5

ESCAPING VIOLENCE THROUGH BELONGING

'People need to feel they belong. To a nation, to a race. Otherwise, who knows what might happen?'

Kazuo Ishiguro[1]

The evolution of status-seeking presented in the previous chapter paints a picture of human interaction plagued by insecurity, one where everyone is constantly jockeying towards the top, and willing to use violence to get there. As we saw earlier, sustained competition, on average, reduces the reproductive fitness of the individual competitors. This means that individual competition creates a selection pressure for some sort of solution to the problem of random violence between individuals over resources, especially status.

Other species also face the problem of competition: they have evolved very clever solutions like marking out territories, adjusting reproduction rates to lower population densities, and mobility over long distances. Humans use some of these, too. But by far the most efficacious individual violence reduction mechanism that has evolved in humans is our ability to build cohesive social groups. These, by definition, have much lower levels of internal, intraspecific violence than would otherwise be present among the same number of individuals.

This chapter will explain how the selection pressure to escape violence—and other selection pressures—created the human desire, and motivation, to belong to groups. Like status-seeking, a desire for belonging motivates certain behaviours that, on average over evolutionary time, have paid off with increased fitness. All humans alive today are descendants of others who were able to survive and reproduce because they belonged to cohesive social groups. As we will see, the bigger the group, the greater these benefits are. For that reason, both the in-group itself and an individual's membership therein must be protected at all costs. Membership of a cohesive in-group is an essential proxy for a continued reproductive life, in much the same way that higher status is a proxy for an increased ability to attract mates. Groups keep us safe, help us use resources more efficiently, and surround us with potential mates—pretty much an evolutionary slam dunk. Let's focus further on each of these benefits.

The advantages of group membership

First, sexual partners. In evolutionary terms, most individuals are looking for the highest number of the best quality mates that they can find. Humans' attraction to others (and hence desire to mate with them) is informed by whether their combination of genes is likely to produce successful offspring in their current environment.[2] As with almost all gene expression, there is not a straight line of causation that runs from genes to mate attraction and selection: there are large environmental and cultural shaping effects. However, in the most basic terms, what is happening genetically is that human males seek as many fertile females as possible (quality is not irrelevant, but it is less important than quantity), whereas females look for high-status males who will be able to provide resources and protection for their offspring (quality more important than quantity).[3]

Staying with genes, attraction signals two things to humans. Firstly, in genetic terms, attractive mates are those who have better-quality genes that contribute more to reproductive fitness. To give some examples, men who are taller, on average, are rated as more attractive by women.[4] On average, taller men are also more dominant in human societies, gain greater access to resources, and have an advantage in conflict. The same is true for strength. On the other hand, research has shown that the female waist-to-hip ratio that men found most attractive was linked to reproductive health, the preferred ratio being 0.7 (with the waist smaller than the hips).[5] Symmetrical faces, for both sexes, are considered an honest signal of a trouble-free developmental period, and so a sign that the offspring are more likely to survive to reproduce themselves.[6]

But there is more to it than general qualities. Attraction, particularly non-visual attraction mediated by pheromones, signals genetic appropriateness of mates, flagging potential sexual partners whose genes, in combination with one's own, would produce offspring more likely to survive in the environment. To illustrate with a fascinating example: humans living in environments with a broad spectrum of disease threat find more attractive potential sexual partners with an ability to defend against diseases and parasites that they themselves cannot fight off. This is because the resulting offspring would have a broader spectrum of disease resistance. Conversely, in environments with a narrow spectrum of disease threat, humans tend to be attracted to potential sexual partners who are able to resist a similar range of parasites. Very elegantly, this is mediated by smell: humans find potential mates attractive or not based on (subconsciously) smelling their resistance to certain diseases.[7]

What this demonstrates is that there is a genetic element to attraction. Therefore, the more sexual partners one has the choice of, the better it is in evolutionary terms, and humans want to mate with the 'best' possible potential partner. This simple rule multiplied twice creates the human marriage market: the job of finding the best possible mate, who also thinks that you are the best possible mate for them.[8] These processes are easier in groups, and much easier in bigger groups. It's a simple numbers game: the bigger the group, the greater the choice of mates, and so the greater the chance of finding a partner whose genetic makeup compliments your own. As anyone who has moved from a small village to a big city knows, a bigger pool will afford better—and more fun—opportunities to date.

Second, there are other resource benefits to living in groups. This is slightly counter-intuitive, because group living implies that individuals live in a higher density than otherwise, which should lead to increased competition. However, living in groups allows access to resources that would otherwise not be possible. In the human prehistoric environment, the most obvious example is the protein that was available from cooperative hunting.[9] This effect has also been demonstrated in other animals like dolphins, who hunt fish by jointly herding them to the surface much as dogs herd sheep (the main difference, of course, being that humans are not directing the dolphins' activity).[10]

The effect of a larger group is dramatic: one study estimated that when a population of hunter-gatherers doubles in density, each individual in the group becomes 15 per cent more efficient in their resource use. In other words, doubling the size of the group means that every individual receives the same amount of resources for the same amount of effort, plus 15 per cent extra.[11] At a slightly larger scale—say, a small village—the blacksmith and the farmer trade the outputs of their labour and both benefit from increased resources. This dynamic continues until we get to mega-cities of millions. What's more, group living does not just enable exchange of objects; it also enables the sharing of good ideas—it facilitates our 'collective brain'.[12] The impact that this has on technology is astounding: one brain on its own is able to produce an excellent flint hand axe. A million brains, working together, are able to produce smartphones. The hand axe changed little in design in hundreds of thousands of years, whereas new smartphones, with hundreds of new features, come out every year.

The process by which this comes about is specialisation, which is enabled by groups and more so by bigger groups. Compare a sole trader, who carries out all business functions themselves, to a modern corporation, with multiple, specialised functions. But the dynamic of specialisation increasing efficiency is not only present in modern economies. Probably the first specialisation—that between pre-human male and female roles—facilitated greater resource accrual, which resulted in more surviving offspring. The greater the possibilities for specialisation, the greater the efficiency with which humans can accrue, produce and distribute resources. If the example of a smartphone increasing evolutionary fitness is too tenuous, think about how complex the first bow and arrow must have seemed, and what an effect that weaponry had on human ability to hunt.

Finally, we turn to the relative security of group living. This is probably the single greatest evolutionary benefit of groups—there is safety in numbers. There are two aspects to it: there is the direct benefit of being able to defend against predators who have a taste for human meat, like bears, or several species of big cat; but, importantly, groups also protect against other human groups trying to steal or dominate resources, whether mates or watering holes.[13] Simply, grouping together with other humans is the best way of staying alive. Once bigger groups began to establish themselves, the lower internal levels of violence therein were another evolutionary advantage to members. Forming groups that were mostly peaceful internally meant that their human members were protected from both external and internal violence. We will look into how groups lower both internal and external violence in Chapter 6.

These three aspects of life—sexual partners, resources and security—have a direct impact on the individual humans whose evolutionary aim is to survive long enough to have children, and resource them well enough that they survive. These strong and obvious benefits to group living led to the evolution of a mechanism, a groupishness module.[14] Those human ancestors who developed this instinct—expressed as the sense of belonging most of us feel towards family, community, country or political system[15]—survived to reproduce more. Firstly, it simply creates a motivation in humans to live in groups. Secondly, it motivates humans to behave in ways that help us to do so.

The benefits of group living to individuals are so great that groups, without exception, develop a membership price; otherwise everyone would join, and destabilise the group. These could be things like tribal marks, dialects, or particular

ESCAPING VIOLENCE THROUGH BELONGING

diets.[16] This price also helps define who is in the group and who is not, and thus who benefits from the group's bounty. The price(s) having been established, the evolutionary benefits of groupishness lead humans to develop a selection pressure for the traits required for successful group membership. A lack of these traits could, say, result in ostracism from the group, or at the very least a reduction in your mating prospects within the group.[17] Those individuals who were drawn to other members of their species, and able to cooperate with them in groups, gained the greatest selective benefit, primarily from the collective security on offer.

Where does fighting come into this? I argue that followers fight in wars in order to maintain the greatest surrogate resource of all: continued membership of their own groups. We fight because losing membership of our in-group— whether because it is disintegrating, or because we're being shunned for not fighting—is evolutionary suicide. We fight to belong to our groups, because group living means living with a lower rate of violence than not living in groups.

Those who fight in wars, or are motivated to fight in wars, are following the statistics of evolutionary averages: ancestors were more likely to die through losing group membership as a result of failing to participate as followers in war than through risking themselves in combat. In evolutionarily terms, then, fighting for group membership is how we escape the greater violence of being outside a group. This does not mean that when people go to war in modern service-based economies they are hoping to avoid being ostracised. It means that the brain has evolved to motivate fighting when others in the group are fighting, so as to maintain group membership. This still drives humans, even though fighting in a large-scale war (except when your family are at risk of

89

death), no longer makes evolutionary sense: in the modern context, group membership is fluid and belonging less vital to individual survival, but that is still how we are motivated. These evolutionary averages mean that groupishness is a human universal, like falling in love. This means that you, the reader, will recognise the standard, innate human behaviours in the evidence supporting the existence of groupishness— outlined below.

The neurological basis for groupishness

Evolution tinkers with already existing biological systems,[18] and so it is with the groupishness module: it evolved through the development of the biological system that motivates a strong pair bond between parents (particularly mothers) and offspring. Pair bonding originally evolved to solve the problem of infant helplessness.[19] This means that those parents and children who remained together so that the child was able to develop successfully into an adult were likely to have more grandchildren and great-grandchildren.[20] As we saw in Chapter 3, this bond between parents and children, particularly in the period around birth, is regulated by the hormone oxytocin.

Originally, it was thought that oxytocin only motivated uterine contraction and milk production around the birth of a child.[21] It was later discovered that there were oxytocin receptors all over the brain, which means that it has an effect modulating and motivating all sorts of behaviour.[22] Oxytocin is a peptide hormone, meaning that it is made of amino acids and is a protein, and is thus transcribed from the genetic code in the normal way (testosterone, by contrast, is a steroid hormone: a chemical rather than a protein). It is produced by the hypothalamus in the brain (whereas testosterone production is controlled by the hypothalamus but produced elsewhere). Oxytocin release motivates physiological changes in the body that are interpreted by our conscious brains as feelings of attachment and love by parents towards new offspring; this facilitates nursing and care.[23] Any new parent will recognise the power of this feeling—remember, feelings and emotions have only evolved to motivate humans to behave in certain ways that proved evolutionarily profitable for their ancestors.

Somewhere along this evolutionary journey, humans (and pre-humans) have co-opted the oxytocin mechanisms that enable this parental bond, to help us build larger and larger groups.[24] We now know that the same mechanism binds us to our closest kin and facilitates families, nations and religions. As groups have continued to grow in size, all the way up to mega-groups of nation states and transnational military alliances, the human groupishness module has become triggered by what anthropologists call our imagined kin: those that are part of our group by dint of interacting with us through social emotions, or because we believe in the same god, or because we come from the same nation state.[25] So how does it work?

Before a child's birth, the existence of romantic love between humans (as opposed to infatuation, or sexual love) correlates with higher levels of oxytocin, and the resulting behavioural patterns include attachment, proximity-seeking (the desire to cuddle) and caregiving.[26] This continues and deepens with the birth of the child, when oxytocin promotes caregiving and other parental behaviour (including lactation in mothers), as well proximity-seeking between both parent and child.[27] Cuddling is important because it helps us understand the two-way positive feedback loops characteristic of oxytocin's functioning: the mother's levels of the hormone are increased by visual and tactile cues given by the infant. The increased oxytocin in the mother then promotes pro-infant behaviour, which in turn increases oxytocin levels in the child.[28]

Not only with mother and child, but also more generally among humans, oxytocin behaviour is reciprocal: if you are treated in a trusting way, your level of oxytocin will rise, which will motivate you to be more trusting towards the other person.[29] You will accept a higher level of risk from social interactions—that is, you will be less worried about people cheating or hurting you.[30] This trust has been shown to remain even when it has been breached several times.[31] Oxytocin increases generosity towards people with whom we identify (as being in our group).[32] It also causes people to conform to group norms, rules, regulations and opinions— in other words, it increases socialisation and groupthink.[33] It even affects in-group hierarchies by reducing in-group aggression from leaders, even whilst they continue to maintain out-group aggression.[34] These processes, guided and facilitated by oxytocin release, are what help groups to form.

Oxytocin interacts with other hormones, three of which I will detail here. It increases dopamine and serotonin— reward hormones that make humans feel pleasure. They, alongside oxytocin, cause the shivers down your spine that one sometimes gets at religious ceremonies, football matches, or when playing in an orchestra—that is, when one is participating in group-bonding activities. Both are linked to many human motivational systems and have evolved to encourage humans toward actions that increase reproductive fitness— in this case, making belonging to groups feel good.[35]

Oxytocin also reduces testosterone levels.[36] So, increases in oxytocin motivate lower levels of status-seeking and, potentially, the violence that goes with it. In fact, these two hormones work against each other in our social cognition: testosterone motivates more selfish, and oxytocin more pro-social, behaviour.[37] With the rise in bonding, there is a decrease in status competition—the major cause of interpersonal violence, as we know. This is an extremely important piece of information that we will return to in Chapter 6, when we look more closely at how human groups drive down levels of internal violence.

The oxytocin 'footprint' is found everywhere. People have greater affinity with their own cultural markers—flags, languages, food taboos, or even shared ideology—when they have been given oxytocin.[38] Regularly practising religious people, for instance, have been shown to have greater levels of oxytocin,[39] as do choral singers.[40] It increases performance in team sports, where higher levels of trust and empathy are vital.[41] Oxytocin is also reflected in our highly kinship-orientated group language: we speak of priests as 'fathers', elders as 'uncles' and 'aunties', comrades as brothers-in-arms, study groups as sororities, and political organisations as brotherhoods; fellow gang members or even young friends call each other 'bro'. These are the social groups for which humans fight and die, as if they were close kin.

However, for every in-group that oxytocin facilitates, there must be a corresponding out-group.[42] To understand why, think back to the circumstances in which the groupishness module evolved from the mother-child bonding mechanism. In this case, discrimination between 'own offspring' or 'not' was vital for the mother to know which child to care for and resource. As evolution tinkered and the scope of the bonding mechanism grew, it maintained the group boundaries between Us and Them. Why did the distinction remain?

Let us imagine a scenario where this were not the case. That would mean that every member of the species would be approached with trust, affinity and proximity-seeking behaviour. It would then be very easy for a selfish individual to evolve who took advantage of all of the trusting group members, such that the trusting genotype would decrease or be removed from the population. But if the in-group/out-group, Us/Them boundary is bound up with the trust mechanism, it is possible to create small groups of trusting individuals, from which those who abuse that trust can be removed.

So, oxytocin differentiates between the in-group and the out-group. It does this by triggering different pathways in the brain when relating to outsiders versus insiders: the fear response for the former (enabling aggressive responses to external threat), and empathy and love for the latter.

In some experiments, participants were sorted into groups by dint of an arbitrary marker, such as whether or not they liked a particular painter. Some groups were given oxytocin, and then their behaviour was tested in a number of ways. Whilst oxytocin promoted increased trust in the in-group, it also increased defensive behaviour towards the out-group.[43] Oxytocin has even been shown to increase dishonesty when it benefits the in-group at the expense of the out-group.[44]

In other words, oxytocin heightens social categorisation: depending on whether the other person is a member of the 'in-group' or the 'out-group', oxytocin motivated different behavioural outcomes towards each.[45] And a higher degree of in-group commitment always correlates with a higher degree of out-group non-commitment: it is a zero sum game.[46] In the words of a prominent scholar in the oxytocin field, the hormone is a 'modulator of parochialism'.[47]

This Us/Them distinction, facilitated and motivated by oxytocin, has wide-ranging effects. For example, it results in information asymmetries between the in-group and the out-group.[48] This happens because people empathise and bond with their in-group. Paying more attention to them gives you more information about them. This occurs whilst you are less able to read the emotional cues of the out-group, pay less attention to them, and know less about them. This leads to group-level ethnocentrism, nationalism and racism—of course, there are many other hormones and cognitive processes involved in these behaviours, not to mention environmental factors, but the fundamental in-group and out-group differentiation originates in the oxytocin mechanism.[49]

The parochialism motivated by oxytocin is triggered by social information—that is, clues as to who is in the in-group and who is in the out-group.[50] These are cultural markers like dialects, tattoos, habits or proscriptions, beliefs in spirits, and even ideologies. They enable us to identify our social groups—those who stand to benefit from membership—as well as identifying everybody else as 'other'. As the evolutionary co-option of the parental bonding mechanism has proceeded, the markers that trigger the oxytocin pathway have changed. At first, it was the ability to recognise one's child, from smell, proximity, similar facial features, and so on. As groups have grown in size, this same pathway has evolved to be triggered by things like flags, anthems and gods.

In the evolutionary security environment, maintaining cohesion of our own groups was as important as disrupting the cohesion of enemy groups. These social markers play an important cohesive role, which is why we consider attacks on our social markers as attacks on our social groups—our imagined kin—to which we respond (both neurologically and behaviourally) as if our kin were being attacked.[51] This is why people become emotive when their religions are attacked, or their flags disrespected. Those ancestors who successfully defended their group cohesion and preserved their cultural markers survived to reproduce another day.

So far, the dynamics motivated by oxytocin will seem horribly familiar. The in-group/out-group dynamic is so basically human—arranging humans into groups of Us and Them—that it is immediately and intuitively recognisable. The groupishness brain module and the oxytocin motivational system provide the mechanism. And it is this simple mechanism, the ability to form groups of imagined kin, that provides the basis for human society and civilisation.[52] But how exactly does oxytocin regulate the responses towards in-groups and out-groups? The mechanism is precise: when confronted with the appropriate in-group stimuli, in-group 'positive' processes—empathy, trust—occur. On the other hand, when confronted with threatening outsiders, oxytocin motivates increased in-group vigilance and cooperation, and actions defensive of the in-group: it 'tightens', as a protective response to the out-group threat.[53]

Oxytocin and increased in-group bonding can also motivate pre-emptive attacks on an out-group. Importantly, the causal pathway is one where offensives against outsiders are motivated not by hatred of the out-group, but rather by the need to defend the cohesiveness of the in-group and the individual need to preserve membership of it.[54] In evolutionary terms, attacking out-groups is motivated by preserving the proxy fitness benefit of group membership, which gives access to security, more or better sexual partners, and greater resources. Of course, hatred of the out-group comes with defence of the evolutionarily important in-group; it is impossible to separate the two, due to the way that the groupishness module and the oxytocin system have evolved.[55]

Finally, it is worth pointing out that there is a wide diversity in the genetics behind the oxytocin system. This means that some people have a stronger genetic basis for being more strongly motivated to belong; meaning that, aside from any environmental factors, they feel a stronger sense of belonging.[56] There is a key underlying gene that transcribes into the oxytocin receptor—the OXTR gene—within which a number of variants have been recognised.[57] These variants lead to differences in the degree to which people trust others.[58] It has also been found that those with particular variants of the gene show an in-group racial bias;[59] this is but one study, but if replicated, it could demonstrate that certain people have a greater genetic predisposition towards racism. There are also variants of the gene that have been linked to autism, which, although a complex condition, could be considered a form of extreme asociality.[60] Other variants have also been linked to more aggressive asocial behaviour, such as getting into fights, hurting others or being angry.[61]

Again, this is not to say that if you possess this gene variant then you will definitely be more aggressive (for example) in your views of other groups. Rather, on average, holders of this gene variant are more likely to be more aggressive—but that also depends upon a huge variety of other factors like childhood environment, as well as interactions with other genetic predispositions. Human behaviour is exceedingly complex. That said, variations like these in the OXTR gene could exist because of an evolutionary stable ratio. In a large population, variations in a social trait often persist because the evolutionary advantages or otherwise of a particular type of behaviour—such as not feeling attached to groups—will fluctuate depending on the proportions of its other variants in the population—such as feeling a strong sense of belonging. For one behavioural leaning to have evolutionary success, we need other individuals in the population to display an opposite or different leaning. The truth is, we don't really know why the variants exist.

The question remains as to whether this is all still true today. Does a sense of belonging really drive people to fight in modern armies? It appears so: as I was writing *Why We Fight* in 2017, the British Army released a recruitment campaign called 'This is Belonging'.[62] The advertising campaign focused on a series of mundane military experiences, like patrolling, or standing guard, or cooking food. But each was painted as an occasion to bond with comrades, and work together in a home-like environment. This emphasis on solidarity and friendship transformed these boring and physically uncomfortable activities into positive reasons to join up. The Chief Creative Officer at Karmarama, the agency responsible for the campaign, said, 'We decided to highlight real and authentic army contexts and moments that clearly show the importance of being part of a strong and selfless family'.[63] The use—one assumes unconscious—of the word 'family' in the context of recruiting for a national army, is fascinating: both activities are underpinned by the oxytocin mechanism.

In summary, the surrogate resource of group membership offers fantastic evolutionary advantages to individuals. If they are members of groups, they can choose from a greater variety of sexual partners, they enjoy more efficient uses of resources and, most importantly, they enjoy a security from which they wouldn't otherwise benefit. Because of these advantages, humans have evolved a groupishness module in their brains that motivates a desire to belong to social groups.

This motivation is regulated by the oxytocin mechanism, which, in turn, has been adapted by evolution from the original mother-child bonding mechanism. Oxytocin motivates us to group together in order to avoid the intraspecific competition trap.

However, by necessity, the oxytocin mechanism creates boundaries between in-groups and out-groups. It has to be this way because a mechanism universally trusting of all conspecifics (individual animals of the same species) would be evolutionarily outcompeted by others taking advantage of it. Thus, implicit in this mechanism that identifies in-groups to be trusted is a degree (sometimes more than that) of out-group hatred: such hatred, and resulting violence, is a logical consequence of humans seeking to belong to groups in order to escape interpersonal violence. In the next chapter, we will look at how these groups grow in size, and the problems that they must overcome to do so.

6

THE GROWTH OF HUMAN GROUPS

'There are not more than five musical notes, yet the combinations of these five give rise to more melodies than can ever be heard.

There are not more than five primary colours, yet in combination they produce more hues than can ever been seen.

There are not more than five cardinal tastes, yet combinations of them yield more flavours than can ever be tasted.'

Sun Tzu[1]

This chapter will explain how the evolution of the groupishness mechanism has resulted in bigger and bigger human groups over time. It will explain the dynamics of these groups, especially when they are at war with each other. It will also look at the relationship between groups and violence through the paradox outlined in the previous chapters: that we seek to belong to groups (mostly) because of the internal and external security advantages inherent to group living. This desire to belong causes us to fight in conflicts with other groups, because we seek to maintain our group membership even at a cost: on average, to lose membership of a group results in an almost assured death sentence (and hence fitness reduction), whereas fighting in wars carries a lower percentage risk of death.

What are groups?

Animals group for a number of reasons, and the 'grouping' trait has evolved a number of times in different parts of the evolutionary tree. There are spectacular examples of group living in insects, for instance. Different species of ants form into super-colonies of billions—although they group because of a peculiar system of genetic inheritance which means that worker ants share 75 per cent of their inheritance with their siblings, as opposed to the 50 per cent in most species, thus massively increasing kin-based cooperation. Most animals group (or flock, or herd) for reasons of security from predation,[2] to make it easier to find appropriate mates,[3] or for species-typical reasons like increased aerodynamics in bird flocks.[4]

In the pre-human lineage, group living in the mammals initially emerged approximately 200 million years ago, stemming from the enhanced care for offspring that mammary glands represent.[5] Primates, and particularly the great apes like the chimpanzees and the bonobos, then developed more complex groups with a greater degree of interaction between non-kin individuals. Humans live in such complex socially interconnected groups of non-kin, with repeated and remembered interactions between the individuals in those groups.[6]

What makes human groups interesting, and different to those of other animals, are the cognitive mechanisms in individuals that enable them to: a) understand that others have different points of view ('theory of mind'); b) remember details of interactions with others and use them to shape future interactions ('memory'); and c) think in three, four or five social dimensions ('recursive mind': that is, Jon thinks that Mary is annoyed, and so Jon will ask Jane to talk to Mary). These cognitive abilities have evolved because of the problems of living in complex groups: essentially, if you live in a high-density social group with many conspecifics, this creates a strong social selection pressure towards being able to interact with others without resorting to violence—that is, to interact with others without falling into the trap of intraspecific competition. As we will see, this evolution towards greater sociality is still continuing: humans are evolving to become more social.[7]

In humans, the size of our groups means that we must use identity markers to recognise our own. As we have seen, these can be things like language, body painting, or wearing team colours. As everyone will recognise from their own lives, humans have multiple, overlapping and occasionally inconsistent identity markers. However, when it comes to conflict, only a very small number of these groups are relevant—there are only a small number of groups that people will fight and be prepared to die for. These are usually close family, tribe, ethnic group, or country, although political parties or movements are a recent addition (in evolutionary terms).[8]

Violence, or the threat of it, very quickly awakens our pre-existing primary group identity, which is latent on a day-to-day basis.[9] This is due to the main function of human social groups: to protect us. When we come under threat, our identities 'activate' and we look for others with similar identities for security. Henceforth, when I use the term group, I mean fighting group; that is, a group an individual would be willing to die for—this is what is evolutionarily most salient.

How do groups grow in size?

The last chapter outlined the benefits to humans of living in groups: increased protection from other humans, greater choice of sexual partners, and a more efficient use of resources. A quick glance at extant rates of urbanisation will show that two of these advantages are still present in 2017—generally, urban environments provide greater access to economic resources, and a greater, more diverse selection of mating choices.[10] What is more, higher-density, larger groups support these dynamics better than smaller, more dispersed groups.

That said, these pressures towards ever-larger group size are partly balanced by opposing forces that increase fragmentation and cause group break-up.[11] These forces of fragmentation stem from high densities of individuals living together without having solved five basic problems—of which more later. Humans, because of their cognitive complexity (which allows for things like language, social emotions, and religion), are better able to minimise these problems than most animals, who do nevertheless benefit (to a lesser degree) from grouping. This allows humans more easily to build, and reap the benefits of, larger and larger social groups. And, as we have seen, there has been a long-term selection pressure for better group players because, summed over evolutionary time, these more sociable individuals are more capable at taking advantage of group benefits.[12]

The entire process of increasing human group size is driven by an external factor: population growth.[13] This increases the density of humans in a given area, which means that people come into contact with each other more often. And, as populations grow, people tend to agglomerate in groups for security reasons, rather than spreading themselves evenly.[14] Even if we discount the ecological influences on grouping behaviours, it makes evolutionary sense—in a fight, two people are better than one, and five people are better than two. Imagine it as an arms race: once initial groups had formed, competition between them, and the perceived threat from other groups, meant that bigger groups were more likely to survive. Bigger groups were better able to defeat smaller ones in conflict (all other things being equal), and this meant that average group size systematically increased. So violence, or the threat of violence, drove ever-bigger group formation, all the way up to groups of millions of humans.

Let us look at a mythical 'war' between two individual people. Of course, this is the same as the intraspecific competition and human homicide that we described in Chapter 4. In this case there are no followers, just two 'leaders'. Individuals partaking in this scale of 'warfare' are taking the risk because they intuit that winning will increase their status. At the slightly larger scale of a small kin group, genetic relatedness comes into play: your relatives share many of your genes, and so from an evolutionary point of view you should be willing to risk your life to enable them to survive and reproduce. You share 50% of your genes with your parents or siblings, 25% with grandparents or aunts/uncles, and 12.5% with your cousins—so, in theory, sacrificing your life in combat (ending your reproductive chances) in order to enable eight cousins to survive and reproduce would be a fair trade.

This is called inclusive fitness—it is not only your genes that you are fighting for, but the copies of the same genes carried by your relatives.[15] At least in early life, almost all individual animals cooperate with their close family, to the point of sacrificing their own lives, because closely related kin are more likely to share genes. As reproduction continues, this creates ever-expanding circles of kinship, with ever-decreasing degrees of relatedness between individuals. This idea leads to the apocryphal biologists' quip that one should die for two brothers, or eight cousins, and is reflected in a saying common in patriarchal tribal societies: 'I against my brothers, my brothers and I against my cousins, my cousins and I against our tribe, my tribe against the world'. It is also why, in wills, people tend to favour closer relatives with greater bequests.[16]

Now, imagine a slightly bigger group—perhaps a small band of early humans, competing with another over a source of water. This band has three options. Firstly, they could fight the other group for the resources, defeat them, and incorporate their women into the group. More difficult would be to cooperate with the other band over sharing of the resource. This would usually entail the swapping of women between the bands, in order to bond them together. Should that continue for a couple of generations, the bands may begin to merge, particularly if the dynamic is reinforced with other resource-swapping or basic trade. The final option would entail an alliance with a third band of humans, in order to defeat the one with which they are in competition—that is, an agglomeration for defence.

In all three cases, security concerns (or realities) cause people to live in ever-larger groups, because larger groups are better able to win in conflict. This dynamic applies from the smallest groups of humans to the largest—it is most often the reason why states form alliances with each other. For example, the Warsaw Pact was formed in 1955, partly in response to the formation of NATO six years earlier. In the short term, violence often creates more violence, but over the (very) long term, violence, or the threat of it, instead creates larger and larger groups.[17]

This is good news because, as we will see later on, all other things being equal, bigger groups have lower rates of both internal violence and intergroup conflict: as our groups have grown in recent history, violence and war have been putting themselves out of business.[18] In other words, the overwhelming majority of people alive today primarily have human social groups to thank for their survival. Underlying this, groups only exist because of the human cognitive complexity that enables us to solve the five group problems without resorting to violence.

The problems of group living[19]

Complex group living, with individuals repeatedly interacting with each other, gives rise to group problems that are inherent to high population densities. Every individual is faced with a balance: they have to avoid the negatives of group living while benefitting as much as possible from the positives.[20] This requires them to solve the five problems inherent in group living. Although they manifest themselves in different ways, it is always these same five challenges that threaten internal cohesion. They emerge once a group has formed, and then humans invent or evolve solutions. This allows groups to grow in size, at which point the same problems re-emerge, and so on. This is equally true of a band of hunter-gatherers and of the current era, when many are trying to construct a global polity.

Failing to solve these problems will lead to the group splintering into smaller groups, ones that are able to do so: in the prehistoric and historic environment, it most probably would have led to violence as well. The key point about these problems is that, in solving them, we establish norms within groups, which a strong majority of people must observe. If there is disagreement on how to approach the issues to the extent that individual members cannot accept others' solutions, then the groups will splinter. The five questions posing this threat are:

- Identity: who is in the group, and who enjoys the benefits of group membership;
- Hierarchy: how it works, and who is in charge;
- Trade: what constitutes fair trade between individuals in the group;
- Disease: the rules to be applied in order to minimise disease stemming from higher densities;
- Punishment: whom the group is allowed to punish, and how much, if they break the rules.

Again, what is important is not that everyone follows all the group's solutions to these problems all the time. What is important for group cohesion is that enough people agree on the solutions, and abide by them enough of the time. As we have seen, humans began to evolve biological solutions to these problems before they began to talk about, and agree on, solutions: the groupishness module helps solve the identity problem, while the social emotions help with others like hierarchy (pride), trade (anger), disease (disgust), and punishment (vengeance).[21]

Further into this book, we will discuss how humans have constructed moral codes, religions and shared ideologies to solve the five group problems—but all of these constructions rest on a strong biological/genetic base. That is not to say that who is or is not in a group is genetically or biologically defined. Rather, what is determined by evolution is the concept itself of differentiating between members and non-members, and the benefits of group membership.[22] Humans then discuss and agree in a dynamic, conscious process where the group boundary lies—what is and isn't acceptable from a group's point of view is constantly changing and evolving.

The first problem of group living is that of identity: the identification of who is in the group, or not—that is, who should, versus who should not, benefit from the advantages of group living. If it isn't solved satisfactorily, then groups can split up and violence can ensue. Consider the cases of some nations that had their colonial-era borders drawn for them. There have been, and continue to be, real problems stemming from the question of what it means to be a national of one of these unlucky countries. Does this or that ethnic group 'deserve' to be part of the national polity? Although most acute in cases like these, all countries suffer from such identity challenges to a degree—the recent vote in the United Kingdom to leave the European Union was, at least in part, driven by questions of identity posed by UK citizens.[23] Are we European? Are we British? What does it mean to be British? So far, however, these questions have not yet led to major violence in the UK.

The costs of membership—membership fees—that prevent all individuals in the environment from joining the group are usually things that cannot easily be faked, or are costly to signal. Tribal markings, mother dialects, food taboos, religious rituals, and social security numbers are all ways of solving the identity problem. Particularly in intergroup conflict, these markers can become what are known as sacred values: things so inextricably linked with the group's identity that they cannot be separated from the group.[24] Examples might include the right of return for Palestinians, recognition of the State of Israel for Israelis, a democratic system of government for twenty-first century European countries, and recognition as a geo-strategic player for

Russia. Critically, sacred values cannot be traded for material gain in order to facilitate peace: apologies, statements and recognition of the other side's values and identities are held to be the only way to achieve peace between two groups each opposed to the other's sacred values.[25]

So, whilst having a defined identity is absolutely essential for a group's coherence, it will naturally clash with that of another group, because of the dynamic between leaders and followers. Leaders espouse their own group's identities in order to enhance the belonging that their followers feel (thereby creating/maintaining the groups that leaders lead, and thus satisfying leaders' demands for status). Followers are attracted to this rhetoric because they seek to belong, but, because of the nature of the oxytocin mechanism's evolution, there cannot be in-group love without out-group hatred.

The second problem is that of hierarchy. Who leads the group? In complex human groups, what is the (majority-) agreed hierarchy that controls the group? In essence, getting agreement on the hierarchy is partly aimed at solving the violence and other problems caused by status-seeking. An agreed hierarchy also enables resources to be spread vertically in the group—those higher in the hierarchy will tend to receive more than their equal share of resources. Exactly how much more is acceptable to those at the bottom is the question to be solved. By 'acceptable', I mean sufficiently accepted so that those at the bottom of the hierarchy are not willing to use violence to subvert it.

History repeatedly tells us that hierarchies tend to be subverted and overthrown when those at the top are taking too many resources, or are perceived to be taking too much of an unequal share of resources: revolutions more often than not stem from inequality.[26] The French and American revolutions were both caused by high levels of dissatisfaction with the hierarchy. But this dynamic does not only occur at macro scales: homicide rates have been shown to be higher in cities where there is a greater level of income inequality.[27]

The third problem is that of trade; specifically, what constitutes fair terms of exchange between individuals. This is independent of hierarchy, and extends beyond mercantile transactions to acts like sharing: if I help you out today, what future help from you would be sufficient for us both to consider that I have been repaid? This has applications in all realms of society, from rules about monogamy and adultery (marriage as a contract) to those governing reciprocity and gift-giving among kin. Mechanisms to address this question are similarly ubiquitous in our societies—from actions like looking people in the eye and shaking their hand to 'seal a deal', to complex legal frameworks that protect commercial contracts. As we saw in Chapter 4, problems over deals gone wrong, or adultery, are the second commonest cause of homicides after status disputes. Solving this problem adequately also underpins altruism in society.

The fourth problem is that of disease. Once animals live in groups, it is much easier for disease to become prevalent, because of the much higher density of genetically-similar individuals (susceptible to the same diseases). The disgust mechanism that reacts to people with lesions on their faces is an example of a solution to this problem, as are manners, food preparation rituals and vaccinations.

The last problem is one of collective enforcement or punishment. In solving the other four group problems, a series of rules or norms will be established that, if everyone in the group follows them, allow the group to function properly. Inevitably there will be transgressors of group norms, as some individuals will deem this more beneficial than their observation. How, then, do we separate those group members upon whom we can inflict violence to ensure rule compliance from those whom it would be inappropriate to punish? How societies treat mentally ill murderers, or what degree of violence we allow in our schools in order to enforce discipline, are examples of agreed group norms that address this problem.

This is an important point: it is not that groups are completely non-violent internally. Rather, violence not sanctioned by the group is kept at a low level or is absent. There may still be plenty of group-mandated violence, but this will be expressed in a way that obeys the group's rules on what constitutes acceptable violence. Modern societies have very clear rules on this: consider how children and criminals are treated (putting someone in jail involves the use of violence, because it is done without a person's will and is forced if necessary). These rules change over time through internal discussion. Hence, the problem: if the group does not agree on who is or isn't a legitimate target of violence, it risks splintering through random fighting.

The five group problems are interlinked and balance each other. Hierarchy and the application of punishment, for instance, often go hand-in-hand. Punishment, after all, enables the persistence of hierarchies that some within the group perceive as unfair. Similarly, strategies for limiting disease and the identity of the in-group often express themselves together. And trade (fairness of resource-sharing) is often in tension with accumulations of resources in hierarchies. All of these problems are solved through discussion that results in enough people accepting solutions to the extent that they are not willing to use violence to overturn them. Often, and as will become clearer throughout this book, humans have developed mechanisms that solve several of the problems of group living at once. The first four problems, if left unchecked, will cause a loss of cohesion and violence within the group. The last, that of the correct application of punishment, is essentially a question of how to use deliberate violence to enforce solutions to the other four, which are causing disputes and violence within the group in the first place.

It is important to keep these five problems of group living in mind. Throughout the remainder of this book, when we talk about the various mechanisms and frameworks that humans have evolved or devised to manage bigger groups, we are talking about different ways of solving these five problems. Indeed, we have already covered how humans first approached solving these problems: the regulation of social interactions by the social emotions. Guilt and shame regulate trade by enforcing fairness; hierarchy is automatically sensed and regulated through anger, humour and the like; disease is kept minimal through disgust, which keeps individuals at a distance from one another; and feelings about group-mandated punishment are based on vengeance. Identity is clearly regulated by the groupishness module and the oxytocin system.

However, the social emotions only help us to regulate interpersonal relationships between a maximum of around 150 people. For human beings, 150 is the average cognitive limit to the number of people with whom one can maintain stable, meaningful and useful social relationships. In other words, an individual human can know every fellow member, and grasp the relationship between any two members, in a group of up to 150. This is known as Dunbar's number, after Robin Dunbar, a British anthropologist and evolutionary psychologist.[28] He spotted that there is a correlation between brain size and average social group size in different species of primate—Dunbar's number for chimpanzees is fifty.[29] Once discovered, the number 150 began popping up everywhere in human organisation. It is the average size of Neolithic farming villages, modern-day infantry and commercial companies, academic sub-groupings, and online social and gaming networks.

It should be stressed that this does not mean that all humans walked (or walk) around in groups of 150. Simply, in a world where security dictates that a bigger group is better, the amount of time required to maintain one-on-one social relationships (at humans' level of cognitive complexity) limits groups of this description to sizes of roughly 150 individuals. Bigger groups would have required bigger brains, but humans had already reached the largest brain size that would fit through the female birth canal, while leaving the mother a pelvis that enabled her to walk.[30] However, beyond groups of 150 there is still pressure for groups to grow in size. The security dilemma still dictates that bigger groups—all other things being equal—are more likely to win conflicts with smaller groups. Resources are still more efficiently used in bigger groups, and sexual partner choice still increases with group size. Humans have circumvented the cognitive limit to group size by consciously thinking about and building both sub-groups and internal structures common to the group as a whole.[31] These internal structures— moral codes, religions, and shared ideologies—essentially solve the five problems at progressively larger scales. This reduces levels of internal violence, thus making groups attractive places to live.

Bigger groups, less violence

There is an intimate relationship between human groups and violence. The two inversely correlate: on average over macro human history, as group size goes up, levels of both internal violence and intergroup conflict go down (in terms of violent deaths per head of population). It is important to note that I am not implying causation: you cannot necessarily point to any particular large group and argue that it should result in lower levels of violence. But, in macro terms, the well-documented decline in human violence over the course of history should be viewed in the context of the overall size of the human population, and the number of political groupings within which it has been arranged. There were many thousands of bands of hunter-gatherers in the Palaeolithic era, each of around thirty people, yet there are currently only 193 nation states in the United Nations, each composed of millions. Thus, levels of both internal and external violence have declined as average group size has increased.[32] Why?

This process is easier to explain in relation to internal violence: as humans solve the five group problems, individual members need not resort to violence in order, for example, to contest hierarchy, or settle problems arising from trade. This is exactly the argument of Thomas Hobbes' *Leviathan*: that life in history and prehistory was 'nasty, brutish, and short ... a warre of all against all', and that the state reduces violence by acting as a supreme judge of disputes between subjects.[33]

The higher number of individuals in a larger group might suggest a greater risk of violence, but it's clear that bigger groups are also more successful in managing it. Due to their greater complexity, they generally necessitate more inclusive ideas (democracy versus absolutism), require greater organisation and administrative penetration into individuals' lives (identity cards versus feudalism), and generate higher levels of technology (the Internet versus the town crier), in order to keep them cohesive—which reduces violence.[34] Many argue that the reason this cohesion was needed was in order to extract taxes, which paid for war with other states (out-groups), but the overall effect was a lowering of internal violence.

Pre-state, of course, other mechanisms like moral or tribal codes or belief in the supernatural served the same function, and allowed human groups to grow slowly. But in the latter stages of development, increases in education and commerce have given people other avenues to achieve status and wealth, thus reducing violence.[35] Education is a product of larger group sizes because of the specialisation permitted by a greater population size, freeing people up from farming, and commerce is both a cause and an outcome of larger groups.[36]

In other words, the same processes that reduce violence internally in groups also allow the groups to grow, hence the inverse correlation. Conversely, groups with too high a level of non-mandated internal violence will splinter and cease to be cohesive groups. The whole process is driven exogenously by population growth, which itself is only so great because of our ability to escape the intraspecific competition trap by living in groups.[37] Individual violence and groups are inseparably related. And as governments get really good at solving the five problems—through the application of law and administration—they can drastically reduce the homicide rate. The best evidence we have for this comes from England, where homicide statistics have been recorded for over 700 years.[38]

In 1300s England, the annual rate of violence was, on average, twenty-three homicides per 100,000 heads. A rate of 25/100,000 means that, in a life span of forty years, an individual would have a 1 per cent chance of being killed—but this is in whole population terms. As men both commit and are victims of the vast majority of homicides, a man in this society would have nearly a 2 per cent chance of getting killed. Even if we take into account underreporting in the historical record (less state control will have meant more unreported homicides), in England the annual figures probably weren't higher than thirty-five homicides per 100,000 individuals.[39] By the 1600s, the rate had reduced to roughly ten homicides per 100,000.

The modern-day annual homicide rate in England is approximately one per 100,000. This means that, in a lifespan of sixty years, a man would have roughly a 0.1 per cent chance of being killed.[40] This sharp decline is mirrored across Europe. In Italy, the Netherlands, Germany, Switzerland, and Scandinavia, annual homicide rates have declined from around 30/100,000 in c. 1300 to 1/100,000 today.[41] This means that, assuming a concurrent doubling of life expectancy, a European today is over fifteen times less likely to be killed during their life than a European in 1300, and a man is now roughly thirty times less likely to be killed than he would have been back then.

It is clear, then, that a higher level of state penetration, particularly in the realm of justice, has the effect of relieving people from the burden of constantly guarding or enhancing their status. Thus, if the state carries out retribution on an individual's behalf (particularly in eras of capital punishment), it removes the need for the individual to do the same.[42]

However, it is slightly more difficult to explain why the war casualty rate declines as group size gets bigger. To a large degree the answer is numerical. Firstly, bigger average group size has tended to mean a smaller number of groups. For example, Europe had 5,000 political units in the 1400s, 500 in the early 1600s, 200 in the early 1800s and less than thirty in 1953.[43] (It is also worth noting that the number of political units in Europe has increased considerably, to approximately fifty in 2018. It is likely that this has happened because the growth of supranational bodies like the EU and NATO have enabled small states to exist without fear of being bullied or invaded by bigger states.[44] As we have seen, the security environment drives group formation; effectively, for the purposes of security, Europe is one group.)

Secondly, there is the curious fact that groups of different sizes—villages, chiefdoms, states, and so on—tend to go to war at approximately the same rate, in terms of numbers of wars per year.[45] This is because of the 'power law' relationship that I described in Chapter 4, which states that leaders of groups fighting other groups behave in the same way irrespective of the size of the group they lead—the same dynamics of escalation, de-escalation and bluff play out at every level. This means that human groups of whatever size tend to go to war with the same frequency. With this in mind, a smaller number of bigger socio-political units going to war must result in fewer wars overall.[46]

Of course, given larger group sizes, the wars that do occur can, individually, result in many more casualties. Bigger groups are able to marshal greater numbers of combatants, and are able to bring higher levels of technology to the fight (although increased medical technology in the most developed states, which saves lives, must offset at least to some extent the increased death rate from more destructive technology). In absolute terms, then, although modern wars, fought between massive states or alliances, can be very bloody indeed—the Second World War had approximately 80 million casualties—in relative terms, bigger groups have lower levels of casualties from war. This is because, as societies get bigger, mobilisation rates decline. Warfare becomes more resource-heavy, and a greater number of people are needed to support those on the front line. This leaves the 'interiors' of the groups untouched by war.[47] Increased absolute numbers of casualties are spread over a proportionally much larger population size.[48]

These two dynamics—going to war at the same rate no matter the group size, and larger groups having relatively fewer casualties—mean that the war casualty rate has dropped in line with the general increase in human group size over the course of history. We can see this argument reflected in the statistics. A study of twenty-seven non-state societies from 1800 to today revealed an average war casualty rate of 524/100,000 per year, as observed by contemporaneous witnesses, rather than inferred from archaeological records.[49] These are small-group societies arranged into tribes, villages and bands. The maximum rate was found among the Kato tribe (from California) in the 1840s: they suffered a casualty rate of almost 1,500/100,000 per year. This amounts to 1.5 per cent of people dying in warfare every year, or 3 per cent of men, assuming it was only men that fought.[50]

By contrast, in early empire populations, such as the Aztecs and Romans, the war casualty rate is far lower: around 250/100,000 per year.[51] This further falls in more developed states of similar sizes, even when they are experiencing very bloody wars. For example, France during the revolutionary and Napoleonic wars suffered a war casualty rate of 70/100,000. Even Western Europe in the sixteenth-century Wars of Religion only experienced approximately 50/100,000 war deaths per year.[52] As for modern times, we can look at the war deaths of the United States. The US both fought many wars in the twentieth century and also is engaged in a large number of security alliances. The combined population of the NATO member countries, for example, is approaching 1 billion. Some caution is in order here, as the US benefits from fighting its wars on other continental land masses, and its armed forces benefit from highly advanced medical care that hugely reduces the death rate from combat. Even so, the US experienced a war casualty rate of 3.7/100,000 per year during the twentieth century.[53] If we take 2007, the bloodiest year for the US during the 'War on Terror', the rate was 0.34 war deaths per 100,000 in the population.[54] Europe has even lower rates.

Thus, zooming out and viewing the process at the most macro of scales, we can see that war between groups causes groups to grow in size for their own security, and that this growth in group size reduces casualties from war. Effectively, the process of warfare, viewed over a long-term scale, is putting itself out of business.[55] We should recall here the relationship between testosterone and oxytocin, which mirrors the relationship between violence and group size: testosterone motivates status-seeking, and so most interpersonal violence, while oxytocin motivates group bonding and lower levels of testosterone, which reduces violence. In other words, elegantly, what is happening at the individual neurological level is reflected at the macro group level.

Human self-domestication

This chapter has looked at why and how humans group together cohesively, and has identified the five problems that they must overcome in order to do so. Chapter 5 introduced the groupishness module, and the oxytocin system underlying it, that enable us to form cohesive in-groups, and to help us build bigger and bigger groups. What's more, because the oxytocin system is a specific mechanism, with releasers and receptors, there are probably many genetically-coded neurological structures that are still evolving in it—with the usual caveats about gene expression being dependent on the environment.

Because of the evolutionary advantages of groups, there is a selection pressure for being able to take that advantage, mainly by maintaining your membership and avoiding being ejected or otherwise ostracised. This means that it is very likely that humans have evolved and are still evolving to become more sociable—that is, more able to get along with other people. This has probably been happening over the last 10,000 years, and may even be continuing today.[56] What evidence is there for this?

Firstly, there is plenty on the speed of the evolutionary change: for example, the ability to digest milk in adulthood (through the enzyme lactase) has evolved in human populations only in the last 10,000 years, and only in populations that practise pastoralism.[57] Concerning the changes around sociability in humans, there is also some evidence that modern humans are less aggressive than their ancestors,[58] perhaps because aggression is seen as a social faux pas that limits individuals' ability to mate. Aggression itself is highly heritable, meaning that the social environment can select it out of the gene pool;[59] most tellingly, variations in the oxytocin receptor gene are linked to the degree to which individual humans are pro-social, and hence less aggressive.[60] However, this simply shows the variation in human populations— what hasn't yet been elucidated is the degree or speed of the selection towards pro-sociality.

That said, it is easy to see how increased pro-sociality might have evolved. Less group-oriented behaviour, as a result of possessing fewer oxytocin receptors (caused by random variation in the genetic code), would result in individuals being expelled from small bands of humans, or villages, and thus making that individual less likely to reproduce. Alternatively, those who were less sociable will have reduced their status through breaking with group norms, which in turn limited their marital prospects. Those with more oxytocin receptors, on the other hand, would have been more strongly drawn to the group, and thus benefited from the advantages of group living. Some self-selection also comes into play here: in each generation, those group members who are more cooperative and social, who are able to work in complex hierarchies, for instance, tend to seek each other out and work with each other, thus making themselves individually more successful in maintaining their own security, attaining resources, and potentially maintaining child-rearing relationships.[61] This is an example of where the cultural environment starts to influence genetic selection and evolution.[62]

Taken together, these dynamics have likely had a subtle but noticeable effect on human evolution. All of a sudden, there may have been a slightly stronger selection pressure to follow societal rules, or norms—to become more sociable. Humans began to self-domesticate for living in groups because this offered a more likely path to increased fitness, a positive feedback loop that would have worked across evolutionary time.

7

FRAMEWORKS

When I first went to Afghanistan, shortly after my twenty-sixth birthday, I was a believer. I believed that we were there to defeat the Taliban. I believed that we were there to fight for the right kind of values—democracy, women's rights, the moral right implied in liberal interventionism, and so on. The Afghan government were our partners in this fight, and they believed in the same things as we did. This was a war of different ideas, about different ways to live, and our leaders said as much.

The enemy in Afghanistan were the Taliban and al-Qaeda. 'They' were guided by a particularly toxic Islamist ideology; they launched suicide attacks, threw acid in girls' faces, closed down schools, and oppressed Afghan civilians. I might have accepted that the Taliban were defending their religion (which seemed odd, as we weren't there to attack their religion), but by that point I hadn't consciously sorted out the difference between an ideology and a religion.

This was a war that was black and white; good and bad. But the longer I spent in Afghanistan, and the longer I spoke with my Afghan counterparts—friend and enemy alike—the more I realised that these ideologies were a very poor description of what was going on, let alone being the driving causes of the conflict.[1]

WHY WE FIGHT

Everyone seemed to think the war was about something different. Ostensibly, for NATO, the war in Afghanistan was an ideological one, fought in defence of democracy, and against the Islamist doctrine of the Taliban and other insurgent groups. For many Afghans fighting NATO (barring those 'driven' by extreme Islamist ideology), it was said to be a religious war, or a war of national resistance against outside invaders, or a conjunction of the two. In the cases where Afghans were fighting Afghans (on whichever side), it was a tribal or familial war caused by land disputes, old feuds, greed, or defence of family honour. In fact, most of the violence was of this type, and the foreigners— us—often got dragged into these internecine struggles.

Gradually, the overt narratives broke down. The stories that the combatants on both sides told themselves, and each other, about why we were fighting seemed to collapse with even the slightest intellectual prod when held up against our behaviours. The Afghan government were no more democrats than the Afghans that we were fighting—in fact, in many cases the government behaved much worse towards the population, because they had (our) outside support. Often, the 'Taliban' were defending their village from the marauding and raping actions of the government police—a cause considered noble by 'Taliban' and villagers alike.

Looking back over the last forty years of strife in Afghanistan, it was ever thus: the conflict, with the same actors, tribes, families, and dynamics, has been described through a multiplicity of lenses, sometimes simultaneously. Some scholars explain this shifting causality by arguing that conflicts are often sparked by one factor, but end up being driven by another. However, *often, wars come to be defined by what defines the groups fighting them. And the Afghan war that started in 1978 and is still ongoing is an example: originally described as an ideological and/or religious uprising against communism, it then was said to have become driven by ethnicities during the 1990–6 civil war, before returning to an ideological war (fundamentalism versus democracy) post-2001.*

But these descriptions were levied by the outside intervening powers—the Afghans doing the fighting mostly described it as a tribal and/or familial war over land and water. This has been consistent over time—the conflict between tribes, families, or individuals endures over the decades, even when the individuals or groups involved take on different ideological labels: communist, mujahed, Talib, democrat, or tribesman (of a particular tribe).

Thus, today, the member countries of NATO frame the conflict as a defence of liberal democratic ideas. NATO itself is at least partly based on these ideas, and it is also true that it is an alliance of America's allies, originally formed in opposition to another type of ideology: communism. In such circumstances it was natural that its member states would consider the war to be about democracy versus Islamism. The same applied to the Soviets when they intervened in Afghanistan in the 1980s: they framed the conflict in communist/anti-communist terms. Conversely, for the Afghans who were fighting in tribal or family groups, it was tribal civil war: that was the basis on which their groups were formed, and so that is how they viewed the conflict.

8

THE CONSCIOUS AND REASONING BRAIN

*'People will do anything, no matter how absurd, in order to
avoid facing their own Soul.'*

Carl Jung[1]

So far, we have explored macro evolutionary processes and
the subconscious, intuitive cognitive mechanisms that have
evolved as a result of these processes. In turn, these subconscious intuitions, emotions and responses motivate human
behaviour and create the dynamics we see between individual humans—all the way up to societal dynamics. We have
also looked at what motivates both individual and group
violence, and how building bigger groups reduces violence
overall. In this chapter, we will explore the role that conscious, reasoned thought plays in human affairs, and particularly how it has enabled us to enmesh subconscious
individual drives within group narratives.

Indeed, it is the application of consciousness and reason
that has enabled us to solve the five group problems at progressively bigger scales, driving down violence, and reducing
war. For a long time, certainly since the Enlightenment, it
has been felt—at least in the West—that reasoning drives
human affairs; that the application of reason brought about

material improvements to human society. This, indeed, is why many of the social sciences rely on variants of the rational actor theory, whereby people (and states) make rational choices that allow them to maximise their individual gain. Advantage and resource gain, therefore, is the product of reason. This chapter is a brief 'time out' to explain how the conscious, reasoning brain works, and how it interprets and justifies our motivations towards status and belonging which cause us to fight in wars.

Consciousness can be defined as one's subjective experience of the world, and awareness of oneself in relation to everyone else.[2] Reasoning has traditionally been defined as the ability to achieve knowledge or make decisions; it is reaching conclusions after analysis.[3] But this traditional view may be changing: some scholars now argue that reasoning evolved in order to help us give others socially justifiable reasons for our actions and decisions and, if necessary, to provide argumentation for others so that our intentions would carry more weight socially—in other words, that these 'decisions' have in fact already been taken at a subconscious, intuitive level, before the reasoning occurs.[4]

Both consciousness and reasoning have been touted as 'the' unique human ability. As we will see below, this may well hold true with respect to reason, but probably not for consciousness. They certainly evolved much later than most other cognitive abilities. Indeed, all of the higher-order human cognitive abilities, also including language and the social emotions, are thought to have evolved due to social selection pressure, rather than environmental selection pressure.[5] This means that, as humans were developing their cognitive abilities, it was the selective environment provided by other humans that affected an individual's fitness. Thus, living in groups with other people who were also developing these abilities provided a competitive selection pressure that progressively improved human qualities of consciousness and reasoning. These abilities were then applied to the physical, non-social world.

Finally, I would like to stress that research into consciousness and reasoning is very fast-moving, and that what follows is an overview of the current thinking, which almost certainly will be modified over the coming months and years.

Consciousness

Consciousness is the topic of much serious research. Yet questions remain over how it evolved, what evolutionary problems it evolved to solve, or even whether it evolved by accident.[6] Consciousness, after all, is hugely energy-intensive, and slows down mental processes. What advantages does it bring if, as I mentioned before and will argue later in more detail, the conscious brain merely 'rubber-stamps' decisions that the quicker subconscious has already made?[7]

Consciousness also poses a challenge to the modular theory of the brain. This is because brain modules have evolved to solve specific evolutionary problems, and consciousness appears to be a general, highly flexible and infinite activity—indeed, this is where the 'blank slate' theories of the mind came from. From the insides of our own heads, it appears that we can think about anything, in any combination. This is supported by the fact that the applicability of human consciousness is ever expanding: what once produced cave art now also writes poetry, and forms political parties.[8] But traits tend to evolve when there is a clear selection pressure: how does natural selection select for such a broad trait as consciousness?

Here, I will argue that social selection pressure created a clear fitness advantage for individuals who were able, cognitively, to model themselves with respect to others, as it enabled them to better navigate complex social networks.

We will return later to why consciousness evolved; first we will look at how it did so. One of the most intriguing ideas is that the conscious brain is still fully modular, but that the different modules are so well connected that it is very difficult to pick apart the inputs and outputs for each module. In other words, the different modules, through their interconnections, are reading each other, and this is what creates the subjective experience of an individual being able to consider his or herself—one bit of the brain is 'reading' another bit. One scholar terms this 'cognitive fluidity', and argues that it was a distinct advantage of Sapiens over other hominid species.[9]

This cognitive fluidity enabled Sapiens to form much bigger groups than Neanderthals,[10] and may be why Neanderthals were outcompeted, driving them to extinction between 25,000 and 40,000 years ago.[11] It may also be why art and evidence of religion begins to appear in the archaeological record slightly before that time: the relatively common occurrence of animals depicted with human heads, for instance, would represent the integration of different modules within the brain, such as those that deal with social cognition and natural history cognition.

It is thought that language was the method for this brain module integration.[12] Language developed primarily as a means of communicating the social emotions. Gradually, other types of information—like natural-historical information about local plants and animals, or technical information about the development of hand axes—became integrated into a speech that, until then, had been entirely comprised of expressions of social emotions. This process may be the origin of how words as arbitrary sounds originated: if I say 'book', and you do not know what one is, you cannot work out the meaning from its pronunciation, whereas many emotions are still expressed vocally as physiological reactions (*ahhh*, for surprise, or *mmmm*, for enjoyment)—which is why we can still communicate to another individual the basics of how we feel without sharing a common language.

Under this theory, language ability developed as an extension of social intelligence, and once language began to be used for other domains of intelligence—like technology or natural history—these domains and modules began to integrate.[13]

In a slightly different version of this idea, consciousness evolved as a development of what is known as the 'theory of mind' ability: the ability to infer mental states in other individuals—that is, to be able to understand that someone else feels differently from you, or has a different set of intentions. Do they want to kill you, or to love you? The ability to use our own minds as a model for others' minds, allowing us to determine their motives, carries with it a distinct survival advantage. Once humans had developed the ability to determine the motives of others, with their newly integrated multi-modular minds, they began to use this ability to interrogate their own minds—the resulting introspective thought is consciousness.[14]

However it came about, the self-regarding ability of consciousness clearly offers an enormous advantage: an idea of self, in contrast to others, enables an individual to cognitively model social situations and networks. It allows one to understand one's social position with respect to others, and with respect to the group—indeed, that is its definition.[15] It allows individuals to interrogate their interests with respect to others; to better understand the effects of their behaviour on others, and so to manipulate them more easily. Without consciousness, it is impossible to operate as an individual in a massive society with impersonal rules.

Consciousness also allows us, via self-interrogation, to look at our basic drives and desires (such as to gain as great a share of a hunted animal as possible), and to assess whether following them will pay off for us socially. Of course, humans avail themselves of this ability of self-reflection to greater or lesser degrees, and some are naturally more introspective than others. But consider that good human leaders are generally acknowledged to be more self-aware, which enables them to understand the effect that they have on others;[16] and that leadership has a clear fitness advantage. Higher levels of consciousness enable individuals to gain the most advantageous positions in their social milieus, with respect to resources and mates.[17]

It appears that other primates do not have the same level of ability to be aware of oneself in relation to all others (although some scholars argue that all animals have a degree of self-awareness).[18] Testing whether an animal has a concept of self, of course, is an inexact science. One of the most replicated ways of doing this is through a classic experiment called the mirror test. First, animals are habituated to mirrors in their environment. Once they are used to the mirror, chimpanzees and bonobos tend to start examining the areas of themselves that they cannot normally see—their gums, or their anogenital area. They are then put to sleep and marked on the eyebrow with a non-smelling pen. Upon waking, chimpanzees and bonobos tend to start examining the marks, touching them and sniffing their hands. Sometimes they try to rub them out.[19]

However, it is hard to say conclusively what mirror self-recognition as a behaviour demonstrates as a cognitive experience. Even if we accept that chimpanzees and bonobos do have a concept of self (it is harder to demonstrate in gorillas, and is not proven in other apes or monkeys),[20] they remain limited in their abilities to express it (language) or to understand their position with respect to a large group of others (theory of mind). And, of course, it is impossible for humans to understand what it is like to be a chimpanzee; indeed, it is impossible for one person to understand fully what it is like to be another.

Reasoning

Traditionally, reasoning has been described as the process by which individuals achieve better knowledge and make better decisions. It is the general ability to process and analyse facts, and is present only in humans.[21] In this telling, reasoning has enabled humans to become the predominant species on the planet, because it has enabled us to think, plan and decide. This view of reason has persisted since the ancient Greek philosophers, through the monotheistic religions, into modern evolutionary psychology—the only difference in these perspectives is in the mechanism through which 'reason' was bestowed upon humans (god versus evolution, for instance).

More recently, scholars have come to the conclusion that this is not how or why reasoning evolved, or even the function that it provides today. This is for two main reasons. Firstly, it is hard to propose a single selection pressure that would develop the overall ability of reasoning. That is not to say that the ability to reason—defined as acquiring and processing knowledge—is not a fitness advantage to an individual when developed. It is. But, as with consciousness, it is hard to demonstrate how it could have developed from a less well-formed into a better-formed reasoning ability. Again, abilities develop best when there is a well-defined selection pressure like predation, gravity, or the deceit of other humans.[22] What could have been the selection pressure for such a generalised ability?

There is a second flaw that is even more telling: humans are not even that good at reasoning.[23] People—as is now commonly accepted—commit all kinds of cognitive fallacies when trying to reason. What about groupthink, which causes people to adopt incorrect answers to questions if the others in their group have done the same? What about confirmation bias, the tendency to search for information that confirms one's preconceptions? Or the bandwagon effect: the tendency to do or believe things because other people do or believe these same things? Or projection biases? This is where people unconsciously assume that others share the same or similar thoughts. There is even an obsequiousness bias, whereby people systematically alter their responses in the direction that they believe is desired by the investigator.[24]

There are many more of these cognitive biases (sometimes called fallacies), and they stem from the heuristics discussed earlier. They were brilliantly explored by the world-famous psychologists Daniel Kahneman and Amos Tversky in the 1980s,[25] who—followed by a host of others[26]—argued that there was a (metaphorical) 'twin track' system of cognition in the brain.[27] In summary, their argument was that the intuitive brain formed quick responses that were right most of the time. These obeyed heuristics or rough rules of thumb—speed is a great fitness advantage. Later to the decision-making process was the conscious, reasoning brain.

This slower, more considered response to stimuli was most often influenced by the decision already made, although sometimes, in the event of it being a deleterious response, it was possible to override the initial intuitive response with reasoning.[28] More often than not though, the conscious, reasoning brain simply arranged itself around the already-formed response, and presented 'reasons' for it, which were not necessarily logical.[29]

Thus, the cognitive fallacies are not problems with reasoning per se; simply, reasoning is influenced by other, quicker intuitive processes, which are subconscious and therefore non-reasoning. Despite being seminal at the time— Kahneman won the Nobel Prize for work related to this insight—these arguments are problematic: how and why have humans evolved a reasoning ability, which operates at great energy cost, if we don't even use it most of the time?

Scholars now argue that reasoning did not develop in order to assess facts and make decisions. Instead, they suggest that it emerged as a means of explaining our already-formed impulses to our social peers. In terms of the evolutionary selection pressure, those individuals who were better able to explain their (selfish) drives, decisions and instincts to others gained a fitness advantage. Reasoning helps us position ourselves socially, and justify our actions both before and after they are taken. It helps us guard, maintain and enhance our reputations within our group.[30] This account also explains why reasons often come out as unreasoned—that is, illogical.

Reasons are the expression of our understanding of our own mental states, injected with a strong dose of social normativity—essentially, 'reasons' are our desires and intuitions, but packaged for social consumption.[31] From this insight, I argue that when humans talk about morals, religion or ideology causing war, what they are actually doing is making a socially acceptable justification of their own subconscious desires. Because war is motivated by desires for belonging and status, the most socially acceptable way for humans to justify war-making is by talking about the frameworks that solve the five problems—including belonging ('identity') and status ('hierarchy').

The two scholars who brought us this insight—Hugo Mercier and Dan Sperber—also argue that there is a reason- ing module in the brain whose purpose is to help us socially justify our impulses and maintain our social reputations whilst achieving as much as possible of what we subcon- sciously desire.[32] This justificatory mechanism does also help groups of humans to make better decisions most of the time, though this is a by-product rather than the purpose or cause of its evolution. This explains why reasoning has been so dif- ficult to analyse and understand until now: scholars have been confusing the side effect (better solutions brought about by reasoned argumentation) with the reason the mechanism evolved (socially justifying our motivations and desires). And as I will also demonstrate below, this argumen- tation between individuals trying to justify their own intui- tive desires has led to the creation of the conscious frame- works of morals, religions and shared ideologies.

Consider two individuals who both want the same thing—say, the entire carcass of an animal that they have hunted together. Parts of their brain will intuitively motivate them towards maximising their individual protein intake from the animal. Perhaps in an extreme case, the two indi- viduals might even fight over it. Through this process, each person will deploy their arguments as to why they think that they alone should get the carcass. Each individual's argument is refuted by the other, and the two eventually settle on a reason for the way the carcass will be divided that is socially acceptable to both of them (and to anyone else who may hear or take part in the discussions). Inevitably, in this case, that will mean sharing the carcass—which is a better fitness outcome in the long term, for both of them, even though they have each lost the possibility of getting 100 per cent of the carcass. This is because sharing now develops the options of sharing in the future, when protein might be scarce; and because sharing helps form alliances that are helpful in situations of competition with other humans.

So, the process of each person attempting to justify socially what they want results in an outcome that delivers an improved utility to both over the long term. Reasoning solves problems of social coordination through a process whereby the parties to the problem justify themselves in an iterative fashion. The only way that one can use reason to guard one's reputation (and so one's status and belonging) over the long term is by reasoning one's desires in such a way that they match—as far as possible—the desires of all group members. This would result in some kind of 'objective', or commonly agreed upon, 'rationality'.[33] The reasons for their desires that people put forward are therefore 'objective'—or as close to objective as is socially acceptable—because they know that this is both the best way to maximise how much they will get of what they want, and also the best way of getting their peers to agree that this is the 'right' thing to do. The process of two or more people doing this results in decisions that are more objective: a long series of experiments backs up the assertion that people collectively reach better solutions when they are able to debate and discuss the possible outcomes.[34]

This process even extends to humans thinking alone about a problem—as I am doing right now, writing this paragraph at my desk in East London. When you work through a problem alone, you are actually working out what the socially acceptable solution is, and arguing with yourself. Through this mechanism, on average you will come to a better, more 'reasoned' decision—that is, a solution or conclusion that is seen to be socially acceptable by as many people as possible.[35] Indeed, researching and writing this book has involved imagining potential criticisms of it and pre-emptively applying these to its reasoning and arguments, with a view—I hope—to improving their quality. Most science, despite what some scientists might tell you, is the result of this process of socially justifying sub-conscious intuitions, and arguing with self and others, thus making that intuition more objective.

Free will

There is a further twist to these arguments that originates in philosophy: individual agency, and consciousness, don't really exist. Free will is an illusion.[36] The 'decisions' that each of us make are ultimately products of both our genes and our environments—reactions to others that surround us, and other random phenomena in the environment. In other words, the 'decisions' that I make can ultimately be traced back to the kind of person I am (genes, upbringing, environment), my current surroundings (luck, series of random events), and what kind of person I think you are (such judgements being influenced by, for instance, whether our bodies motivated us to have an adequate breakfast this morning).

At each point that we make a 'decision', what is actually happening is a series of chemical reactions in the brain, in certain synapses rather than others—exactly which is dependent on chemistry, physics and biology. This is the physical cause of the action when our body carries out a decision the brain has made.[37] Where, then, does our 'free will' come into it? Fascinatingly, it appears that our brains have evolved the specific ability to impose an illusion of free will onto a reality that we do not, in fact, control—we have evolved to create a parallel reality.[38] This chapter has laid out the evolutionary advantages of such a development: free will enables us (roughly) to plan and understand our environments, and to impose some order on them by imagining ourselves in relation to our environments (particularly our social environments), and vice versa.

Ultimately, solving the five problems at a macro scale occurs when the individual members of the group converse (argue) until they come to a solution that is acceptable to as many people as possible. This has occurred over thousands of generations and tens of thousands of years.[39] Human moral codes (and religions and shared ideologies) are the product of a process of reasoned argumentation between millions of individuals and their multitudes of intuitions and desires; the process has produced ways for us to express our subconscious motivations towards status and belonging in socially acceptable ways, which ultimately reduces internal violence.

However, it does mean that when we talk about violence being driven by the conscious frameworks of morals, religions or ideologies we are not correct in implying causation—we are simply justifying the true driving instincts, which were there first. It also means—viz the argument that free will doesn't exist—that those conscious frameworks have no intrinsic value in and of themselves—they are purely constructs that exist within and between our brains. However, because individuals are not aware of the subconscious drives that are post facto reinterpreted by the reasoning brain, they interpret their reasoning as causal.

Moral codes, the supernatural, and shared ideologies

In conclusion, humans have individual drives towards status and belonging. These desires, and the violence that we use to achieve them, need to be socially justified if they are to be pursued successfully. To do this, humans use their consciousness to position themselves socially, and their reasoning module to frame their drives within socially agreed frameworks, which are themselves the process of reasoned argument over thousands of generations. Because others—both on your side and on the other, in a war—are also trying to justify their own drives, and guard their own reputations by subsuming their drives within socially acceptable frameworks, people have long understood war as being *caused* by those frameworks. But, technically speaking, these frameworks are illusions, because they rely on conscious reasoning, or free will—which, some philosophers argue, is itself an illusion.

The next three chapters will look at these three stages of group development in humans. Roughly speaking, moral codes helped us assemble in groups of hundreds and thousands; belief in the supernatural helped us assemble in groups of thousands and millions; and shared ideologies (which include the large-scale religions) helped us assemble in groups of millions and billions. Together, these frameworks have allowed nascent human society to grow in size beyond the personal; beyond the level where each individual recognised and knew everyone else; beyond Dunbar's number (see Chapter 6). In fact, the initially resulting regional groups of forager bands, of around 500 individuals each, represented the first distinctly Sapiens scale of social organisation.[40]

Such human groups are based around shared markers and shared ideas of how to solve the group problems. The process of their early formation was one of individuals recognising those who believed in the same moral, religious or ideological group-organising principles and identifying them as being in the in-group. Those who differed in their beliefs were in the out-group. There was a strong evolutionary justification for this: living in a group where individuals behave in predictable ways is better than otherwise, and so these organising principles and beliefs became both identity markers for groups, and prices of membership.

These socially constructed frameworks are like scaffolding erected by consciousness and reason around the foundations of our subconscious, emotional brain modules. Consider, for instance, romantic love. The biology, in the form of brain modules, is almost completely the same—all humans get butterflies in the stomach. It is how we socially construct 'rational' narratives to explain these emotional yearnings that changes—think of how 'love' is portrayed socially in different parts of the world, or even how differently love was viewed in Victorian Britain from its treatment in present-day British society.

This reality—that moral codes and religions are social constructions built through argumentation over intuitions—is why humans practise a plethora of religions, and disagree strongly over what is right and wrong, yet all human societies and cultures have moral codes and religions which all offer solutions to the five group problems of identity, hierarchy, trade, disease, and punishment. To put it overly simply, there is a cognitive module for identity, and one for judging hierarchy, and so on; different cultures will fill these boxes in different ways, resulting in different solutions to the five problems.

Critically for our argument, it means that these frameworks do not cause war, but that differences in these frameworks correlate with the conflicts that exist between groups. In strict fact, they do not actually exist as things in and of themselves, and so it is impossible for them to cause anything. The next three short chapters will demonstrate that morals, religion, and shared ideologies do not cause war, but rather help to build groups that fight one another, and help to justify such violence.

9

MORAL CODES

'Morality binds people into groups. It gives us tribalism, it gives us genocide, war, and politics. But it also gives us heroism, altruism, and sainthood.'

Jonathan Haidt[1]

Moral codes can be defined as the unwritten rules of small groups of humans, backed up by feelings of right and wrong, that solve the five group problems. They are ideas in a society about what is right, and what is wrong; this translates to rules about what to do and what not to do, including how to interact with other people in the group. Moral codes have a long evolutionary history in humans.

One assumes that what we now recognise as morality evolved around the time of the human cognitive explosion (roughly 50,000–100,000 years ago, although the dates are contested). There is also evidence that the roots of this early morality lie even further back in our primate ancestors. Its modern-day echoes can be seen in the unwritten tribal codes of groups like the Pushtun (Pushtunwali) or the Somalis (Xeer).

This chapter will explain how moral codes help humans to build internally non-violent groups by solving the five group problems. Through this, it will show that moral differences only correlate with the opposing sides in a conflict, rather than causing it—as argued earlier, conflict is motivated by status-seeking among leaders and desires to belong among followers, and morality is used as a way of framing and justifying these drives for both parties. This chapter will demonstrate not why we fight, but why we don't fight, and also why we think we fight.

When I was researching the UK's involvement in the Libyan campaign of 2011, it became clear to me that the then Prime Minister David Cameron's main aim was to 'get' Col Gadhafi, the Libyan leader, to the exclusion of almost anything else.[2] I was working in the UK Ministry of Defence during the conflict, and had been tasked to write a paper about the post-conflict aspects of the war. This involved speaking to tens of officials at the centre of the British war effort, in order to assess what the likely effects of the war would be. At the time, the war was ostensibly being prosecuted for moral and legal reasons, with David Cameron describing the war as 'necessary, legal and right',[3] but it was obvious to many in the MOD that the prime minister was focused above all on killing Gadhafi. Ministry officials had tried to seek further guidance on the prosecution of the war from 10 Downing Street, but there was very little forthcoming beyond protecting the civilians in Benghazi from the Gadhafi regime, and killing the man himself.

Once the status of the civilian population in Benghazi was assured, the conflict aims became centred on killing Gadhafi, to the consternation of the MOD officials tasked with carrying out the war. They were confused as to why such a complicated conflict and post-conflict environment was being boiled down to the killing of a leader, and puzzled by the complete lack of centrally directed planning (from David Cameron) for what would happen should that event occur. Sadly, my understanding of this situation at the time has since been borne out by a September 2016 report on the intervention published by the House of Commons Foreign Affairs Committee.[4]

Interestingly, according to an official who had been in meetings with the prime minister about the conflict, this was not a subterfuge: Mr Cameron apparently genuinely believed that the conflict was as he described it. But his actions were different from his words. Why was he talking about rights and wrongs, operating within the law, and protecting the population of Benghazi, when all he was truly interested in was the other leader?

The evolution of morality

Moral codes are sets of rules detailing behaviour that are accepted by the majority of a group of people. These rules are focused on the five group problems: identity, hierarchy, trade, disease and punishment. In each area, you, like the vast majority of other humans on the planet, will feel that certain things are 'just right' or 'just wrong'. (Remember, feelings are only your brain motivating you to carry out a set of behaviours that, on average, enhance evolutionary success.) For example, the ideology (not the practice) of extreme modern Liberalism aside, it feels right to treat people in the in-group differently from people in an out-group.[5] This is for very good evolutionary reasons: in the Palaeolithic, your survival depended on the small group of which you were a member.

These rules are critical for successful group living. In all cases, for example, there will be rules on who you can and can't kill, who you can and can't have sex with, who is in charge, what is considered fair and just, and what other behaviour is expected of you as a group member. The notion of morality and the specific moral code at large are pre-requisites for living in groups that extend beyond those people you know personally.[6] The fact that, as fundamental concepts, right and wrong do not exist[7] (have no inherent meaning) does not change the fact that, as one of the bases for extended group living, they are among the most important behavioural adaptations that humans have evolved. But in evolutionary terms, shared individual behaviours that support group membership 'feel' right, while those that do not 'feel' wrong. When we say that a behaviour is wrong, what we really mean is that it is not conducive to group living and so, critically, is not conducive to maintaining group membership—our evolutionary goal.

The roots of morality, the pre-moral sentiments, lie in the social emotions. These emotions—love, envy, gratitude, vengeance, pride, anger, trust, guilt and disgust—were originally either deployed as signals toward another individual, or triggered through interactions with one other individual.[8] With more individuals and hence more social interactions, it was of great evolutionary advantage to be able to separate your thoughts from others', and to understand how one person feels about a third—that is, to understand how their (illusion of) reality differs from yours. For example, it is easy to understand the benefit of someone in the group seeing you demonstrating gratitude to someone else who has helped you: they will be more likely to help you in future. Similarly, an individual observing the action of vengeance means that they will not treat the avenger badly, for fear of receiving the same punishment.[9]

In a further, more complex example, humans evolved the ability to express shame that could either influence person A in order to have an effect on person B, or even appease whole groups of individuals after personal wrongdoing. Thus, the social emotions became multi-dimensional—these are the pre-moral sentiments. As we will see, moral codes rest on a series of (groups of) emotions modules that guide intuitive behaviour around the concepts of identity, trade, hierarchy, disease, and punishment.[10] These moral systems allowed us to manage reputations, build alliances, recruit helpers in disputes and maintain predictable behaviour.[11] This in turn helped us build bigger groups, and drive down rates of violence.

The evolution of moral codes from the social emotions has left footprints. Consider that being moral and good is often equated linguistically with cleanliness. Morally bad behaviour is 'unclean'. Our language describes it as 'disgusting' behaviour—an obvious derivation from the disgust mechanism that protects us from toxins and pathogens.[12] Similarly, consider behaviour around trade. Within the concept of fairness, there is a feeling of different acts being equivalent (say, stealing a loaf of bread and being sentenced to death—once considered a fair deal). This is a direct derivation from the social emotion of vengeance, whose purpose was to raise the cost of acts that benefited the perpetrator at the expense of their object.[13] Gradually over evolutionary time, these one-on-one emotions became one-to-many and many-to-one feelings: human beings evolved universally applicable feelings about what was right and wrong.

These common moral instincts guided behaviour to discourage individuals, for instance, from committing adultery, or cheating on a trade of foodstuffs. Following these behaviours meant that they were more likely to survive and reproduce,[14] because they were less likely to have conflicting issues with other individuals in the group, and so were more likely to avoid being ostracised or losing status. Of course, the briefest look at any society will tell you that not everyone behaves in a 'moral' way, and even those who do will not always do so. Rather, these cognitive developments mean that, on average, people have these feelings which motivate 'moral' behaviours—a sense of morality. Whether they choose to act on it is another question, but clearly most people do mostly act, and have ever acted, on moral feelings. At times, of course, it is of much greater benefit to deviate from the strict moral path. These dilemmas are encapsulated in those problems posed to first year ethics students, like whether it is wrong to steal a loaf of bread if you are starving. On average, however, it is more beneficial to abide by the code.

This code will differ between groups of humans because, whilst we share almost all the cognitive modules to help us solve the five group problems,[15] these modules interpret different ecologies in different ways, producing different behavioural outputs.[16] This generates different moral codes, as each aspect of the group's problems is given differential importance within the system. For example, one system may feel that group identity is the most important thing and should come before the individual, even at the risk of generating 'unfair' outcomes for some individuals. In another system the opposite may be true—equality over trade between individuals might be the most important thing.

These cultural differences mean that the basic schema of these modules had arisen by 70,000 years ago, when Sapiens left Africa, if not earlier.[17] There is evidence that before this primates had already evolved the rudiments of hierarchy, punishment and trade: primate hierarchies are well

described, and there is clear evidence that primates understand them and act accordingly.[18] When it comes to trade,
chimpanzees are more likely to make unfair deals if they can
get away with it, and fair deals if they are likely to be pun-
ished by another chimpanzee. In one experiment, monkeys
who were rewarded unfairly for work (they got cucumbers,
when co-workers got grapes) stopped working.[19] The roots
of 'human' morality run very deep indeed.

In summary, human morals are like other human behaviours: they have developed from genetically determined
brain modules (very similar for everyone) that respond to
the cultural environment (different for different groups).
Also like other behaviours, moral responses are motivated by
unconscious intuitions that are then explained by our reasoning brains. Whilst the brain modules at play have their
evolutionary roots in pre-hominid species, the major difference is that, as far as we know, only humans shape their
moral responses differently from group to group depending
on culture. It is also worth stressing that the genetic variation
between individuals in one ethnic group is as great as that
between different ethnic or cultural groups, and that these
differences are just like individual differences: not binary, but
on a spectrum.[20] (Of course, our groupishness module nevertheless causes us to interpret such differences through a
binary, in-group/out-group lens.)

It is not for me to comment on whether any particular cultural interpretation is 'better' for humanity. Indeed, I argue
that each of human society's different moral codes should be
considered as a product of the particular ecologies in which
different groups of humans have lived, particularly since set-
tling in small villages around 12,000 years ago. Of course, to
argue that one or another is morally 'right' or 'wrong' does not

make any sense—moral codes developed to be appropriate for their milieu (and are, in any case, products of genetic predisposition, ecology and constructed reality). All, by definition, were appropriate for particular times and places, and all are flexible and change—sometimes very fast, as with the shift in many countries' approach to homosexuality over the last fifty years. This is because our current moral codes are historical hand-me-downs adjusted from—but born of—the original ecologies facing our different ancestral groups.[21]

Consider, for example, the degree to which a group of humans is collectivist or individualist—that is, the balance between the group and the individual. The extent to which individuals feel that their own interests should trump those of the group and vice versa have a direct bearing on at least two of the five group problems—those of identity (not only who is in the group, but also how firmly those boundaries are delineated), and of hierarchy (its relative importance and flexibility, and whether we should follow its rules). This becomes a key question as groups increase in size—generally, bigger groups have bigger hierarchies, which absorb more resources per capita, both affecting trade and changing the application of group-mandated punishment. Scholars call this the collectivist/individualist spectrum,[22] and it has long been recognised in human societies. There is, for instance, a widely accepted broad difference between East Asian and European societies: the former are seen as more collectivist, and the latter as more individualistic.

One study has attributed this difference to the underlying agriculture; this, in turn, is a product of the differing availability of locally domesticable plant species between and within the two regions.[23] Thus rice, which is irrigation fed, and highly labour-intensive, requires greater cooperation, nurtured by a collectivist mind set. Terracing and irrigation over a wide area requires a much greater reliance on hierarchy to regulate which fields get watered when, and to solve disputes between individual farmers: because run-off water is more salty and affects yields downstream, the actions of individual farmers have a large impact on their neighbours. Conversely, crops like wheat that were domesticated in the Levant and Europe are rain-fed. Here, the actions of individual farmers were confined to their own land. Water was a resource equally available to everyone, because it fell out of the sky. This resulted in a more individualistic style of thinking, one that many in both the East and West see as the foundation for modern European behavioural norms.[24]

It would be too far-fetched—not to mention reductive—to lay the differences between East Asian and European cultures at the feet of a single factor, but it seems logical that these ecological differences have had a differential impact on moral codes and behavioural norms.[25] Other ecological factors have also been linked to such differences from group to group. For example, regions with greater endemic diseases have been found to contain more collectivist societies with a stronger in-group bias: poor out-group relations tend to limit contact with strangers, who are more likely to carry diseases.[26]

Similarly, regions of climate extremes have been shown to produce societies whose behavioural norms tend to be more collectivist. In very hot environments conducive to the spread of disease, following group norms on food and sanitation enabled pathogen avoidance,[27] while societies that emerged from cold—and so resource-poor—environments have been found to be less xenophobic. There, the benefits of trading with out-groups were strong, whereas the risk of disease was minimal.[28] In this example, we can see that the priority and solutions attributed to group problems (identity, hierarchy and disease resistance) varied between, and directly depended upon, the groups' different ecologies.[29] Thus, groups descended from herders are more individualistic than those descended from farmers, who need to organise on a greater level. By the same logic, fishermen appear to be more individualistic than herders.[30]

We can see, then, how the different moral codes in evidence around the world today developed. Their high degree of variation reflects the large number of differing ecological factors impacting on specific groups of humans. But what of the brain modules? What are the shared aspects of human cognition underlying these different codes?

As we know, every moral code on the planet addresses the same five group problems. Each problem is addressed by cognitive moral foundations—collections of brain modules that shape behaviour in that area. The nature of the shaping differs as outlined above, but all moral codes, therefore, are based upon the same five moral foundations.

The five moral foundations[31]

The first of the five moral foundations is that of identity. Most obviously, this is developed from the groupishness module, which helps shape who is in the in-group and who is in the out-group. As we discussed in Chapter 5, this idea of identity and groups mainly comes from the oxytocin system, but there are a number of other supporting modules involved in foundation. For example, the emotions associated with loyalty and betrayal—pride and anger—motivate humans to form and maintain stable coalitions. The roots of the foundation can be seen in pre-hominids grouping together, although no species approaches identity in as complicated a way as Sapiens (with consciously designed identity markers, group narratives, and so on).

The emotions that make up the identity foundation have evolved under very strong evolutionary selection pressure— those individuals who were able to build stable coalitions were able to survive. Whether in early human history or today, giving away information about your group to another, competing group will lead to anger, while symbols of your own group, like flags and territory, will inspire pride. The ideas of loyalty and betrayal still play a key, although different, role in modern life. The current expression of this foundation includes sports teams and companies, and legal punishments for treason.

Secondly, we come to the moral foundation of hierarchy. This foundation evolved as groups of pre-hominids formed bigger and bigger groups—this can be seen most clearly in chimpanzee troops, where an alpha male takes a leadership position and other males in the group signal submissiveness. Human approaches to hierarchy are not as linear as chimpanzees'—for example, two humans can have equivalent statuses in a group—but everyone understands intuitively what a hierarchy is and everyone's place in it. This foundation is developed from the basic emotion of fear, or its lack: trust. Adequately solving the group problem of hierarchy helps to minimise status disputes, which cause interpersonal violence and homicide.

For human leadership to endure, it cannot only be about raw power backed by force—the leader must provide certain services to the group, usually centred around order, distribution of resources, or care of subordinates. In other words, there is an element of reciprocity. Thus, the brain modules underlying this foundation recognise and understand signals of hierarchy and respond appropriately. This allows an unequal division of resources across the hierarchy—for example, an alpha male will have access to more females in oestrus (primed for reproduction)—without the group descending into violence (his greater access is recognised as fair, because he provides leadership services to the group).

The hierarchy foundation is a fundamental part of what makes groups work: all groups need leadership. For that reason, we are all able to intuit when a hierarchy has been subverted or is exerting unfair influence, even if we ourselves have not been directly affected.[32] Humour, sarcasm and cynicism are some of the responses triggered by followers' perceptions of an excessive or unfair application of hierarchy. By unfair, we do not simply mean an unequal allocation of resources, but one that violates the notion of 'fair enough' (which is usually backed by the threat of corrective violence). On balance, therefore, it is better to stay in the hierarchy than to attempt to subvert it. The concept of an individual's social position within the group allows the same (low) levels of internal violence to be maintained even when bigger groups are formed.

The third moral foundation is that of trade. Similarly to the others, the trade foundation is present in all moral systems, but how or with whom trade is fair will differ. Feeling that an exchange (of food, time, effort) is 'right' means that if individuals were to repeat the terms of that trade over evolutionary time, they would receive an overall survival and reproductive benefit. Conversely, those individuals who made trades that were not in their interests—because they didn't have the cognitive machinery to judge that it felt wrong—suffered a fitness cost. This foundation, and the feelings that it generates, are what guide reciprocal altruism in humans: the ability to give something to someone in the expectation that you will receive something equivalent in future—not necessarily from the same person, but from the group. This is neatly encapsulated in the phrase 'what goes around, comes around'.

This foundation rests upon the emotions of trust, gratitude, anger, shame and vengeance, combined with an ability to remember different individuals in the group. Again, as we saw above, the foundation of fair trade most probably evolved in the pre-hominid line, and it probably evolved, like most social emotions, from individual-on-individual interactions. It first enabled two people to trade, share and swap with each other. Once everyone in the group had this ability, further developments of theory of mind (the ability to understand what others are thinking) and recursive thought (the ability to nest thoughts about yourself within other thoughts) led these abilities to become socially multi-dimensional. Individuals were then able to regulate trades and deals involving multiple people. At this point, the moral foundation becomes a group norm to which all individuals in a group subscribe. The feeling of fairness, of what constitutes an unfair trade and of what should be done about it are the evolutionary motivators for individuals to adopt the correct behaviour. This ability to judge what is or isn't fair better regulates the increased number of interests in a bigger group.

The fourth moral foundation is that of disease prevention. This foundation originally evolved from the disgust emotion that helps animals to avoid contaminants and parasites. A calibrated sense of disgust is essential for survival—too strong and an animal will eat nothing, considering everything to be 'dirty'; not strong enough and the individual will put themselves at risk of a fatal parasite load, or of poisoning themselves. Originally the module evolved to flag up those things that probably exemplify unsafe-to-eat items, or sources of disease: particular smells, other people with visible marks or injuries, or other animals known to have 'dirty' lifestyles (for example, scavengers).[33]

The original disgust mechanism was then appropriated for a much wider social use: we began to feel disgusted when individuals in our groups displayed behaviour that made the group more susceptible to disease, like incestuous sex. Similarly, outsiders, foreigners and newcomers to the group (immigrants) were seen as 'dirty' precisely because they were close enough to us genetically to share parasites that could affect us, but new enough that we hadn't yet had time to develop resistance to those parasites. Even today, disgust is commonly used to frame out-groups as 'impure' against the 'pure' in-group.[34]

Originally, then, the disgust mechanism became co-opted into social disgust as a way of reinforcing the first moral foundation: identity and groupishness. Thereafter, actions and behaviours could be taken to be disgusting irrespective of whether they carried with them an increased chance of disease or toxin. For example, refraining from eating certain foods—a group identity marker—is socialised from birth.[35] People commonly feel disgusted when presented with food-stuffs that their culture deems disgusting, but which other cultures delight in eating.

Other examples of such 'social' disgust include Hitler's characterisation of the Jews, or the Hutu majority's charac-terisation of the Tutsi minority in Rwanda as 'cockroaches' before and during the 1994 genocide: cockroaches are detritivores and carry disease, and so the thought of them triggers the disgust response even if the invocation is meta-phorical. Clearly, our moral foundations can be used to frame out-groups as targets of violence, even though we are actually triggering a mechanism that encourages peaceful group living.

As the basis for this moral foundation, the disgust mechanism allows us to rank in a hierarchy those things that are impure and that we shouldn't go near, but also those things that are sacred and good. Moral disgust allows us to keep our in-group 'pure' and 'clean', through rejection of people who commit taboos like incest or infanticide.[36] These morally disgusting individuals are outcast for the safety of the group as a whole—once outcast, they can no longer 'infect' the rest of the group. At the very least, they would be ostracised until their behaviour improved.[37] Conversely, those individuals who had an appropriately tuned sense of disgust were better group members; their groups were healthier, and so better places to live from an evolutionary point of view. This was particularly true further back in time when disease was more widespread, but may not actually be true now, when the problems that we face are mostly man-made. These problems require heterogeneous, mixed groups that inspire diversity of thought and hence solutions. Today, the social disgust mechanism may be working against us, discouraging us from forming the diverse groups that we need in the modern age.

The last of the five foundations is that of group-mandated punishment. Moral codes, like the social emotions that evolved before them, allow us to modulate and channel violence within groups, which enables groups to remain cohesive. The key question, developed from the emotions of vengeance and love respectively, is who within the group is worthy of punishment and who is worthy of being cared for.

Is it acceptable to inflict violence on any member of the group? Under what circumstances? The roots of the love that inspires protection of group norms (including punishment of their transgressors) lie in evolution of mammals who nurtured their offspring more than reptiles did, suckling their young. Likewise, the social emotion of vengeance developed from a one-on-one emotion to a concept whereby violation of group norms would result in punishment or ostracism from the group, both enforced by organised—or demonstrative—violence. This would be achieved through either internal coalitions, or the acquiescence of the transgressor and their relatives in the face of group-norm-enhancing violence. Over evolutionary time, a commonly-evolved moral feeling that norm-observing people within the group should not be subject to violence has made groups much better places to live. Those individuals who had evolved such a sense were able to maintain access to group living.

The way in which the moral foundations evolved, then, is intimately linked to their evolutionary success. Specific behaviours were not hard-wired by evolution. Rather, areas of behaviour, equating to the five group problems, were outlined. Evolution did not leave humans with brains that dictated a particular hierarchical structure; our brains only evolved a guiding principle: 'make sure you understand the nature of hierarchy in your group, and follow the rules'. These broad rules of thumb meant that groups, as they grew in size and experienced changing ecologies, could continue to prosper, so long as they had the moral foundations to develop behaviours and rules addressing the five group problems. This is a fantastic example of how cognitive evolution works, by providing us with genetically determined brain modules that produce different behavioural outcomes in the different social and cultural environments in which we developed and live.

Finally, as with every brain module, the moral foundations do not operate independently.[38] They interact with each other, and with other modules in the brain. (This is why moral discussions are so vexing. Often you are trying to weigh up one foundation against another, but they do not invite easy comparison, as they have developed from different modules.) For example, social and moral disgust interacts with the groupishness module. This creates the essentialism and xenophobia that lead to racism, and enables the active dehumanisation of the enemy that makes war easier. Hierarchy and disease often run parallel to each other—think of the lowest castes in India and how they are 'untouchable'. Concepts of who is clean or dirty (disgust), and where a group draws it boundaries (identity), often dictate who should and should not be the recipients of group-mandated violence (punishment).

The development of moral foundations—the idea of group behavioural norms—was the key moment of evolution in the building of human groups. It is the point at which all of the social emotions began to interact and work together, whereas hitherto they had evolved as individual, one-on-one modifiers of behaviour. The social emotions were only able to develop in this way because of the continued evolution and integration of theory of mind ability, recursive thought, language and consciousness. In other words, moral codes are the culmination of many cognitive developments coming together, and represent the point at which group behaviours started being more than a collection of actions between individuals, and began displaying multidimensional interactions between group members. It was here that our socially constructed illusion of reality began to get much more complicated.

But what about our original question: what was David Cameron doing when directing the war in Libya? As we have seen in this chapter and the last, the moral—and legal[39]—frameworks that he cited are frameworks that reduce interpersonal violence. They help us build groups and are the product of genetic evolution interacting with ecology, and of reasoned argumentation, over thousands of generations, between individuals with conflicting desires and motivations. Because of this, when a leader expresses their desire to achieve status over another, they do so in terms of the moral frameworks that provide a social justification for that desire. By the terms of this argument, Mr Cameron's conscious brain was socially justifying his subconscious intuition that Gadhafi should be killed.

10

BELIEF IN THE SUPERNATURAL

'I was told it was all about Islam; I can see now that they were lying. It was all about power.'

Afghan jihadi commander[1]

Religion can be defined as the extension of human morality by adding supernatural belief: beliefs in animal spirits, in the abilities of inanimate objects like mountains, or in powerful gods. This supernatural belief (or rather its object—the spirit or god) acts as the central point of the extended moral code, which helps to cohere large groups of individuals by providing solutions to the five group problems: identity, hierarchy, trade, disease and punishment.[2]

The last chapter discussed the evolution of moral codes, and how different ecologies interact with otherwise similar brains to create different moral codes. The next chapter will look at shared ideologies—among them the major religions and theologies. But the subject of this chapter—human belief in the supernatural—acts as a critical bridge between small-band-scale moral codes, and mega-scale societies organised around shared ideologies. The evolution of a belief in the supernatural enabled humans to extend the scale of their moral codes, and marks the dawn of wider religious

161

thought. It is not understating the case to say that this development underpinned human civilisation as we know it.[3] Of course, there are many individual humans without religious belief—but they have evolved to harbour such beliefs, and, on average, this has been beneficial.

Here, I will outline how belief in the supernatural helped humans to build larger groups. Through this, I will show that, as with moral codes, differences in supernatural belief correlate with opposing sides in a conflict, rather than causing that conflict. Belief in a god, spirit or demon pond is an excellent justification that humans can claim for their intention to commit violence and warfare; it is also a fine group identity marker, of which more later. That said, because religions underpinned by supernatural beliefs have enabled human mega-societies, with the related decline in violence outlined in Chapter 6, I would strongly argue that they have done more than any other factor to reduce violent human deaths. Like the presence of a moral code, belief in the supernatural makes groups evolutionarily more attractive places to live.[4]

When I was working in Afghanistan, I often spoke with people who had fought for the mujahedin, or the Taliban, or any one of a number of ostensibly religious groups.[5] Although an atheist, I presented myself as a Christian, which I am culturally. This was for the simple expediency of encouraging them to talk to me—an atheist might have been too far removed from their reality. Conversations naturally turned to religion, and to God. In one such conversation, similar to many others, a mullah who had worked in the Taliban movement of the 1990s told me that he had joined to defend the honour of God.

In his telling, the horrible depredations of the mujahedin warlords on the innocent population were displeasing and dishonouring God. This is a slight blending of the Pushtun tribal code—heavily based on honour—and the concept of God, but this is what a religion is: an extension of morals with the addition of supernatural belief.[6] Utterly genuine in his beliefs, he had wanted to please God by driving the mujahedin from his area, and thence from Afghanistan (the mujahedin, incidentally, also saw themselves as warriors fighting for God). If he could work to achieve this, then God would reward him, in this life and the thereafter. This was because God wanted a peaceful and Islamic Afghanistan.

At other times, especially when talking to young Talibs, I was often probed and asked questions about my own (Christian) God. To them, this was a point of difference between us: they had Allah and I had God. My pointing out that, scripturally, we had the same God, and my bringing in older Afghans, generally more aware of their own religion, to back me up, often left them confused. If we were on opposite sides, how could we have the same God?

At these times, 'God', was a moral justification made much stronger by the invocation of a supernatural being that—at least in the realms of science—neither of us could prove existed. It was, in a sense, the trump argument: if one cannot prove or refute that God exists, or what he or she might be thinking, then one has the ultimate un-respondable-to justi-fication for one's drives and actions. Belief in this particular God was also a large part of Talib identity.

This brings me to a very important point: the vast major-ity of people who believe in the supernatural must truly believe it to be true. If they were lying in proclaiming their belief in the tree spirit, or God, then, by definition, religion as a mass phenomenon could not exist. Supernatural belief is not a cynical elite manipulation created in order to control human populations, although that may occur occasionally. Even then, as a strategy, cynical manipulation would only work if the majority truly believed in the thing or being they were using as a tool.[7]

The evolution of supernatural belief

The evolution of supernatural belief originally led to animist and spirit beliefs: this tree, this water hole, that animal, has special powers that will protect or guide us, or that are a force to be avoided. Such beliefs were tightly geographically focused and so only allowed small groups to form.[8] Broadly speaking, and tens of thousands of years later, polytheistic pantheons of gods emerged that supported the development of more complex societies. These allowed different gods for different groups, but also allowed for some shared beliefs between them; different groups could operate in a shifting mosaic, sometimes aligning, and sometimes fighting.[9]

Much later, and well into the period of recorded history, these polytheistic traditions were followed by monotheistic religions like those of my Taliban interlocutors and my own culture. These tended to integrate ideas around universality (God is everywhere), conversion (all humans can become members of X religion) and the incorporation of morals such as infinite justice (to allow large-scale cultures where people regularly interact trustingly with strangers).[10]

Interestingly, and as with moral codes, different types of religions tend to be reflective of the differences in their original underlying societies, which themselves reflect the underlying ecologies.[11] Deserts—harsh, exacting environments—tend to lead to monotheistic gods, whilst rainforests—bountiful, diverse environments—produce polytheism. Agriculturists have gods who tend to influence the weather. Moralising gods tend to be associated with large-scale, anonymous societies. As human societies have developed, they have often changed their religions, to ones more suitable for the environments that those societies have come to inhabit. Such shifts occurred because our reasoning brains interpreted our intuitive belief in the supernatural within the new environment, and a new religion was born. All religions, however—from tree beliefs to those with churches—are underpinned by a belief in the supernatural. In line with how we understand the reasoning module to work, religions offer a post-facto justification for a subconscious instinct. So how did this subconscious belief in the supernatural evolve?

At first sight, this is an evolutionary puzzle. What was the reproduction or survival advantage to an individual of believing in things that are at times invisible and—in some cases—increasingly demonstrably untrue; things that necessarily violate the natural laws that permeate the world?[12] These natural laws have shaped our brains' evolution so that different cognitive domains understand aspects of the world with what is called folk intuition: the result is our understanding of folk physics, folk biology and folk psychology, to name just three. Thus, human brains intuitively understand the properties of the natural world—the fact that rocks fall when dropped, or that similar plants and animals are related and share properties. This is possible because these attributes of the natural world have remained unchanged throughout our cognitive evolution and therefore have helped to shape it.[13]

To give a few examples of these natural law violations: supernatural beings are often all-powerful and exist everywhere at once, and assume different forms; they enable objects to change from one thing to another; describe environments that have never been seen or reported on (the realms of the afterlife); and allow dead bodies to return to life or, in the case of reincarnation, personality essences (spirits) to change species. They even support miracles—which are actually defined as events that do not obey natural laws, or at least our understanding of them. How, then, did believing concepts that disobeyed our own evolved cognitive domains offer an evolutionary advantage to individuals?

It gets more complicated. Humans invest significant time and effort into the supernatural: time that could otherwise be spent increasing survival and reproduction, by looking for food or sexual partners, for instance. Consider the amount of effort that goes into building gigantic religious structures; the amount of time spent praying and observing other rituals like keeping one day of the week non-productive; or, perhaps strangest of all, the common imposition of celibacy or abstinence on certain types of people (such as priests or the unmarried)—the ultimate counter-evolutionary activity. Belief in the supernatural very often has direct evolutionary costs to the individual that are never repaid.[14]

There have been multiple, quasi-evolutionary reasons advanced for the existence of supernatural belief. For example, it helps humans with their fear of death, or explains our highly changeable environments, full of weather events like storms and volcanoes that, for most of human history, seemed random. Intuitively, these accounts are explanatory; belief in the supernatural does do those things.[15] But so could many other cultural phenomena. For instance, many descriptions of the afterlife imply a judgement, which requires the existence of a supernatural being to do the judging. It is not immediately apparent why this is necessary for an afterlife to exist, or what the evolutionary advantage of this would be. Generally, explanations such as these for the origins of supernatural belief can be considered functionalist; in other words, they suggest that this belief evolved for the functions for which it is now used—a circular argument.[16] Another example of a functionalist argument is that supernatural belief brings people together in groups, therefore that is why it evolved.

The implication is that the identified purpose or function of belief is enough to explain the deficits of function created by the high evolutionary costs of religious ritual and sacrifice (among other things). But these types of explanations do not help us understand why an individual would make individually evolutionarily costly commitments to a group in the name of the supernatural—this is the group selection argument that we argued against in Chapter 1. It is even more difficult to understand when we consider how such beliefs grew from a single believer to become shared across the group. Beliefs must reach a tipping point in populations—a certain percentage of people must harbour them for it to make sense for the group generally to adopt them. How could that point arrive given that, when belief in the supernatural initially evolved, there would have been a negative selection pressure against any behaviours involving costly time and energy commitments?[17]

Agency

A clue to these puzzles is that the beginning of human supernatural thinking was linked to the dawn of consciousness. Recall from Chapter 8 that scholars believe consciousness to have evolved either when humans began to integrate their different brain domains (the social, natural history and technical intelligences), or as an extension of the theory of mind module, when humans began to use their own minds to model the minds of others, or as a combination of both. This integration of different brain domains laid the context for the initial beliefs in the supernatural.

The next piece of the puzzle is that a key part of hominid social intelligence is theory of mind: the ability to determine the agency and intentions of others, and see them as different from our own thoughts and intentions.[18] In essence, this allows us to detect what others want to do—in actual fact, to determine whether and how their illusion of reality differs from our own. This has a key survival benefit.[19] If, for example, we are able to determine that other humans 'mean' us harm when they come at us with an ox bone raised over their heads, or when we see two of them talking quietly while looking at us askance, then we are more likely to survive and reproduce.

In Chapter 1, we learnt that cognitive evolution is full of modules that were strongly selected for by one set of environmental stimuli, but are also triggered by other, related stimuli. This is because brain modules, if too specific, would miss triggers slightly outside the evolved target stimulus. The advantages of broad application are clear. In the case of, say, predators or threats, too narrowly defined a module that missed real threats would have serious survival consequences when individuals failed to react. In evolutionary terms, it is better for brain modules to have false positive reactions (overreactions) than false negative reactions (under-reactions).

Other human beings are the evolved target stimulus for the theory of mind module. What if the theory of mind module began to (over-)attribute motivations to other stimuli like animals and trees? All it would have taken is slightly human-like 'behaviour'—say, trees 'sighing' in the wind, or animals looking like they are 'plotting'. These phenomena, easily explainable by modern knowledge (acoustics and biology), could have been understood by the first humans with theory of mind ability as actions or expressions driven by an underlying desire or belief. This is exactly how the theory of mind module extrapolates internal beliefs from other people's actions, and vice versa: future actions are then extrapolated from those beliefs, allowing prediction of behaviour.

The theory of mind module is overactive. This may have caused it to intuit desires in objects or animals even when our other folk intuitions tell us that they should not have such motivations,[20] leading to spirit animals, animal worship and animals with human behavioural characteristics. This is backed by the archaeological record, such as evidence of a bear-worshipping cult in the Middle Palaeolithic.[21] At around the same time, cave art flourished with half-animal, half-human beings depicted regularly.[22]

Humans also attribute(d) motives to the recently dead, or more distant ancestors, without an explanation for this agency within human understanding of natural law. We know that Palaeolithic people often decapitated corpses and decorated the skulls. Ascribing motives to the dead would reinforce the hierarchies of the present, and would be an excellent way of ensuring land rights: 'this was my ancestor, and this is his land'. In fact, in a very useful spinoff of the overactive theory of mind module, the more complex societies of the later Neolithic were probably underwritten by powerful, active ancestors or beings.[23] This is a highly effective extension of the moral codes of early societies.

This explanation for the evolution of supernatural belief appears to be borne out in research: when believer participants in experiments were asked to think about god, brain scans showed that they were using the parts of their brain used for theory of mind and social cognition.[24] This overactive brain module is also the basis for the anthropomorphisation widespread in daily life—attributing human motivations, characteristics or behaviours to inanimate objects, such as computers that 'refuse' to work, or pets.[25] To bring this back to our main thesis, when we describe supernatural thought like this, it is very hard to demonstrate how it can 'cause' conflict.

Attributing agency to humans—that is, understanding how their illusion of reality differs from yours—was incredibly helpful and drove the evolution of the theory of mind module.[26] Thus, the agency detection module was very strongly selected for, and spread quickly as an evolutionary adaptation. Belief in supernatural beings was simply a by-product of this, rather than being directly selected for. This makes it the most useful evolutionary by-product in human history, because it enabled humans to form much larger groups than ever before. However, the resulting anthropomorphisation of animals, rocks and mountains, for example, was also beneficial to our survival—likening the physical to the social environment made it easier to navigate, injecting agency and so predictability into natural phenomena as part of humans' conscious illusion of what reality was like. Once such belief in the supernatural had come about, it was maintained in the population due to the unequivocal advantages that agent detection (of other humans) brought to individuals, as well as its lesser advantages for individuals living in bigger and more cohesive groups as a result of moral codes infused with supernatural belief.

Thus, we return to the origins of all human behaviour: our reasoning brain rationalises non-conscious, intuitive responses, building conscious scaffolds over innate, emotional foundations. All religions have supernatural agents, and this part of religious theology comes from the intuitive 'feeling' of agency in the environment, tied to either living organisms or inanimate objects.

Religion from supernatural belief

These supernatural agents—animals, spirits, dead people, gods—are then interpreted by our conscious brains, the result being religious thought and, later, organised religion. Eventually, supernatural beings are given a place on the hierarchy (leading to a tiered cosmos); they have views on fairness, act as the ultimate source of group-mandated punishment, and pronounce on disease and identity, much as (leader) individuals in our societies do. This is how the scaffold of religion has been created from an initial attribution of agency to non-human objects.[27]

Even complex theologies—the Muslim or Christian faiths, for example—are the products of our conscious reasoning brains further rationally 'explaining' the theory of mind module's automatic, emotional attribution of agency, within the context of the local ecology. Thus, religious belief systems are frameworks consciously created to explain 'feelings' of supernatural agency, even when they contradict our cognitive domains of folk knowledge—just as every culture has foundational identity myths, or stories and ideals about falling in love.[28]

It is difficult to separate the (co)evolution of supernatural belief and moral codes. In fact, once belief in the supernatural had evolved by the end of the Middle Palaeolithic (approximately 50,000+ years ago), there is evidence that there was no separation in daily life between the supernatural and the 'real', or tangible, world.[29] Both had similar effects on nascent human societies, in that they enabled groups to grow beyond those based on personally knowing all the individuals therein. Both are also specific, socially constructed scaffolds for common cognitive mechanisms, as all societies believe in the supernatural.[30]

A religion is simply a moral code, with the addition of belief in the supernatural. This extends the moral code and adds otherworldly qualities: deities are the highest on the hierarchy, the purest on disease/disgust spectrum, exact the greatest group-mandated punishments; in later, moralising religions, they have infinite justice (fair trade), and, in monotheistic religions, define groups of humans depending on whether they believe in a particular deity (identity). All of the moral foundations were altered by the concept of the supernatural. Religion is the group problems solution *par excellence*, and therefore enhanced all five of the moral foundations, resulting in their further selection. In other words, is likely that humans would not have such well-defined moral senses were it not for the evolution of supernatural belief.[31]

Then, as with many other aspects of evolution, what evolved for one purpose—or by accident—was hijacked for another purpose in later generations. This is how overactive agency detection grew in scale into a shared belief in one supernatural landscape; that shared belief has in turn become an incredibly useful marker of group identity, including in conflict.[32] This happens when individuals need to be able to demonstrate to other members of the group that they share the group's beliefs. With moral codes, the costly signalling commitment—showing the rest of the group that you follow the same code—is adherence to behavioural norms. The signalling is implicit in the act—if you behave 'well', you are a member of the group. But with supernatural belief, this is much more difficult: you have to prove something that is unproveable, or at the very least hard to demonstrate. How do you display your honest belief in a particular supernatural being?

In the main, and similarly to other signalling in animals,[33] honest signalling of supernatural belief must be costly, and hard-to-fake. Beyond the relatively minor time and energy involved in working on the Sabbath, or praying collectively, more extreme religious signalling—human sacrifice, or suicide bombing (more on this later)—can be exceptionally costly, and very hard to fake; the assumption by those who witness the signalling, therefore, is that it must reflect an honest belief, because the behaviours involved are simply too costly to be worth faking.[34]

Signalling that you believe in the same supernatural objects or beings as others demonstrates that you are part of the same community, and therefore these signalling behaviours are often heavily policed.[35] This is the best way to ascertain, as far as possible, that the other people in your group actually share your supernatural beliefs, and are therefore worthy of group membership. Those believers who cut themselves with knives or chains in the Shia Muslim Ashura rituals, for instance, are powerfully demonstrating their group commitment. And in a study of eighty-three communities, those with more costly religious rituals proved to be more likely to survive as cohesive communities.[36]

So where does this leave my young Talib interlocutors with whom we started this chapter?

Certainly, on both sides, our Gods were identity markers; for the believers amongst us, there were expectations about God's desires and wishes that had to be satisfied, and actions that could be interpreted as signalling group membership. Of course, the fact of different religious groups fighting each other and claiming justification from god is commonplace, and elicits responses from neutral observers ranging from cynicism (the fighters don't really believe in god but are just using him as an excuse) to bewilderment (they don't correctly understand what god is about). Yet, given its costliness, we must assume that for the majority of those engaging in such signalling—whether a group or an individual—their belief is genuine.

As the ultimate identity marker, belief in a god becomes the proxy for group belonging and identity for which individual humans are motivated to fight, and even die. It is one of the most socially acceptable justifications for our subconscious drive to wage war. In other words, supernatural religion is often why we say we fight—but that does not make it why we fight. In fact, like the other frameworks, belief in the supernatural helps us to build bigger groups, which, as we know, in fact drives down levels of violence. In short, one could even argue that, without religion, the vast majority of us would not be alive.[37]

11

SHARED IDEOLOGIES

'In an age when it is common for progressive cosmopolitan intellectuals ... to insist on the near-pathological character of nationalism, its roots in fear and hatred of the Other, and its affinities with racism, it is useful to remind ourselves that nations inspire love, and often profoundly self-sacrificing love.'

Benedict Anderson[1]

In Neolithic Britain, around 6,000 years ago, people stopped eating marine food, and changed their diets to meat and vegetables. This was not driven by simple ecology, or a shift from fishing to agriculture. The ancient Britons continued to use fish and seafood as burial goods, placed around dead bodies to accompany them into the afterlife. Rather, this dietary switch appears to have signalled a food taboo, and possibly a shift in the wider relationship between man and the sea.[2] What was going on?

This chapter is about shared ideology enabling humans to build large groups—potentially up to and including all members of the species—and, in so doing, driving the greatest reduction in violence and war in the history of our species. It leads directly on from the last chapter: the shared ideologies that we are going to consider are universal solutions to the five problems.

These include Neolithic religions like the one described above, and ideologies that emerged during the Axial Age (in the middle of the first millennium BCE) like Zoroastrianism, Judaism, Confucianism, Buddhism and classical Greek philosophy.[3] They also include the major world religions that came slightly later, like Christianity and Islam (technically open to all who wish to convert), as well as secular ideologies like nationalism, communism and democratic capitalism, and modern-day reactionary ideologies like anarchism, (Islamist) jihadism, and (Christian) fundamentalism.

However, this is not a chapter about ideology per se. We will only briefly explore what an ideology is, before going into some detail about how individual brains process ideologies. Finally, we will look at how ideologies spread across and cohere groups, turning to the rather elegant series of within-brain mechanisms that allow humans to harness shared ideology for group-building, including of mega-societies of millions and billions. As with moral codes and religious belief, outlining this cognitive processing will lead to the argument that these ideologies correlate with opposing groups rather than motivate war.

To return to Neolithic Britain, the start of this period marked the forging of a new identity, or at the very least a repudiation of the previous Mesolithic identity (hence archaeologists' separation of the two periods). This was a time of great change, when the previous foraging lifestyle was being replaced by farming, and consumption of fish was abandoned in favour of meat. A similar shift away from fish and seafood also occurred in southern Scandinavia, and in Brittany and Spain.[4] This was despite the diversity of ecologies, subsistence practices and material cultures between these four areas. Not eating fish was an assertion of a new identity, and possibly a new religion.[5] The Neolithic was the beginning of the age of shared ideologies—in this case, one marked by a food taboo.

At first glance, food taboos may appear to be reflective of an ecological concern—for instance, the idea that early Muslims and Jews didn't eat pork because of the large number of diseases that pigs carry. In that case, however, the proscription should be to cook pig meat thoroughly, rather than not eat it at all. Rather, food taboos help delineate groups of humans, like dialects and tattoos: we don't eat pig, because they do.[6] In other words, in evolutionary terms, food taboos represent an identity marker and a membership price, because individuals must forsake otherwise perfectly good calories, in potentially food-scarce environments, in order to maintain their group membership. When we also consider that collective hunting and sharing meat around a campfire was a strong selection pressure for human sociality, is there any better way to separate different groups of humans than to stop them from eating together?

Other areas experienced the Neolithic transition even earlier. In what is now southern Turkey, rituals saw thousands of people gather from hundreds of miles around at Göbekli Tepe—a series of T-shaped megaliths (stone pillars)—to feast on wild animals and, it appears, drink vast amounts of beer. Astonishingly, this complex structure was built around 11,000 years ago by hunter-gatherers (rather than the usually more technically accomplished farmers). Some of the stones were 50 tonnes in weight and 6 metres tall,[7] their assembly representing quite a feat of organisation—hundreds of people needed to be fed whilst they worked for months.[8] So, why was this done?

It was about this time that human regional groups began to grow in size beyond 500 individuals.[9] The underpinning of this increasing group size was the establishment of shared ideologies across mass populations: in this case, a Neolithic religion. It is probable that Göbekli Tepe was a religious complex, as no traces of accommodation have been found there. No one really knows what this particular religion was about, but some have hypothesised—due to carvings of vultures on the rocks—that a central tenet was the role of carrion birds in carrying dead people to the heavens.[10] Whatever they were, the temple was a physical enactment of these shared beliefs.[11] In fact, participating in its construction was most probably a signal of individual belief, the group's membership price. This should be considered similar to Stonehenge, an ancient stone circle in southern Britain, where thousands of people came—and small numbers still come—for winter and summer festivals. Initial work on Stonehenge began roughly 5,500 years ago—approximately 500 years after the establishment of non-fish-eating identity in Neolithic Britain.[12]

What is an ideology?

This is much debated in scholarship.[13] Its intended meaning is also often pejorative; indeed, the seeds of this book lie in the overuse of the word 'ideology' by Western politicians at the beginning of the twenty-first century. But, quite simply, an ideology is a system of ideas that define or delineate social and political questions.[14] Of course, similarly to moral codes and supernatural thought, they do not in actual reality exist—they are part of the socially constructed illusion through which humans understand reality. Nevertheless, an ideology provides the rules for living, and the organising principles for the lives of a group of humans.

By definition, therefore, an ideology needs to be shared and accepted by a majority of the group for it to be effective in framing social and political questions—although the exact percentage differs from group to group, depending on things like the degrees of group punishment used, and the presence or absence of ideological alternatives. Inevitably in a book on war, this chapter will focus on those ideologies that humans are willing to die for, rather than, say, the political ideologies of political parties—though I accept that, as history has shown, it is hard to draw a strict line between the two.

Shared ideologies have their roots in the moral codes and supernatural belief explored in the last two chapters, and likewise seek to solve the five group problems: identity, hierarchy, trade, disease and punishment.[15] Thus, ideologies are systems of interlocking ideas that address these challenges, and must therefore be capable of cohering groups. This means that, while ideologies that people are willing to die for will factor into war-making, they all must also ultimately reduce internal violence, solving the five problems in order to deliver evolutionary benefit to individuals. Given this role in maintaining group cohesion, shared ideologies will come with identity markers—such as flags or slang—and also membership costs—from tax and citizenship tests to holy war or rituals like fasting. They will also tend to involve clearly defined hierarchies, with somebody in charge—whether a group of elders, a deity, a high caste or an elected leadership.

Shared ideologies will have definitions of what constitutes fairness in internal exchange or even adultery and monogamy—whether that is based on divine justice or secular contract law. Note that, given the relationship between status and polygyny (see Chapter 4), rules about monogamy are also about hierarchy. Finally, ideologies will have positions on disease control—proscriptions on incest and other sexual relations, rules on what to do with sick people, ideas about whether the sickness was caused by sinning or witchcraft, rules on food preparation—and group-mandated punishment, such as religious laws warning of hell, legal systems and prisons, rules about how to treat children or the mentally ill, and notions of who is the rightful recipient of compassion (the opposite of group-mandated punishment).

But before exploring this further, we need to consider whether anything else could be responsible for facilitating mega-groups of humans. Yes, population pressure and conflict create ever-bigger groups, but is there anything other than shared ideology that could then sustain them? The two most obvious answers are strong and effective government—Hobbes' famous *Leviathan*[16]—and commerce—a substitute for strong government during the Neolithic period.[17] Both are mutually supporting: the modern state, for example, becomes more effective when it has greater tax revenues, while commerce can only generate these tax revenues in a stable environment if the government provides enforced rules and basic public goods, like roads, enforced weights and measures, and mass standardised education. The latter is particularly important as it offers a way of reinforcing the sharing of ideology across entire populations. It is as much about socialising people as it is about the acquisition of knowledge.[18]

However, there is a problem with this point of view. Arguing that effective government and commerce underpin human social groups confuses the emergent dynamics of said groups with their underlying frameworks. Effective government and commerce are dynamics of large groups, but shared ideology is the basis for large groups. Of course, to a great extent, shared ideology, technology, commerce and effective government have developed in symbiosis and parallel. Shared ideology, for instance, underpins the trust required to trade and organise society effectively. Thus, if an ideology is shared amongst the individuals in a group, it will strengthen both commerce and governance. For example, Islam spread into Africa along early modern trading networks, and often the first people to adopt it were merchants, as it meant that they were able to trade with a much wider network, the identity marker of shared faith allowing them to trust with a transaction people they had never met before. With prosperity fuelling the development of in-groups (and vice versa), shortly after came government—whether by home-grown rulers as in northern Nigeria, or by foreign sultans as on the Swahili coast.[19]

Furthermore, shared ideologies are codified in legal systems—which also underpin both government and trade. The first legal systems developed out of moral codes and early religions,[20] and all laws answer one of the five group problems. Take, for example, the Sumerian-language Code of Ur-Nammu, which dates from around 2,100 BCE—the earliest legal system of which we have a partial copy.[21] Its substance is immediately recognisable to modern readers, establishing who comes under the purview of the law (group identity) and laying out (group-mandated) punishments for a multitude of crimes, such as flooding other men's fields. It details a social hierarchy, identifying and naming different classes of people and establishing the king's divine authority. As for fair trade, it specifies compensations after injury, externalising the need for vengeance and insult—it seems that status disputes leading to homicide were a problem then as well. Amazingly, standard weights and measures are also enshrined, to aid with fair contracting. The only foundation not discussed is that of disease prevention. The Code had fifty-seven laws in total.[22]

At its most simple, the incredibly complex societies that exist today can be boiled down to the shared ideas that groups of humans have formed in answer to these five questions. This is how it has always been—the same problems facing our mega-societies now also existed in groups of thirty individuals and were solved by the evolution of social emotions, much as moral codes and early supernatural belief helped solve those problems in larger groups. Indeed, the reason for the universal existence of shared ideological solutions to the five group problems is their basis in the underlying moral foundations.[23]

But what is the precise cognitive underpinning for this, beyond the moral foundations already explored, and how does a group of millions of individuals (mostly) agree on what constitutes a shared ideology? How do individual minds join together to create shared group ideologies? This final section will explore how individual brains seek to minimise dissonance within themselves, and how this cognitive process causes individual brains to seek coherence with others. We will then explore how ideas spread though populations, before finishing with how the groupishness mechanism causes us to cluster into groups of like-minded people.

Cognitive dissonance

Cognitive dissonance is the stress that an individual feels when they hold simultaneously in their head two contradictory thoughts or beliefs.[24] All conscious thoughts are coloured by emotional valences (feelings), and contradictory beliefs are those that are emotionally inconsistent. For example, if you believe that the absolute right to life is a good thing, then you may subconsciously attribute a negative valence to abortion. This means that it would be inconsistent for you to see capital punishment as a positive thing (to experience positive emotional valence), providing that you agree that capital punishment is an absolute right to life issue.

Maintaining inconsistent internal beliefs takes more energy than maintaining coherent beliefs, so human brains naturally seek to reduce their internal cognitive dissonance. The greater the dissonance, the greater the psychological pressure to reduce the stress.[25] How do individual brains do this?

Consider the contradiction in wanting to eat a fried breakfast and wanting to lose weight. Both are thoughts with positive valence, yet have opposite effects on the body. In circumstances like these, people reduce their cognitive dissonance in four well-recognisable ways. Firstly, they make a decision that removes the dissonance: 'I will not eat a fried breakfast'. Secondly, they will self-justify: 'every so often I am allowed a fried breakfast'. Thirdly, people add new thoughts to regain the coherence: 'I will eat the breakfast, but I will go for a run this evening'. Lastly, they deny the cognitive conflict: 'fried breakfasts are not that fatty'.[26]

It is this cognitive dissonance minimisation, as well as other biases like groupishness, that allow us to support political parties where multiple beliefs are shoehorned into a binary choice.[27] To go back to the original example, some people are both anti-abortion and pro-death penalty because they also believe that, for example, the right to life is forfeited once an individual has killed or raped another, or because certain religious views legitimise killing killers ('an eye for an eye'). Here, new thoughts have been added in order to regain internal cognitive coherence.

These are simple examples involving just two contradictory thoughts. In reality, people hold hundreds or thousands of thoughts in their heads at the same time. As far as possible, the brain will try and keep these different thoughts emotionally coherent with each other. Thus, if one 'adds' a new contradictory thought to a brain, then the already existing concepts and thoughts (as well as the new thought) must shift around, using the above four mechanisms, until emotional coherence is restored.[28] Clearly, this is happening endlessly and, most of the time, subconsciously. This leads to what are known as ideological basins of attraction, where emotionally coherent beliefs cluster together and incoherent beliefs are discarded or otherwise altered.[29]

These clusters of self-reinforcing ideas—such as the linked nature of the ideas of democracy, capitalism and plural political systems—support each other and create stable ideological systems with maximum coherence and minimum dissonance. This is also the reason for the phenomenon whereby people are more likely to believe in an idea if they have been prepped or primed with another, similar idea first: the first idea causes a shift in the coherent structure of the basin of attraction, which then means that the second, related idea is more likely to 'fit'.[30]

Coherence-seeking within individual brains leads to coherence at the social level. This is because our brains are ultimately neural representations of the outside world, which includes other brains. Thus I have a concept, for example, of the desk that I am writing at, and the screen that I am looking at. Other people's brains, being external to mine, are also part of that outside world. As we seek to understand the outside world, including other people's thoughts, new information enters our brain, which then acts to reduce cognitive dissonance and re-establish internal coherence. Because each individual brain is doing this, there is a society-level tendency to establish coherence not only within but also between brains; this occurs when individual brains conduct the same dissonance-reducing processes while sharing information.[31] Coherence between brains is an emergent property of the internal cognitive dissonance reduction mechanism. However, as the next two sections briefly demonstrate, sharing information between brains does not make everyone think the same.

Social networks

In basic terms, social networks are formed of hubs (people) and links (relationships). Information, in our case ideologies, spread from hub to hub along the links. But not all hubs, or people, are the same: some have a greater number of links than others. We all know someone who seems to know everyone, while at the other extreme we have people whom everybody knows, like St Paul the Apostle, Gandhi or Martin Luther King Jr.[32]

As with so many human systems, the relationship between hubs and links displays a power law configuration, like that we met in Chapter 4 when looking at the scale of conflicts versus their frequency (a conflict that causes ten times the causalities of conflict X is approximately three times less likely to occur).[33] In social networks, there are a very large number of people (hubs) with a small number of relationships (links), and a very small number of people with an extremely large number of relationships (super hubs). This is also true of the

185

number of other webpages to which a website links,[34] and even the number of Facebook friends that people have.[35]

The important thing about super hubs is that an ideology can spread very rapidly if they disseminate it. This is because super hubs have so many more links than the 'average' person in the population. (This is also why sexually transmitted infections spread quicker in particular populations: there are some people—like sex workers—who have sex with many more partners than 'average' people.[36]) Beyond the number of links that a person has, the degree to which they exude prestige or influence also helps determine the spread of ideas. Humans are more likely to listen to and adopt the ideas of prestigious humans—that is, those with a higher status. This is the basis for product endorsement by celebrities, even when they are endorsing products that have nothing to do with why they are famous.[37]

Intriguingly, social network-related qualities are highly heritable: accepting, as ever, the large degree of environmentally derived variation in individuals' behaviour, the variation displayed in the human population—between being Billy No-Mates and Mrs Popular—is 46 per cent heritable. In other words, how many friends you have is almost half based on your genetic inheritance.[38] This also goes for the traits that correlate with leadership—such as intelligence[39] and personality traits like extroversion or conscientiousness[40]— are also around 40 to 50 per cent heritable. In effect, what this means is that as well as people being partly predisposed toward certain types of ideologies, there are also certain people predisposed to spread them.

At a slightly larger scale, and ignoring the differences between individuals, ideologies reach what are known as tipping points as they spread through populations. Once enough individual brains have heard an idea, and sufficiently reduced their internal dissonance to accept it as their own, a tipping point is reached. Some studies posit this to be 10 per cent of the population.[41] After this point, the new ideas are highly likely to be adopted by the majority. This is because, at around this percentage, it becomes exponentially more likely that an individual will hear of a new idea, largely because the density of 'super hubs' in that small sample will be very high: they are more connected, and so more likely to receive and pass on new ideas. Ultimately, this is how all now-dominant ideologies that we know—like Islam, or Judaism—started and spread through populations.

Clustering

As we saw in Chapter 1, we all start from different genetic predispositions towards particular types of ideologies like conservatism or liberalism (though these characteristics, like all others, are also shaped by environment and learning). In the previous section, we saw that there is a heritable component to the roles—hubs, leaders, influencers—that people assume within social networks.

Two concurrent processes then act upon this population-level heterogeneity: people seek coherence with other people's ideologies through cognitive dissonance reduction, whilst they are drawn into in-groups and out-groups because of their groupishness mechanisms latching onto ideologies as markers of group identities (and rejecting those of out-groups). This is how ideas, and the people who hold the ideas, cluster in groups.

In other words, different ideological predispositions, when combined with coherence matching and groupishness, cause people to sort themselves into groups of individuals who think in similar ways and believe similar things, much like thoughts with similar emotional valences cluster around basins of attraction within individual minds.[42] These processes, evolved on the African Savannah tens of thousands of years ago, now operate in hyper-drive on social media, with echo chambers of like-minded individuals reinforcing each other. They are also reinforced by cognitive biases (like in-group bias), which cause individuals to adopt positions that are similar to those held by others in the in-group, and antithetical to those in the out-group. Furthermore, other cognitive biases make this even easier, and cause us to think that our thoughts are even more coherent with our in-group than they really are.[43]

In one fascinating study, Christian believers of the same congregation were asked to write down the meanings of the Ten Commandments. It became clear that, despite the participants' expectations of coherence amongst themselves, there was none—despite the fact that the Ten Commandments have been cited as one of the most widespread cultural norms of all time.[44]

All told, this ideological self-selection creates landscapes of ideological attraction,[45] where people are drawn together around different groups of (internally coherent) ideas in each other's individual heads. These idea systems represent different ways of solving the five group problems.[46]

The easiest way of visualising this is by imagining a physical landscape with lots of rivers cutting through it, and with groups of people clustering at the bottom of the valleys (the basins of attraction). Visualising it this way makes it easier to see why it is so difficult to move people from one 'river valley', or coherent ideological basin, to another—to turn someone from a right-winger into a left-winger, or vice versa. It is very hard for an individual to accept an emotionally incoherent idea (with respect to their pre-existing basin of attraction), because this requires them to change their entire ideologically coherent system.[47]

Groupishness plays a further role in clustering. One of the characteristics of the groupishness mechanism in humans is our response when our groups, or our group markers, are attacked: tightening the in-group.[48] We do this because of the evolutionary importance of group living, and of the maintenance of our membership in coherent in-groups. So too with ideology: suppression of an accepted idea causes those who believe in it to reinforce the in-group's coherence of ideas, because this amounts to reinforcing the group identity.

As we learnt in Chapter 5, this has a related negative effect on out-group feeling (and hence on the amount of contact between groups). Attacking the ideologies of particular groups causes them to separate themselves from the majority ideological standpoint. And, as we have learnt in this chapter, tighter groups full of stronger adherents are more likely to be better influencers, which has a related impact on how far and how fast an idea spreads. We have seen these dynamics throughout history. Ideologies that are now dominant were once new and had minority status. Early Christianity spread, in part, because of the repression it faced in the Roman Empire.[49] So too Christianity may have reinforced the survival of Jewish ideology by repeatedly repressing Jews in the Middle Ages.[50] Today, several commentators have identified the increasing prominence of the Muslim headscarf as the reassertion of a group identity signal, reflecting the perception of an attack on Islam by the West and its foreign policy.[51] Humans cannot help but act on an in-group/out-group basis any more than they can stop themselves falling in love.

This chapter has been the briefest of looks at how our brains treat and share ideologies. As with moral codes and belief in the supernatural, there are two conclusions that we can draw. Firstly, shared ideologies, spread by hubs and shared cognitive coherence, allow us to create social groups, which reduce violence. This was as true of Neolithic Britain as it is of the major world religions today. Writ large, the processes described in this chapter are those that have enabled us to form mega-societies using shared ideology. Secondly, there are a variety of mechanisms that cause us to cluster in groups, and to arrange ourselves into in-groups and out-groups, and none are to do with 'rational', conscious thought, or consideration of particular political ideologies. Emotional valence, and who else holds particular ideas, are much more useful indicators of whether or not an individual will adopt a point of view.

Reviewing the evidence in this chapter, it is hard to argue that ideology causes people to commit violence, or, for instance, that it is ideology that needs to be defeated in the case of terrorism. This, in part, is the story of the book's Conclusions.

12

REFLECTIONS

It took me a long time to work out what was going on in Afghanistan. What I saw in front of me—everyone's behaviour—did not match any of the narratives describing the war. This mess was thrown into stark relief when I observed British company commanders in charge of the predominant fighting unit, a company of approximately 120 soldiers. My job was to train and advise such commanders, and I often worked with them from pre-deployment to the end of their tours in Afghanistan.

Before going to Afghanistan these men[1] spoke, and mostly believed, in an ideologically defined war. By this I mean the contemporaneous ideology in the army, the organising principle to our actions: counter-insurgency. The population was the prize to be won, and the Taliban were a scourge on that population. In other words, they felt it really was about democracy, women's rights, and defeating the extreme Islamist ideology of the Taliban.

This idealism never, except in very rare cases, survived the first casualty. Then, subtly, the rhetoric would change, and the war would be stripped back to its essentials: killing the other side, and making sure that your comrade had not died in vain. The war became more visceral. I also saw something else: teams pulling together in a way that I have not seen before or since.

This dissonance also extended to the people trying to kill us. It was most obvious with so-called insider attacks, when the Afghan army or police that we were trying to train and mentor turned their guns on us. At first, we explained these as ideologically motivated: the Taliban had 'got to' certain recruits, and their ideology had caused them to attack us.[2] But, in all the instances that I investigated, there had always been a previous incident involving the killer. Perhaps one of their trainers had slighted them, or they had endured some other humiliation; perhaps revenge had been inspired by something, like their brother's accidental killing in a coalition airstrike.

More widely than this, the people who shot at us daily were described as Taliban who, to a greater or lesser degree, were motivated by either religion, or Islamist ideology.[3] Yet, again, when I looked into it, I would find that small groups were motivated by feuds over land, or were avenging a dead relative. Militias were fighting to keep the police out of their areas because the police stole their opium; people fought because the rest of their village was fighting. The ideology of jihad was merely a justification for a multiplicity of disputes over more immediate concerns.[4]

This dissonance between what we said and what we saw was clear to many who fought the war. But, in a classic case of cognitive dissonance minimisation, we ignored evidence that did not fit our prisms for understanding the war. The UK ambassador to Afghanistan at the time, Sir Sherard Cowper-Coles, described it to me as 'self-deception'—he felt that we all saw what we wanted to see. We all self-deceived to a greater or lesser degree.[5]

For all the combatants, the frameworks of the Afghan war(s) (1978–) represented an ideological landscape of attraction. For the NATO soldiers, had they unpicked a foundational premise of the war—for example, that we and the Afghan government were on the same side, and that appalling police behaviour was an aberration rather than the norm—this would have led to the unravelling of a whole host of other narratives about the war, including our position within it in support of the Afghan government. I term this the self-psychological security argument. It was impossible to question the explanatory frameworks surrounding the war without removing our own raison d'être for being there.

The ideological narratives fitted the essence of the war extremely loosely, and actors on all sides cherry-picked evidence from their respective ideological frameworks. Truly, the underlying driver of the war remained the survival of each actor and their immediate group. So how did all these frameworks, narratives and ideas interact with the main point of the war: to survive? Essentially, the character of the war was one of manipulation, specifically four manipulations used by pretty much all of the Afghan actors: side-switching, betrayal, denunciation, and collaboration.[6]

This meant that—during every era of the conflict—Afghans pursued their own personal and group interests, yet justified them in the dominant ideological narrative of the outsiders. Thus, an old personal enemy would be described to the foreigners as a Talib, or a Mujahed, in order to get the foreigners to kill them. When actions of the foreigners were deemed to impinge upon the interests of a particular Afghan actor, appeals would be made to the defence of Islam. In short, pursuit of personal interest—accruing power (status) and allies (belonging) in order to survive—was always justified by the prevailing ideological framework.

CONCLUSIONS

'The true soldier fights not because he hates what is in front of him, but because he loves what is behind him.'

Gilbert Chesterton[1]

Why We Fight argues that humans wage war because they have evolved to subconsciously seek—and fight for—status and belonging. It further argues that our reasoning, conscious brains interpret these intuitive desires through the conscious frameworks of moral codes, religions and shared ideologies. These conscious frameworks are illusions, albeit very powerful and very useful ones. Their value is that they help humans to build bigger and bigger social groups by solving the five group problems of identity, hierarchy, trade, disease and punishment. Bigger social groups reduce levels of internal violence and group conflict, and make groups evolutionarily even more attractive places to live.

These basic ideas—buttressed by the fact that human cognition is extraordinarily similar across different individuals and cultures—outline the 'essence' of war, first set out by Carl von Clausewitz in the 1800s, and embraced by scholars ever since.[2] Furthermore, although technological advances such as cyber attacks and drones are changing the mode of warfare, human cognition is and will remain the same for the foreseeable future. That means that any military commander or strategist must always seek to influence what lies between the ears of the opposing leader. This is, and always has been, the enduring essence of war.

That war is a conflict with the 'other' is only true insomuch as it represents a competition between leaders for status, or leaders' attempts to maintain their status within their own groups. Similarly, mass mobilisations of fighters occur because we are shaped by evolution to seek belonging in an in-group, particularly when there is a lack of cohesion within that group. Leaders and fighters both explain socially their subconscious drives through the reasoned frameworks of morals, religions and shared ideologies—in fact, these frameworks are the product of thousands of generations of reasoned argumentation between individuals who have been trying to justify socially their individual subconscious drives and motivations. Furthermore, these frameworks are but a conscious illusion that we have laid over reality to explain it to ourselves and to others—a reality, remember, that also includes our subconscious motivations and desires.

Why We Fight reframes violence, conflict and warfare. So, too, we need to reframe our approaches to conflict, war and other types of violence like terrorism. This concluding chapter will explore the wider implications of the book's ideas and their application to civil wars, insurgencies and terrorism, including the policy changes they demand. Before that, however, I will outline some directions for future research.

Future research

Why We Fight offers both micro and macro assertions about the cognitive basis for warfare. Reflecting the way our brains work, this book started out with an intuition that was later reasoned through deliberate, conscious contemplation. My instinct was that the way many were describing warfare did not match the lived experience. I have spent the last ten years justifying that instinct through the research that went into both my first book, *An Intimate War*, and the book now in your hands, *Why We Fight*. But both books are limited in different ways—the first was a micro study of one small conflict, and the second could hardly have a larger scope. These ideas need to be tested further, refined and extended, or replaced.

One of the key themes in this book is the prominence of belonging in conflict. This can be studied both at a macro scale through the social sciences, but also at the micro scale. Several studies, for instance, have shown that men score better on measures of cooperation when their group is in competition with another group (there is no difference for women). This is most likely related to the oxytocin mechanism, but we need to know more.[3] What happens, for instance, to oxytocin levels of soldiers? What about in the run-up to conflict, or during periods of mobilisation, or training? Does this extend to other types of combatants like terrorists? What is the exact hormonal landscape of someone experiencing the rush of combat? Do people who fight in wars or become terrorists have more oxytocin receptors than average, making them more sensitive to a lack of belonging?

To my knowledge, the role of oxytocin in war has not yet been tested. But the circumstantial evidence is there. The segmentary nature of military organisation (squads, platoons, companies, battalions, then lieutenants, majors and colonels) reflects kinship organisation (immediate family, then cousins, then second cousins, fathers, grandfathers and great-grandfathers), much like the kinship terminology employed when discussing relations within the military— bands of brothers, and so on. Military leaders have recognised forever that combat success correlates strongly with small unit cohesion—people fight for their friends, and their brothers. Then there is the extreme hormonal exhilaration of combat. Most interestingly, oxytocin levels in chimpanzees rise both in anticipation of, and during, combat.[4] Does the same happen to humans? And is this merely a correlation, or is it a causal relationship?

The second theme in this book is the importance of status for humans as a proxy for the requirements of life: sustenance and mating partners. This displays itself in those military leaders who seek status, and it seems as if this is reflected in the highly status-conscious military environment, with ranks, saluting, insignia and parades. An interesting line of research would be whether men drawn to military service, or other forms of organised violence, have a higher propensity to seek status—the same goes for elected politicians who lead us into war. The corollary of this is the question of whether such status-seeking can be sated by other activities or positions, so as to divert leaders from war—as we saw in Chapter 4, status-seeking is motivated by testosterone, which will only result in aggression if that is what the environment rewards.

There is some evidence for links between status and organised violence, beyond those already presented in Chapter 4. For instance, a person's measure of their preference for hierarchy, and for maintaining differences in status, has been shown to correlate with their level of support for the military—but caution is in order here: the sample was composed entirely of US college students and is therefore not representative of wider humanity.[5] Furthermore, what was studied was behaviour in talking about conflict, rather than leading it; it remains to be seen whether valuing status as important amounts to having a propensity actually to seek it.

All of these points signpost interesting areas for further investigation. I would argue that this needs to come from the cognitive and/or genetic angles: do those with more testosterone receptors approach conflict or organised violence differently? What about participation in the military, or in terrorist groups?

The basis of these themes is that leaders and followers are motivated by different things in conflict: status and belonging, respectively. But—especially as we will see below, when we explore terrorism in more detail—it is often not clear where to draw the line between leaders and followers. Indeed, I have deliberately left it undefined. In truth, for most people who fight in conflicts, there is almost certainly a blend of the two motivations, the balance perhaps depending on environmental factors and roles. Strictly, the data tell us that the evolutionary benefits of pursuing high status only pay off if you are a leader—for instance, only the top leader in a band of pre-modern foragers would have two women. Conversely, the evolutionary benefit of conflict for followers is that of belonging to a coherent in-group. Nevertheless, the distinction merits further investigation in psychology and neuroscience.

The third big argument in *Why We Fight* was that our reasoning brain socially justifies our subconscious, intuitive drives towards status and belonging (and hence war) through conscious group-building frameworks. War is thus emotional and subconscious, not rational nor conscious. This argument about reasoning is novel, although the broader argument that our conscious brains make decisions often predicated on already-made subconscious instincts is well accepted. What is less novel is the argument that consciousness is an illusion—but this does not negate it as an avenue for research. Quite the opposite, in fact—the usefulness of the illusion in reducing violence delivers real-world fitness benefits, and the very fact that it is an illusion may mean that we are more able to influence it than we might think.

With respect to war and conflict, the most pertinent line of inquiry is whether, once we have justified our drives using these socially acceptable frameworks, the conscious 'reasons' then shape our or others' response to the intuition. In other words, once we have explained our motivations for status and belonging through religion, for example, do the theological aspects of that religion truly shape the actions then taken? In reality, I suspect it will be very hard if not impossible to tease apart these processes.

Furthermore, and I will link this to my experiences in Afghanistan, when those fighting say they are fighting to regain their land, it appears that this conscious, reasoned explanation matches the subconscious drive to obtain resources (note that in evolutionary terms status is also a resource); yet when they argue that they are fighting for 'religion', it appears that this is a conscious, reasoned misinterpretation of the subconscious drive to belong. How do we separate these processes? Is it even possible fully to distinguish them when the neurones involved are so interlinked?

The last major argument in *Why We Fight* is that groups remain cohesive when they solve the five problems of identity, hierarchy, trade, disease and punishment. Exploring the degree to which ideologies or religions solve the five problems, and whether this impacts on people's willingness to fight 'for' (under) those ideas, is a promising although difficult question to investigate. Similarly, it would be interesting to see if the degree to which threatened identities 'activate' (in a civil war, for example) is a function of the degree to which that ideology adequately solves the five problems. Do people consider their primary identity the one that they would fight and die for, the one that best solves the five problems for them? Tangentially to this line of inquiry, the degree to which oxytocin drives people to work cooperatively in groups is already well described. But does oxytocin 'prime' people to solve the five problems? Does it 'prime' them to be receptive to accepting solutions to the five problems?

To relate this directly to fighting, both established armies and terrorist organisations rely on small groups training together in adversity to form strong bonds (see below). The evidence in this book leads one to assume that this is in some way regulated or motivated by oxytocin. But does this rise in oxytocin levels also prepare the recruits to receive and accept solutions to the five problems? Is this what we mean by indoctrination or brainwashing (depending on your perspective)? What, in short, is the relationship between oxytocin and the five group problems?

I believe very strongly that the next frontier for research into conflict and war lies not in the social and political sciences. War, a human activity, has its roots in our biology, and especially our cognition. This is where we must look if we wish to minimise, or even eliminate, war.

Wider implications

The arguments in this book have a number of wider implications. Here I will look briefly at how they inform our understanding of interstate war, civil war/insurgency and terrorism, although these ideas can be applied to many aspects of conflict studies, conflict resolution, or peace studies, and offer— I would argue—a novel way to understand, interpret, and resolve conflict.

The major implication for the study of interstate wars is that conflict between groups may actually be more about internal group dynamics than about the actions of the other side. Thus, much as groups will fight back when threatened by others, if war is motived by a threat to individuals' sense of belonging to a cohesive group, then they will fight to re-establish their own group's cohesion. The same goes for leaders seeking to reinforce their internal status in their groups. If the five group problems are not being adequately solved in a particular group, then war is about re-establishing coherence, or 'order', around the solutions—re-establishing the group's internal cognitive clarity. In this argument, the enemy is in fact tangential to the motivating force of the war.

I would like to highlight two current trends that further illustrate this argument. The first is the feeling in many parts of the increasingly globalised world that cultures and religions are being disrupted by technology and/or migration.[6] This has resulted in people flocking to new global movements, like revivalist religions, as old structures break down. Groups can now be arranged horizontally across the Internet, rather than vertically in the real world.

In many cases, this loss of identity is keenly felt and has contributed to some of the turbulence in (especially) European and American politics in the second decade of the twenty-first century. We can find analogous events in human history, such as the Wars of Religion in seventeenth century Europe, when Protestantism and Catholicism vied for supremacy in small part because of the disruption wrought by the printing press. This technological innovation had democratised religion, allowing more widespread vernacular translations of the Bible.

The second trend is that described in Thomas Piketty's *Capital in the Twenty-First Century*. Piketty amasses a wealth of data to show that, over the long run, the rate of return on capital (for example, the rent received from land) outstrips the growth rate of the economy (GDP growth). This means that capital accumulates over time in the economy, and thus the ratio of capital to income gradually increases, so that the society becomes more unequal (because capital is more likely owned by those with high status). Eventually, the ratio will be reset—and the major activity that resets the capital to income ratio is war. Military expenditure and taxation to pay for it completely disrupt this accumulation of capital—money is fired into the sky and blown up on the battlefield. By definition, then, war reduces inequality in the societies fighting it, because it destroys the peacetime accumulation of capital—resources—among those with high status. The previous peak—when capital reached up to 700% of annual income—was just before World War One. During the war itself, it declined to around 300–400%, and then again during the 1930s Depression and World War Two to around 200–300%. The ratio has been climbing ever since; it sat around 500% in 2010, and has now risen beyond that level.[7]

These two trends have a bearing on two of the five group problems: identity and hierarchy. Dislocations in the internal solutions to those five problems correlate with the outbreaks of war. But what if war were in fact a way of addressing internal failures to solve the five problems, rather than anything to do with the enemy? This may be happening now, and I will further explore the notion that we may be entering a period of increased global conflict in the Postscript.

The arguments in *Why We Fight* also have implications for our understanding of the dynamics of civil wars. The definition of a civil war is one between two groups that were, until just before the start of hostilities, previously one group, or subject to the same overall leadership (sovereignty). In the modern day, the two sides will fight each other whilst remaining part of the same legal entity (nation state). Civil wars are known for their particular barbarity, brutality and viciousness.[8] Why?

I argue that this is because, in a civil war, people lose the membership of their primary group—the group, we might assume, that solves the five group problems for them. Humans are very strongly motivated to belong to a social group, and so when nations collapse they turn elsewhere.[9] This usually occurs while their new group, be it ethnic, religious, tribal, ideological or geographical, is under attack. They then have to confirm their membership of one of the groups party to the civil war, and prove to others in their new group that they are worthy of group membership. For the groupishness mechanism, this is the most challenging situation possible—not being a member of any group—and requires motivating the individual to carry out desperate (~brutally violent) measures to re-establish belonging within a new group.

In terms of how our brains process shared ideologies, the language of ideological basins of attraction offers us a further insight (see Chapter 11). In a civil war, individuals have to move from one group identity to another. These identities will be defined by shared ideologies, which are collections of ideas that cohere together in cognitive basins of attraction; for instance, liberal capitalism, rule of law and democracy are coherent with one another. A shift in identity thus means moving from one basis of attraction to another, like moving from one river valley to another by crossing the watershed. It is this journey, through the discarding of the old group iden-

tity and the attempts to prove ourselves worthy of membership of the new identity, that makes civil wars so violent.[10]

As has long been recognised in the so-called Elite
Manipulation theories of civil wars,[11] civil war leaders who
are suddenly unshackled from their pre-war overarching
group have an opportunity to increase their status, and
become leaders outright. Thus they are motivated to seek
status over leaders of other groups fighting the civil war, and
are partly able to do this by articulating the (religious, ethnic,
etc.) frameworks of the group that they aspire to lead.[12]
These conscious frameworks, in line with the reasoning
module's socially acceptable justifications, enable us to per-
petrate appalling violence in civil wars in the name of a particular group. As elsewhere in conflict, in civil wars, leaders
and followers unconsciously work together, each providing
the other with what they seek.

Suicide terrorism

We are now back to where this book started: terrorism. I
include suicide terrorism in this survey of conflicts because,
although it appears a solitary act (at least in the actual
moment of execution), it is commissioned by, and perpe-
trated in the name of, a social or political group.

Terrorism is notoriously hard to define. This is because of
the widespread emotive and agenda-led usage of the word,
which makes it hard for different governments to agree on a
single definition. However, this is a good one for our purposes: terrorism is the use of violence, especially against civilians, in the pursuit of political aims.[13] What follows can only
be the most cursory survey, compared to the immense volumes written on the subject, but I would like to highlight

where terrorist violence can be linked to the arguments in this book.

In doing so, I will draw on the examples of suicide terrorism in various Palestinian groups, some Afghan groups and the Islamic State (or IS). I do not do this to highlight Islamist terrorism. It goes without saying that lots of groups use or have used terrorism—from the Irish, to the Peruvians, to the Tamils—hence why it is so difficult to come to an accepted definition. I do this because of the larger body of research that has studied the psychology of post-2001 terrorism, and especially Islamist terrorism committed on Western soil.[14] This is particularly true of suicide terrorism, which I focus on because it offers the greatest challenge to *Why We Fight*: killing yourself, particularly before having children, is the ultimate anti-evolutionary act.[15] Also, without the act of suicide, it is hard to separate terrorism from insurgencies or civil wars where there is often deliberate targeting of civilians. What is the difference, for instance, between terrorism and terror tactics in an insurgency?

Western jihadi suicide terrorists do not come from any particular socioeconomic profile, nor from any particular geographical area. They are not mentally ill.[16] They usually have jobs.[17] Often they are married with small children. They are hardly ever pious, or attend mosques. In fact, suicide bombers have often absented themselves from their local communities and families.[18] Of those born in European and American society, 60% are second-generation migrants, and 25% are converts; in the US, more than 65% of those who plan Islamic State attacks are recent converts.[19] Most are 'born again' to some degree, having lived a secular life of drinking, drugs, and pre-marital relationships, before becoming radical.[20]

But how is it that they become radical? Traditionally it has been assumed that suicide terrorists are radicalised by extremist ideology, but only a tiny percentage of those who hold extremist views go on to act. This means there is a very weak link between the two.[21] In fact, some scholars are now even advocating an analytical separation of radicalised thought from radicalised action.[22] Radicalised thought is necessary, but by no means sufficient, for radical action, and as such is a very poor predictor.

On the other hand, looking at several in-depth studies of suicide bombers, it appears that both belonging- and status-seeking play a role in their actions, depending on the examples studied. I assume that this is because of the abovementioned imprecision in how leaders (who seek status) and followers (who seek belonging) are defined in the context of terrorism. For example, how do we define the so-called 'lone wolf' terrorist—is he a follower of a wider group, or is he a leader in his own right, simply one without followers? The following paragraphs will briefly outline the wider evidence for the role of belonging- and status-seeking in suicide terrorism.

First, belonging. Suicide terrorists, particularly perpetrators of the so-called 'lone wolf' attacks that have recently become more prevalent in Europe and America, incubate their thoughts of suicide attacks in small groups of friends. These can be childhood friends, acquaintances from prison or a training camp, or soccer buddies. Groups of siblings are also over-represented in the sample, and where they are not full blood siblings, they are often brothers- or sisters-in-law.[23] Up to 80 per cent become jihadis through a peer-to-peer relationship, usually with a family member or friend; they self-generate, rather than being directed centrally.[24] These small groups of close friends—fictive kin—are reminiscent of methods that all militaries use to train people, namely, subsuming them into small teams; note also the prevalence of self-sacrifice in small military units. Presumably, the small groups trigger the oxytocin mechanism, which further motivates individuals' desire to belong, and makes them more susceptible to jihadi interpretations of the solutions to the five group problems (remember also kin selection where individuals die for close kin).

To this data we must add the context of the high proportion of converts and second-generation migrants amongst suicide attackers operating in the West. Second-generation immigrants are, of course, often trapped between the cultures of their parents and those of Europe or America, belonging to neither.[25] Converts face having to prove that they belong in their new religion. And both face a rupture with the culture and religion (~conscious frameworks) of their parents. Most are young men, who are at the age when an individual moves from the family realm to the public realm and consequently experiences a stronger need for identity and belonging.[26]

These contextual factors create in the individual a subconscious (or conscious) feeling that they do not belong. In other words, they feel that their sense of identity is not reflected in the society at large. They do not feel that the society solves the five problems for them. Thus they seek an alternative social identity.[27] Islamist ideology is a solution to their disenfranchisement, offering them a group to belong to. In short, ideology is not the radicalising cause of their actions. It is a route to belonging—a group narrative, describing a successful high-status group to which they can belong.[28] The clearest example of this was the flocking of Europeans to the Islamic State movement in 2014–15, when it was at its most successful. Incidentally, many IS self-recruits had previous histories of gang membership, which is considered in criminology to be about family replacement, generating a sense of belonging.[29]

Finally, there is a fascinating strand of novel research into jihadi culture—music, poetry, cinematography, and even dream interpretation. Cultures, in biological terms, fulfil several functions, like reinforcing group identity—pining or worrying for your culture is your evolved sense of belonging motivating you to remain a group member—and creating a membership price, where cultural practices are time-consuming to learn or hard to fake. In short, cultural practices help individuals to identify those in their group, against everyone else.[30]

Jihadi culture—particular a cappella songs and chants linked to specific locales where jihadis have been active, for instance—is complex to outsiders. So much so, in fact, that counter-terrorism officers cite jihadi culture as one of their main difficulties when trying to infiltrate terrorist groups.[31] As such, it represents a price of group membership, as well as an appealing enhancement of the sense of belonging created by living and fighting with comrades—in Raqqa, Syria at the time of writing, for instance.[32] These places, replete with strong cultures, are where old identities can be abandoned, and new ones embraced.[33]

Some scholars believe that the act of suicide marks the ultimate in signalling commitment to the in-group. It is the ultimate way of proving that you believe what you say that you believe. Remember, in cognitive terms, and as we explored in Chapter 10, belief is a non-provable group identity marker.

For that reason, mainstream religions often involve costly signals of commitment—of shared belief among believers, to

WHY WE FIGHT

prove that they are worthy of group membership. Among these costly signals, humans have developed ingenious ways of showing their devotion, including observing the Sabbath, fasting, and self-flagellation. Jihadi terrorists are on the extreme end of this: in suicide cases, they sacrifice their lives to demonstrate that they are true believers, and thus worthy of belonging to the group.[34]

This idea leads us onto the role of humiliation and status in creating suicide attackers. Humiliation is simply the experience of others pointing out to you—often repeatedly—that you are of low status. There are a multitude of ways that this can occur, but obvious examples in the present day include coming under attack and not being able to respond, the authorities regularly searching your house, family or person, or not being allowed to work or travel sufficiently to lead a normal, modern life. When someone has their low status highlighted in public, they will probably feel shame, but also anger, which motivates them to improve or increase their status.[35]

In a ground-breaking study of Afghan suicide bombers, the well-respected Afghanistan scholar David Edwards remarks that, contrary to the so-called IS-inspired lone wolves discussed above, the suicide bombers in the Afghan Taliban have absolutely no hope of getting married; they cannot afford it. Rather, the various jihadi groups and their associated Islamist schools (*madrasahs*), as well as an intense culture centred on songs and joint activities, create a feeling of family, belonging and 'love'.[36] So far, this is similar to the IS bombers we considered earlier, and even more so when you consider that the war in Afghanistan over the last forty years has destroyed traditional tribal, religious and governmental structures—which provided previous frameworks for belonging.

But what is striking and different here is the number of Edwards' interviewees and observations that come back to

210

the shame and humiliation induced by foreign troops in their country.[37] The nature of the Afghan conflict is such that the force protection measures employed by foreign troops—indeed I was one of them—made it very easy for foreigners to inflict violence on Afghans, but not vice versa. In a culture that privileges honour and reciprocity in all things from hosting guests to deadly feuds, being attacked and killed by an enemy without being able to respond naturally invites shame and humiliation.[38]

The extreme example of this is encapsulated in the drone warfare used predominantly by the US and the UK: having a drone loiter over your village for twenty-four hours and there being nothing you can do about the fear that this creates in your community. This is the humiliation even before it launches a missile and kills tens of people, regardless of their innocence. In these circumstance, Edwards advances the argument that the only way to repay the debt of honour, wipe out the humiliation, and regain one's status in the eyes of the community is to blow oneself up.[39] His findings are also replicated among studies of Palestinian suicide bombers, where humiliation is a main motivating factor. Specifically, it is male witnesses to the humiliation of others close to them who are more likely to become suicide bombers.[40] For female suicide bombers, who often act alone, revenge for the death of relatives at the hands of an occupying power is the most likely cause.[41]

These examples are highlights in a growing body of research that underlines belonging and status as motivating factors for suicide attackers. Naturally, not everyone who lacks in belonging or seeks status becomes a suicide terrorist. In the same way that some people are genetically predisposed to become left- or right-wing, it is likely that there are individual psychological factors that lead to a greater likelihood of carrying out a suicide attack: a more collectivist mind-set, or a more sensitive oxytocin mechanism, or a greater number of testosterone receptors.[42] Because of this variation, many Afghans feel humiliated by the presence of British and American troops, but a very tiny number blow themselves up. All of this would make an excellent avenue for further research, especially to determine under which circumstances belonging- or status-seeking plays a greater role.

Finally, a caveat: I am not saying that status and belonging are the only factors involved in suicide attacks. Rather, these are the individual cognitive drivers for suicide terrorism. Those who commit it are facilitated variously by recruitment into jihadi organisations, and media or social media providing or describing a group identity that they latch onto. At base, however, it comes down to a sense of a lack of belonging and/or a need for status in the individuals who kill themselves—a sense that is becoming more and more prevalent as many in the contemporary world feel dislocated by the pace of change and the disruption of societies.[43]

The ideology merely facilitates the expression of these subconscious desires; indeed, that is how our reasoning brain works—it socially justifies our subconscious motivations and desires.[44] This is exactly what is happening with the recent increase in prevalence of far-right (AKA 'alt-right') ideology. A far-right system of ideas doesn't cause people to act; it merely makes it socially acceptable to act in particular ways to which they had already been motivated. Precisely how such conscious group frameworks interact with subconscious desires and motivations is not well known, and is deserving of further study.

CONCLUSIONS

Policy

So, what does this all mean for the countries or organisations seeking to reduce levels of intergroup conflicts? Whilst detailed policy proscriptions would be well beyond the scope of this book, I will offer some general comments.

Ultimately, group violence is emotive and subconscious, rather than the product of conscious reasoning. As science begins to tell us more and more about our subconscious brains and our cognition in general, I would argue strongly that policies relating to conflict, and particularly terrorism, should be based on the scientific understanding of how our brains work, rather than our 'reasoned', or socially justified, idea of how our brain works. This is not as big a leap as it seems: we accept the role of the subconscious in other areas of our lives and aim to mitigate it—think of the now-ubiquitous unconscious bias training in the corporate world—and legislation and policy-making should be no different. *Homo economicus*, or *Homo politicus*, along with other variants of the rational actor model, must cease being the basis for political and social policy.[45]

Beyond this, the main insight is that solving the five group problems internally, and particularly making populations feel like they belong to the group, may be the single best long-term strategy for reducing war: building cohesive societies stops both internal violence and intergroup conflict. This applies as much to interstate wars as it does to civil wars. If the causes of civil wars lie internally within groups, rather than being driven by 'ethnic hatreds' between subgroups, and if their particular violence reflects attempts to re-establish groups after having them disrupted, then the current practice of other actors on the international stage—funding one or the other of the groups on the ground—will simply extend the war. This is akin to putting fuel on a fire—an observation borne out by the escalation seen in conflicts where this practice is adopted.

Finally, an understanding of the groupishness mechanism, and the excellent reasons behind why it evolved as it did, illustrate much better the relationship between in-groups, out-groups and security.

If we are truly exiting the age where groups replace other groups—that is, where one group wipes out another through conflict; the story of much of humanity—then we need to understand better how to build bigger and bigger groups. This will only be done by adopting fewer ideologies, and sharing them over a greater population, in a way that inherently recognises the very real groupishness mechanism common to us all. The beginnings of this—regional bodies, international trade agreements, and security alliances—all have a role to play in helping us build bigger, functioning groups of humans.

But perhaps the easiest and most realistic policy proscriptions are those related to terrorism. Recognising that suicide attackers are driven to belong to a group would turn counter-radicalisation policies on their head. Those currently in force attempt to counter the ideology that is 'causing' such attackers' actions, or work through 'moderate' Muslim voices—imploring converts and second-generation immigrants to join or serve a particular, 'moderate' society of which they may not actually feel part.[46] Instead, governments should focus on fostering an ideology that encapsulates young diaspora members and makes them feel—cognitively—like their five group problems are being solved, especially the first one: their identity.

Current policy in several countries seems designed to alienate some minorities living within their borders. It is extraordinary that governments who seek to diffuse tensions with minorities first set out to define those minorities as 'Muslim', 'Jewish' and so on.[47] Such policies may well increase the internal status of the leader announcing them, but the groupishness mechanism will see to it that the result is more, not less, tension. One example is the UK government's *Prevent* programme, part of its overall counter-terrorism strategy.[48] This policy rests on several false premises, not least that extremist thought leads to extremist action, and that people need 'protecting' from extremist ideology if they are at risk of being 'radicalised'.

The language of the entire report on which *Prevent* is based reflects the implicit assumption that ideology is like a sickness that infects people and causes them to do wrong. In fact, the initial 2003 *Prevent* programme drew upon the policy work that the government had done to protect vulnerable young people from paedophiles.[49] This approach sees radicalisation as something that comes from without, rather than something that is sought from within. However, the two most damaging aspects of the policy are an explicit separation of government activities that promote integration from those that prevent terrorism, and the recruitment of teachers, social workers, charities, healthcare workers and the like to report to the government any activity that they consider representative even of extremist thought.[50]

The link between extremist thought and action is one of necessity rather than sufficiency: an overwhelming majority of those with extremist thoughts, more than 99 per cent, do not commit violent actions.[51] Extremist thought, even were it adequately definable in a society that values free speech, is a very poor predictor of violent action; defining extremism in this way lumps the supposed thinkers of extremism together with those targeted by the government for their criminal activity—actors of extremism.[52] By seeking to find and punish those who harbour extremist thought, the actions of the government cause people to question their place in British society, when they might not have done so before. In short, it creates or exacerbates a crisis of belonging, even where one might not have existed.

Further, due to the way that the groupishness module works, actions that suppress thoughts, ideas or identities are in fact likely to reinforce them, to create stronger in-groups. If discussion in open spaces is shut down—and the classroom is the very definition of an open space where free speech should be protected—then it will be pushed into the sub-public space, where it cannot be moderated through debate and comparison with other ideas.

This criticism is well articulated in the British press. Examples abound such as the young child infamously referred to the *Prevent* programme for talking about eco-terrorism in class,[53] or the four-year-old who was referred for talking about a 'cucumber', misheard by the teacher as 'cooker-bomber'.[54] More depressing are the blogs of teachers in the predominantly Muslim area where I live: Tower Hamlets in East London. These report that Muslim students now hold back on what they say in school, and have stopped engaging in classroom debate when it relates to politics; some have even been arrested for praying in the park with friends.[55]

Thus, overtly attacking or clamping down on ideas speeds up their spread through society, because if ideas are identity markers, then oppressing them amounts to oppressing the groups that hold them; the oxytocin mechanism then provokes a tighter adherence to those same ideas, to protect in-group cohesion. In other words, we fight back with the force we'd use if our close kin were under attack; it is the same cognitive mechanism. The European and American societies leading the so-called 'War on Terror' cherish the individual, and don't tend to look at—still less understand—groups of humans. Yet, groups are how conflict and ideology are linked.[56]

This is a policy based on politics rather than cognitive science, and there is a strong possibility that it is making things worse: there is a strongly established link between lack of social connection and a propensity to think in extremist terms, or act in extremist ways.[57] Stigmatising people reduces their ability to form social relationships. This is even recognised by senior officials working on the programme, who are privately very critical. A very senior army officer rolled his eyes when discussing *Prevent*, and lamented that it was creating more of a problem than it was solving. A Home Office official actually working directly on *Prevent* told me that the best way to reduce terrorism was to fund local sports clubs and community centres—which foster belonging—rather than 'criminalising an entire community'.

Policies that make people feel like they don't belong should be avoided, because they will drive people to fight, or even willingly die. Policies that force people to 'choose' between one identity and another, or one country and another, should be shunned. Binary narratives reinforce extreme groups.[58] This is as true for Islamist jihadis as it is for the far right, white supremacists, and neo-Nazis. Universal identities should be promoted that gather the broadest groups of people together. Attacking these small groups and their ideas merely makes them more resistant.[59]

Terrorism reflects the world that we live in. Globalisation has detached people from the groups they once belonged to, their proxy families.[60] To counter this, individuals seek belonging in small groups of friends and family, and these groups react to their environments. If they feel as a group that they don't belong, they are more likely to reach out for something that will offer them that sense of identity. And the Internet provides access to one such group identity.[61] This is the context in which so-called lone-wolf suicide attackers operate.

In place of Islamic State or al-Qaeda, it is up to governments, civil society and even religious organisations to provide that sense of group belonging, preferably online. The precise nature of this identity—a non-violent version of Salafism, for instance, or emphasis on the group's position as a diaspora, or a universal identity for all—is a matter for debate, but it is clear that governments should be offering alternative group narratives, rather than trying to counter ideologies that they see as threatening.[62]

There is a very high cost to following jihadi ideologies all the way—that is, killing yourself. In theory, it shouldn't be too difficult to co-create a shared ideology that satisfies people's desires to seek status and belong. Nor, in theory, should it be impossible to change the frameworks around which we order our lives, given that these conscious frameworks are illusions that simply make sense of reality. In summary, counter-terrorism is a battle of ideologies, but not in the way that many governments and politicians understand it. It is not a war against an ideology—that type of war is likely to have too many unintended consequences, and is likely to make the problem worse. It is, or should be, a war to promote an inclusive shared ideology to which all can subscribe. This is the challenge of the next twenty years.

POSTSCRIPT

A GLOBAL GROUP

There have been three seismic advances in communications technology during the Anthropocene. Each has enabled the average human group size to increase. This, in turn, has created the need for a new set of shared ideologies in order to manage the increased complexity that stemmed from increased group size.[1]

The first two great leaps in human technology were the invention of writing (c. 3000 BCE) and the printing press (c. 1450 CE). These technologies ushered in and enabled new forms of socio-political organisation: the ancient city-states and empires in the case of the former, and the nation state in the case of the latter. Writing enabled the resulting mass ideologies to spread during the Axial Age (approximately the eighth to the third centuries BCE): Buddhism, Zoroastrianism, Platonism, Jainism, and Confucianism. These ideologies were the beginnings of universalism, and introduced new ideas of fairness and justice.

The printing press allowed a flourishing of literacy and supported a common vernacular language.[2] Thus, the technology enabled the first 'imagined communities' of nation states based on nationalism, initially after the Treaty of Westphalia of 1648, but increasingly so in the 1800s. This in turn laid the foundations for the strong nation states of the twentieth century, which delivered great benefits to their citizens.[3] These factors—backed up by a common education system—allowed all members of the nation state to take part in shared ideology and narratives. Legal systems and administrative functions created a sense of belonging because they solved the five group problems in the same way for all group members.[4] Countrymen thus became part of an 'imagined community',[5] a development that later enabled many of the '-isms', such as liberalism, communism, and fascism.[6]

The third major communications advance of the Anthropocene has been the Internet, which is currently having seismic effects on human society. The Internet and the tools it enables—social media, online shopping, maps, translation software, vast knowledge repositories—represent the foundational technology for the next stage of socio-political organisation. Humanity is on the cusp of a global grouping made possible by the Internet.

We were already on that cusp throughout much of the twentieth century, as conflicts forced us into ever bigger groups: regional pacts like ECOWAS, the AU, NATO, the EU, and ASEAN, as well as global mechanisms like the UN and its associated agencies and treaties. To this we can add multiple global structures like the banking system, universal human rights (as enshrined in the UN Declaration of Human Rights) and international law. Pre-Internet, this progression was sustained by other advances in communications technology. However, that we are still only on the cusp of a global group after several attempts at creating it is because we have failed to solve the same five problems adequately.

The position of the UN and its lack of power against the sovereignty of the nation states is not, for example, an adequate resolution of the hierarchy definition problem that humans face at every group size. We have not adequately settled—to the acceptance of the majority—how, and to whom, we dispense group-mandated punishment. Other obvious manifestations of this failure to solve the five group problems on a global scale include anthropogenic climate change and transnational terrorism; or, broadly, any problem that sits between the nation state (the largest successful group size) and a potential global group. Consider also the activities of multi-national companies in minimising their tax burdens through legal structures positioned in different countries.[7] Like climate change, this is a problem of basic resource fairness—the 'trade' problem.

However, there is more happening than just failing to fulfil the promise of a global group. Our quasi-global structures, enabled by the Internet, are disrupting the nation state to such an extent that our imagined communities do not exist as they used to. This subverts and undermines the legal systems and governance ability of nation states. Meanwhile, communications and global mobility have disassociated the elites of many countries, so that leaders are no longer bound in a social contract with their followers. As *Why We Fight* has shown, humans need to form groups and belong, but we are beginning to do it on the basis not of nations or gods, but of horizontal interest tribes, or pressure groups.[8] These same factors subvert and undermine the legal systems of nation states. Inequality levels, in terms of the wealth ratio between richest and poorest, have soared, with stupendous wealth accruing to those able to exploit the gaps between nation states and the globalised system. Ironically, this activity is increasingly clear to all those with access to the globalised Internet-based media.

Shared ideologies—whether jihadism, human rights law, or Christian revivalist religions—are now dislocated from the territories and ethnicities of the nation state.[9] Shared ideologies now move horizontally across the planet rather than vertically. The cohesiveness of a primary human group—one for which you would fight and die—relies on it being impossible to leave and join another, and on all the group members needing to settle on common answers to the five problems. For an increasing proportion of the global population, these conditions no longer apply. In short, the Internet is a prerequisite for a global group, but is not sufficient: as with all seismic advances in communications technology, on its own it creates problems as well as solving them.

These problems mean that we need a new shared ideology that solves the five group problems on a global scale. How long will this take to come about? It took ~2,000 years for the ideologies of the Axial Age to gain purchase after the invention of writing, and ~200 years for nationalism to be born after the printing press. Does it follow, then, that the ~20 years from 2017's global mainstreaming of the Internet[10] will be critical in the birth of a new ideology that solves the five problems on a global scale? If so, our future global structures should explicitly be based on what we know of human cognition. We need to think critically about the frameworks with which we organise ourselves: we have enough evidence about the ways in which our brains work, and plenty of directions for future research where we do not know enough.

There will be challenges. The same Internet that is driving the need for globally shared ideology and structures also reinforces the individual, and can remove the accountability that has been present in traditional social structures or groupings.[11] Although there have been some solutions to this question, such as ratings on sites like eBay and Amazon, this is a direct challenge to the first and third group problems:

those of group identity and (fair) trade. Furthermore, the Internet revolution is partly driven by the idea of liberating the individual from their group. But humans need groups. New apps that facilitate local sharing, such as Olio,[12] may offer a promising start, but we are yet to address the question directly: how do you stimulate oxytocin online in a way that reinforces societal structures?

To illustrate the scale of the challenge of forming a global ideology, we can look at three problems. Firstly, global education will need to be harmonised so that all in the world learn the same cultural reference points; without identity markers, there is no identity. Secondly, economic inequality is a huge issue which, when resulting in perceptions of status inequality, drives violence and conflict. Whether our shared global ideology drives down or cranks up the Gini coefficient (a measure of income inequality) will determine its success in reducing conflict and violence. Finally, perhaps the greatest challenge: all human groups to date have had an out-group to help them frame their identity. We don't know whether it is possible to form a global 'Us' without an opposing 'Them', whereas we certainly know that it is significantly easier to bond groups when such 'others' are present. Who will provide the out-group if all the humans on the planet are in the in-group?

Assuming that forming a global group is possible, this does not mean that we will remove all violence worldwide; but it does mean that we should bring an end to major inter-group conflict. Individual violence will continue for as long as some human beings perceive that their status differs from that of some others. Reducing levels of inequality will therefore be beneficial, as will other structures enabling a sense that individuals belong and that their status is respected.

Ultimately, as we have seen, humans are naturally driven to form bigger and bigger social groups, and have evolved to become more social over the millennia—this domestication, more than anything else, will lay the foundations for the global community.

It is clear that such a shift would take decades, if not generations, to complete. It is by no means certain that it would be possible for the multitudes of human identities to be subsumed into one global human identity. It is also by no means certain that the nation state would disappear, even though it is under significant threat at the time of writing. This, however, may be a moot point—for, following the innovations of writing, the printing press, and the Internet, we are now facing another, fourth monumental leap.

This time, it is being brought about by two technologies coupled together: artificial intelligence and brain-computer interface devices. Artificial intelligence—particularly so-called 'strong' artificial intelligence, which could surpass human intelligence by improving itself—may be with us by 2040.[13] (Shortly after, it would take off and self-grow in intelligence quality and quantity to infinite levels of intelligence, but that is the story of another book.) Brain-computer interface devices will come even faster:[14] in 2014 researchers managed to get two human brains to send simple binary signals to each other over the Internet, communicating using only conscious thought.[15]

What this means is that, before we are likely to have constructed our global group, our cognitions may well be interfacing with each other over an 'Internet' that will steadily grow in intelligence until it surpasses our own. Humans do not need a shared ideology for one physical global group; we need a shared ideology that solves the group problems in a globally and cognitively networked virtual society. But what do the five problems look like in such a society? And will the same solutions be applied online and offline?

For instance, how does the fact that our brains seek belonging and status play itself out in the virtual world? How do we structure our online community? What does a virtual hierarchy look like? Should the computer intelligence be at its top? Is disease about solving computer viruses, and can these spread to biological systems? As for punishment, can we expel people from this virtual world? What do the emergent properties of that system—like consciousness being an emergent property of interconnected brain modules, or politics being an emergent property of individual humans living in groups—look like? The answers to these questions will determine what our world looks like in 2050.

Overall, human macro history is a trend towards ever-larger group sizes and ever-decreasing violence. But history is a row of saw teeth; periods of disaggregation follow periods of aggregation. And unless we urgently solve the five group problems on a global scale, the resulting disaggregation and conflict will see us on the downward slope of a tooth—if we are not already there. Whether this slope will last ten years or fifty is unclear, but in light of the forthcoming cognitively networked global society, it may be an unwelcome distraction.

NOTES

PREFACE AND ACKNOWLEDGEMENTS

1. '*Prevent* Strategy', HM Government, presented to Parliament by the Secretary of State for the Home Department by Command of Her Majesty, June 2011, https://www.gov.uk/government/uploads/system/uploads/attachment_data/file/97976/prevent-strategy-review.pdf, last accessed 29 Aug 2017.
2. Martin, Mike, *An Intimate War: An Oral History of the Helmand Conflict*, London: Hurst, 2014, p. 9.
3. Hollande, François, 'Speech by the President of the Republic before a joint session of Parliament', Versailles, 16 November 2015, transcript available from France Diplomatie, http://www.diplomatie.gouv.fr/en/french-foreign-policy/defence-security/parisattacks-paris-terror-attacks-november-2015/article/speech-by-the-president-of-the-republic-before-a-joint-session-of-parliament, last accessed 29 Aug 2017.
4. The title of a 1973 essay by Theodosius Dobzhansky published in *American Biology Teacher*.
5. Clausewitz, Carl Von, *On War*, Princeton, NJ: Princeton University Press, 1989, p. 61.

INTRODUCTION

1. Sun Tzu, *The Art of War*, CreateSpace Independent Publishing platform, 2014, p. 5.

2. Pinker, Steven, *The Better Angels of our Nature: The Decline of Violence in History and its Causes*, London: Allen Lane, 2011, p. xxiv. This is also explored in more detail in Chapter 5.

3. Kahneman, Daniel, *Thinking, Fast and Slow*, London: Penguin, 2012, p. 98.

4. Morris, Ian, *War: What Is It Good For?*, London: Profile Books, 2015, p. 67.

5. Kahneman, op. cit., pp. 24–5.

6. Mercier, Hugo and Dan Sperber, *The Enigma of Reason: A New Theory of Human Understanding*, London: Allen Lane, 2017, pp. 176–7.

7. As do others, for example: Atran, Scott, *Talking to the Enemy: Violent Extremism, Sacred Values, and What It Means to Be Human*, London: Penguin, 2010, p. 39.

8. Ibid., pp. 473–501.

9. Thucydides, *History of the Peloponnesian War*, CreateSpace Independent Publishing Platform, 2017, p. 26.

10. Martin, Mike, *A Brief History of Helmand*, Warminster: Afghan COIN Centre, 2011.

11. Collier, Paul and Anke Hoeffler, 'Greed and grievance in civil war', *Oxford Economic Papers* 56 (2004), pp. 563–95.

12. Gat, Azar, *The Causes of War and the Spread of Peace*, Oxford: Oxford University Press, 2017, p. 93.

13. Gat, op. cit., pp. 95–6.

14. Malešević, Siniša, *The Rise of Organised Brutality: A Historical Sociology of Violence*, Cambridge: Cambridge University Press, 2017, p. 85.

15. Gat, op. cit., p. 97.

16. See, for instance, Harris, Marvin, 'Animal Capture and Yanomamo Warfare: Retrospect and New Evidence', *Journal of Anthropological Research* 40:1 (1984), pp. 183–201.

17. Chagnon, Napoleon, 'Life histories, blood revenge, and warfare in a tribal population', *Science* 239.4843 (1988), pp. 985–92.

18. Walt, Stephen, 'International Relations: One World, Many Theories', *Foreign Policy* 110 (1998), pp. 29–32.
19. E.g. Ross, Michael, 'What do we know about Natural Resources and Civil War?', *Journal of Peace Research* 41:3 (2004), pp. 337–56.
20. E.g. Kunovich, Robert and Randy Hodson, 'Conflict, religious identity, and ethnic intolerance in Croatia', *Social Forces* 78:2 (1999), pp. 643–68.
21. E.g. Dasgupta, Aditya, Kishore Gawande and Devesh Kapur, '(When) Do Antipoverty Programs Reduce Violence? India's Rural Employment Guarantee and Maoist Conflict', *International Organization* (2017), pp. 1–28.
22. E.g. Christie, Daniel and Noraini Noor, 'Humanising and Dehumanising the Other: Ethnic Conflict in Malaysia', in Seedat, Mohamed, Shahnaaz Suffla, Daniel J. Christie (eds), *Enlarging the Scope of Peace Psychology*, Springer International Publishing (2017), pp. 109–57.
23. E.g. Braithwaite, Alex, Niheer Dasandi and David Hudson, 'Does poverty cause conflict? Isolating the causal origins of the conflict trap', *Conflict Management and Peace Science* 33:1 (2016), pp. 45–66.
24. E.g. Gurr, Ted, *Why Men Rebel*, Abingdon: Routledge, 2012, p. viii.
25. E.g. Fearon, James and David Laitin, 'Ethnicity, Insurgency, and Civil War', *American Political Science Review* 97:1 (2003), pp. 75–90.
26. Wilson, David Sloan, 'A theory of group selection', *Proceedings of the National Academy of Sciences* 72:1 (1975), pp. 143–6.
27. Abbot, Patrick et al., 'Inclusive fitness theory and eusociality', *Nature* 471.7339, (2011).
28. For instance, France during World War One. See Pison, Gilles, '1914–2014: A century of change in the French population pyramid', *Population & Societies* 509 (March 2014).
29. Ayling, Ron and Kimberly Kelly, 'Dealing with conflict: nat-

ural resources and dispute resolution', *The Commonwealth Forestry Review* 76:3 (1997), pp. 182–5.

30. Saddington, Denis, 'Under the centurion's boot: corruption and its containment in the Roman army', *Acta Classica: Proceedings of the Classical Association of South Africa*, Supplement 4 (2012), pp. 122–30.

31. Sapolsky, Robert, *Behave: The Biology of Humans at Our Best and Worst*, London: Bodley Head, 2017, p. 314.

32. Churchill, Winston: 'Never ... was so much owed by so many to so few', *Hansard* HC Deb., vol. 364, col. 1159 (20 August 1940), https://www.parliament.uk/about/living-heritage/transformingsociety/private-lives/yourcountry/collections/churchillexhibition/churchill-the-orator/human-conflict/, last accessed 19 Dec 2017.

33. As in France after the French Revolution, for instance.

34. De Quervain, Dominique et al., 'The neural basis of altruistic punishment', *Science* 305.5688 (2004), p. 1254.

35. Konner, Melvin and S. Boyd Eaton, 'Palaeolithic nutrition: twenty-five years later', *Nutrition in Clinical Practice* 25:6 (2010), pp. 594–602.

36. Johnston, Victor S., *Why We Feel: The Science of Human Emotions*, New York: Perseus Publishing, 1999.

37. Pison, op. cit., p. 1.

38. Including Jonathan Haidt, Edward Wilson and David Wilson.

39. Traulsen, Arne and Martin Nowak, 'Evolution of cooperation by multilevel selection', *Proceedings of the National Academy of Sciences* 103:29, (2006), pp. 10952–5.

40. Abbot et al., op. cit.

41. Foley, Robert, 'The adaptive legacy of human evolution: A search for the environment of evolutionary adaptedness', *Evolutionary Anthropology: Issues, News, and Reviews* 4:6, (1995), pp. 194–203.

42. Hibbing, John, Kevin Smith and John Alford, *Predisposed:*

Liberals, Conservatives, and the Biology of Political Differences, Abingdon: Routledge, 2013, pp. 212–7.

43. Ibid., p. 212.
44. Pinker, op. cit., pp. 616–7.
45. Mock, Steven and Thomas Homer-Dixon, *The Ideological Conflict Project: Theoretical and Methodological Foundations*, Waterloo, ON: Centre for International Governance Innovation, 2015, p. 7.
46. See, for instance, Spain, Sarah et al., 'A genome-wide analysis of putative functional and exonic variation associated with extremely high intelligence', *Molecular Psychiatry* 21:8 (2016), p. 1145.
47. Vasquez, John, *The War Puzzle Revisited*, Cambridge: Cambridge University Press, 2009, pp. 23–4.
48. Daly, Martin and Margo Wilson, *Homicide*, New York: Aldine de Gruyter, 1988, p. 14.

1. EVOLUTION AND THE HUMAN MIND

1. Dobzhansky, Theodosius, 'Nothing in Biology Makes Sense except in the Light of Evolution', *The American Biology Teacher* 75:2, (2013), pp. 87–91.
2. Fuentes, Agustin, *Evolution of Human Behaviour*, Oxford: Oxford University Press, 2008.
3. Hedges, S. Blai, and Sudhir Kumar, 'Genomic clocks and evolutionary timescales', *Trends in Genetics* 19:4 (2003), pp. 200–6.
4. Ohta, Tomoko, 'Very slightly deleterious mutations and the molecular clock', *Journal of Molecular Evolution* 26:1, (1987), pp. 1–6.
5. Hibbing, John, Kevin Smith and John Alford, *Predisposed: Liberals, Conservatives, and the Biology of Political Differences*, Abingdon: Routledge, 2013, p. 215.

6. Amemiya, Chris et al., 'Analysis of the African coelacanth genome sheds light on tetrapod evolution', *Nature* 496.7445, (2013), p. 311.

7. Dunbar, Robin and Susanne Shultz, 'Evolution in the social brain', *Science* 317.5843, (2007), pp. 1344–7.

8. Knight, Richard, 'Are North Koreans really three inches shorter than South Koreans?', *BBC News Magazine*, 23 April 2012, http://www.bbc.co.uk/news/magazine-17774210, last accessed 29 Aug 2017.

9. Sapolsky, Robert, *Behave: The Biology of Humans at Our Best and Worst*, London: Bodley Head, 2017, p. 248.

10. Emilsson, Valur, et al., 'Genetics of gene expression and its effect on disease', *Nature* 452.7186, (2008), p. 423.

11. Sapolsky, op. cit., p. 175.

12. Rose, Hilary, and Steven Rose, *Alas Poor Darwin: Arguments against Evolutionary Psychology*. London: Random House, 2010.

13. Pinker, Steven, *How the Mind Works*, London: Penguin, 1999, p. 42.

14. Wilson, David Sloan, 'A theory of group selection', *Proceedings of the national academy of sciences* 72:1 (1975), pp. 143–6.

15. See, for instance, Payne, Kenneth, *The Psychology of Modern Conflict*, New York: Palgrave Macmillan, 2015, p. 78; LeBlanc, Steven and Katherine Register, *Constant Battles: Why We Fight*, New York: St Martin's Press, 2003, p. 90.

16. Hamilton, William, 'The evolution of altruistic behavior', *The American Naturalist* 97.896, (1963), pp. 354–6.

17. Foster, Kevin, Tom Wenseleers and Francis Ratnieks, 'Kin selection is the key to altruism', *Trends in Ecology & Evolution* 21:2 (2006), pp. 57–60.

18. Wilson, op. cit..

19. Williams, George and Austin Burt, *Adaptation and Natural Selection: A Critique of Some Current Evolutionary Thought*, Princeton, NJ: Princeton University Press, 1996.

20. Pinker, Steven, 'The False Allure of Group Selection', *Edge*, 18 June 2012, https://www.edge.org/conversation/steven_pinker-the-false-allure-of-group-selection, last accessed 29 Aug 2017.

21. Abbot, Patrick et al., 'Inclusive fitness theory and eusociality', *Nature* 471.7339 (2011).

22. Henrich, Joseph and Richard McElreath, 'Dual-inheritance theory: the evolution of human cultural capacities and cultural evolution', in Dunbar, Robin and Louise Barrett (eds), *Oxford Handbook of Evolutionary Psychology*, Oxford: Oxford University Press, 2007, pp. 555–70.

23. Henrich, Joseph, 'Cultural group selection, coevolutionary processes and large-scale cooperation', *Journal of Economic Behavior & Organization* 53:1 (2004), pp. 3–35.

24. I am ascribing a correlation rather than a causation here; this is a subject of debate.

25. For criticisms of Cultural Group Selection see Soltis, Joseph, Robert Boyd and Peter Richerson, 'Can group-functional behaviors evolve by cultural group selection?: An empirical test', *Current Anthropology* 36:3 (1995), pp. 473–94; Driscoll, Catherine, 'The evolutionary culture concepts', *Philosophy of Science* 84:1 (2017), pp. 35–55; and Mace, Ruth and Antonio Silva, 'The role of cultural group selection in explaining human cooperation is a hard case to prove', *Behavioral and Brain Sciences* 39 (2016).

26. Harari, Yuval, *Sapiens: A Brief History of Humankind*, London: Vintage, 2014, p. 12.

27. 'Evolutionary Psychology', *Internet Encyclopaedia of Philosophy*, n.d., http://www.iep.utm.edu/evol-psy/, last accessed 29 Aug 2017.

28. Anderson, Peter and Walter Schwab, 'The organization and structure of nerve and muscle in the jellyfish Cyanea capillata (Coelenterata; Scyphozoa)', *Journal of Morphology* 170:3 (1981), pp. 383–99.

29. Aunger, R and Valerie Curtis, *Gaining Control: How Human Behavior Evolved*, Oxford: Oxford University Press, 2015, p. 40.

30. Marlowe, Frank, 'A critical period for provisioning by Hadza men: Implications for pair bonding', *Evolution and Human Behavior* 24:3 (2003), pp. 217–29.

31. Storrs, Carina, 'In the Swiss Army Knife of the brain, the ability to recognize faces may be a specialised tool', *Scientific American*, 7 January 2010, https://blogs.scientificamerican.com/observations/in-the-swiss-army-knife-of-the-brain-the-ability-to-recognize-faces-may-be-a-specialized-tool/, last accessed 29 Aug 2017.

32. Fodor, Jerry, *Modularity of Mind: An Essay on Faculty Psychology*, Cambridge, MA: MIT Press, 1983.

33. Scholars delineate a number of different types of modules. For a useful review see Samuels, Richard, 'Massively modular minds: evolutionary psychology and cognitive architecture', in Carruthers, Peter and Andrew Chamberlain (eds), *Evolution and the Human Mind: Modularity, Language and Meta-Cognition*, Cambridge: Cambridge University Press, 2000, p. 13.

34. Mesulam, Marsel, 'Large-scale neurocognitive networks and distributed processing for attention, language, and memory', *Annals of Neurology* 28:5 (1990), pp. 597–613.

35. Samuels, op. cit., p. 13.

36. For criticism of the 'blank slate' notion, see Pinker, Steven, *The Blank Slate: The Modern Denial of Human Nature*, London: Penguin, 2003.

37. Samuels, op. cit., p. 13.

38. Ellis, Bruce, 'The evolution of sexual attraction: Evaluative mechanisms in women', in Barkow, Jerome H., Leda Cosmides and John Tooby (eds), *The Adapted Mind: Evolutionary Psychology and the Generation of Culture*, New York, NY: Oxford University Press, 1992, pp. 267–88.

39. Öhman, Arne, 'Fear and Anxiety: Overlaps and Dissociations', in Lewis, Michael, Jeannette Haviland-Jones and Lisa Feldman Barrett (eds), *Handbook of Emotions*, 3rd edn, New York, NY: The Guildford Press, 2008, p. 711.

40. Sapolsky, op. cit., p. 29.

41. LeDoux, Joseph and Elizabeth Phelps, 'Emotional Networks in the Brain', in Lewis et al. (eds), op. cit., p. 169.

42. Williams, Lawrence and John Bargh, 'Experiencing physical warmth promotes interpersonal warmth', *Science* 322.5901 (2008), pp. 606–7.

43. Pinker, *How the Mind Works*, p. 42.

44. Mercier, Hugo and Dan Sperber, *The Enigma of Reason: A New Theory of Human Understanding*, London: Allen Lane, 2017, p. 207.

45. Kahneman, Daniel, *Thinking, Fast and Slow*, London: Penguin, 2012, pp. 97–8.

46. Hogg, Michael and Sarah Hains, 'Friendship and group identification: A new look at the role of cohesiveness in groupthink', *European Journal of Social Psychology* 28.3 (1998), pp. 323–41.

47. Atran, Scott, *In Gods We Trust: The Evolutionary Landscape of Religion*, Oxford: Oxford University Press, 2002, pp. 60–1.

48. Atran, Scott, *Talking to the Enemy: Violent Extremism, Sacred Values, and What It Means to Be Human*, London: Penguin, 2010, pp. 13, 39.

49. Eagleman, David, *The Brain: The Story of You*, Edinburgh: Canongate Books, 2015, pp. 6–7.

50. Brown, Donald, *Human Universals*, New York, NY: McGraw Hill Inc., 1991, pp. 92–4.

51. Chomsky, Noam, *Aspects of the Theory of Syntax*, vol. 11, Cambridge, MA: MIT Press, 2014, p. 25.

52. Brown, op. cit., p. 85.

53. Atran, Scott, *Cognitive Foundations of Natural History: Towards an Anthropology of Science*, Cambridge: Cambridge University Press, 1993, p. 110.

54. Carey, Susan and Elizabeth Spelke, 'Domain-specific knowledge and conceptual change', in Hirschfeld, Lawrence A. and Susan A. Gelman, *Mapping the Mind: Domain Specificity in Cognition and Culture*, Cambridge: Cambridge University Press, 1994, p. 169.

55. Atran, *Cognitive Foundations*, op. cit., p. 17.

56. Carey and Spelke, op. cit., p. 169.

57. De Cruz, Helen, 'Why are some numerical concepts more successful than others? An evolutionary perspective on the history of number concepts', *Evolution and Human Behavior* 27:4 (2006), pp. 306–23.

58. Sperber, Dan and Lawrence Hirschfeld, 'The cognitive foundations of cultural stability and diversity', *Trends in Cognitive Sciences* 8:1 (2004), pp. 40–6.

59. Adolphs, Ralph, 'Social cognition and the human brain', *Trends in Cognitive Sciences* 3:12 (1999), pp. 469–79.

60. Sapolsky, op. cit., p. 235.

61. Note that heritability is not technically the same as whether a trait is due to genes or environment; rather, it is about the degree of genetic influence on the variation in the trait's expression across the population. Ibid., p. 241.

62. Heutink, Peter, Frank Verhuls, and Dorret Boomsma, 'A longitudinal twin study on IQ, executive functioning, and attention problems during childhood and early adolescence', *Acta Neurol. Belg* 106 (2006), pp. 191–207.

63. Lewis, Gary and Timothy Bates, 'Common genetic influences underpin religiosity, community integration, and existential uncertainty', *Journal of Research in Personality* 47:4 (2013), pp. 398–405.

64. Kandler, Christian, Wiebke Bleidorn and Rainer Riemann, 'Left or right? Sources of political orientation: The roles of genetic factors, cultural transmission, assortative mating, and personality', *Journal of Personality and Social Psychology* 102:3 (2012), p. 633.

65. Fowler, James, Laura Baker and Christopher Dawes, 'Genetic variation in political participation', *American Political Science Review* 102:2 (2008), pp. 233–48.

66. Cesarini, David et al., 'Heritability of cooperative behavior in the trust game', *Proceedings of the National Academy of Sciences* 105:10 (2008), pp. 3721–6.

67. Orey, Byron D'Andra and Hyung Park, 'Nature, nurture, and ethnocentrism in the Minnesota Twin Study', *Twin Research and Human Genetics* 15:1 (2012), pp. 71–3.

68. This is not the same as support for a particular political party, which is much more environmentally determined, especially in countries with a high number of political parties. Alford, John, Carolyn Funk and John Hibbing, 'Are political orientations genetically transmitted?', *American Political Science Review* 99:2 (2005), pp. 153–67.

69. Saad, Lydia, 'Conservatives Hang On to Ideology Lead by a Thread', *Gallup*, http://www.gallup.com/poll/188129/conservatives-hang-ideology-lead-thread.aspx, last accessed 30 Aug 2017.

70. Alford et al., op. cit., pp. 153–67.

71. Jost, J. T., Glaser, J., Kruglanski, A. W. and Sulloway, F. J., 'Political conservatism as motivated social cognition'. *Psychological Bulletin* 129:3 (2003), pp. 339–75.

72. Hibbing et al., op. cit., pp. 221–3.

73. Ibid., p. 226.

2. *DRIVES*

1. Rose, Damon, 'The Hidden Burden of War Injuries and Other Stories', *BBC News Ouch Blog*, 3 January 2014, http://www.bbc.co.uk/news/blogs-ouch-25581022, last accessed 30 Aug 2017.

2. Combat was once so described to me by a very experienced infantry colonel, with whom I was reminiscing in London about our tours in Afghanistan.

3. THE SUBCONSCIOUS

1. Rubin, Gretchen, 'Feeling Lonely? Consider Trying These 7 Strategies', *Gretchen Rubin Blog*, 6 November 2013, http://gretchenrubin.com/happiness_project/2013/11/feeling-lonely-consider-trying-these-7-strategies/, last accessed 30 Aug 2017.

2. Johnston, Victor, *Why We Feel: The Science of Human Emotions*, New York: Perseus Publishing, 1999.

3. Sapolsky, Robert, *Behave: The Biology of Humans at Our Best and Worst*, London: Bodley Head, 2017, p. 672.

4. PankSepp, Jaak, 'The Affective Brain and Core Consciousness: How does Neural Activity Generate Emotional Feelings?' in Lewis, Michael, Jeannette Haviland-Jones and Lisa Feldman Barrett (eds), *Handbook of Emotions*, 3rd edn, New York: The Guildford Press, 2008, p. 54.

5. Bick, Johanna et al., 'Foster mother–infant bonding: associations between foster mothers' oxytocin production, electrophysiological brain activity, feelings of commitment, and caregiving quality', *Child Development* 84:3 (2013), pp. 826–40.

6. Nesse, Randolph and Phoebe Ellsworth, 'Evolution, emotions, and emotional disorders', *American Psychologist* 64:2 (2009), p. 130.

7. Tooby, John and Leda Cosmides, 'The Evolutionary Psychology of the Emotions and Their Relationship to Internal Regulatory Vairables', in Lewis et al. (eds), op. cit., p. 117.

8. Atran, Scott, *In Gods We Trust: The Evolutionary Landscape of Religion*, Oxford: Oxford University Press, 2002, p. 11.

9. Lang, Peter et al. (eds), *Attention and Orienting: Sensory and Motivational Processes*, New York, NY: Routledge, 2013, p. 49.

10. Fischer, Agneta and Anthony Manstead, 'Social Functions of Emotion and Emotion Regulation', in Lewis et al. (eds), op. cit., pp. 456–65.

11. Kalin, Ned and Steven Sheltona, 'Nonhuman primate models to study anxiety, emotion regulation, and psychopathology', *Annals of the New York Academy of Sciences* 1008:1 (2003), pp. 189–200.

12. Aureli, Filippo, 'Post-conflict anxiety in nonhuman primates: The mediating role of emotion in conflict resolution', *Aggressive Behavior* 23:5 (1997), pp. 315–28.

13. Wallin, Nils Lennart, Björn Merker and Steven Brown (eds), *The Origins of Music*, Cambridge, MA: MIT Press, 2001, p. 77.

14. Urquiza-Haas, Esmeralda and Kurt Kotrschal, 'The mind behind anthropomorphic thinking: attribution of mental states to other species, *Animal Behaviour* 109 (2015), pp. 167–76.

15. Matsumoto, David et al., 'Facial Expressions of Emotion', in Lewis et al. (eds), op. cit., p. 211.

16. Aunger, R and Valerie Curtis, *Gaining Control: How Human Behavior Evolved*, Oxford: Oxford University Press, 2015, p. 61.

17. Aron, Arthur et al., 'Reward, motivation, and emotion systems associated with early-stage intense romantic love', *Journal of Neurophysiology* 94:1 (2005), pp. 327–37.

18. Buss, David et al., 'Sex differences in jealousy: Evolution, physiology, and psychology', *Psychological Science* 3:4 (1992), pp. 251–6. Although the jealousy emotion was originally geared towards reproduction and based on gendered roles in offspring care—and therefore produced gender-differentiated responses in relation to heterosexual pairs—studies have shown that, on average, men (as opposed to women) approach romantic/sexual relationships in a particular way, regardless of sexuality. See also Buss, David, *The Evolution of Desire: Strategies of Human Mating*, 4th edn, New York, NY: Basic Books, 2016.

19. Van Kleef, Gerben, 'How emotions regulate social life: The emotions as social information (EASI) model', *Current Directions in Psychological Science* 18:3 (2009), p. 184–8.

20. Pinker, Steven, *How the Mind Works*, London: Penguin, 1999, pp. 412–4.

21. Ibid.

22. Atran, op. cit., p. 136.

23. Fischer and Manstead, op. cit., p. 457.

24. Keltner, Dacher and Brenda Buswell, 'Embarrassment: its distinct form and appeasement functions', *Psychological Bulletin* 122:3 (1997), p. 250.

25. Haidt, Jonathan, Clark McCauley and Paul Rozin, 'Individual differences in sensitivity to disgust: A scale sampling seven domains of disgust elicitors', *Personality and Individual Differences* 16:5 (1994), pp. 701–13.

26. Pinker, op. cit., p. 412.

27. Smith, James, 'Socioeconomic status and health', *The American Economic Review* 88:2 (1998), pp. 192–6.

28. Sapolsky, op. cit., p. 291.

29. Ibid., p. 314.

30. Bowles, Samuel and Herbert Gintis, 'The evolution of strong reciprocity: cooperation in heterogeneous populations', *Theoretical Population Biology* 65:1 (2004), pp. 17–28.

31. 'Transcript: President Bush's Speech on the War on Terrorism', 30 November 2005, *The Washington Post*, http://www.washingtonpost.com/wp-dyn/content/article/2005/11/30/AR2005113000667.html, last accessed 30 Aug 2017.

32. '"A Crusader-Zionist-Hindu War Against Muslims": Edited translation of an audiotape attributed to al-Qaeda leader Osama bin Laden', *Outlook*, 23 April 2006, https://www.outlookindia.com/website/story/a-crusader-zionist-hindu-war-against-muslims/231048, last accessed 30 Aug 2017.

4. COMPETITION AND STATUS

1. Hobbes, Thomas, *Leviathan* (revised student edition, ed. R. Tuck), Cambridge: Cambridge University Press, 1997, p. 88.

2. 'Competition', *Untamed Science*, n.d., http://www.untamed-science.com/biology/ecology/interactions-among-organisms/competition/, last accessed 30 Aug 2017.

3. Primarily between same-sex individuals due to gender-segregated roles like hunting, dealing with out-groups, care for offspring and so on; these ensure that same-sex group members have more closely aligned goals.

4. Townsend, Colin R., Michael Begon and John L. Harper, 'Glossary', in *Essentials of Ecology* (3rd ed), Oxford: Blackwell Publishing, available online at http://www.blackwellpublishing.com/Townsend/Glossary/GlossaryS.asp, last accessed 30 Aug 2017.

5. Gat, Azar, *War in Human Civilization*, Oxford: Oxford University Press, 2006, p. 72.

6. Chauvin, Christophe and Carol M. Berman, 'Intergenerational transmission of behavior', in Thierry, Bernard, Mewa Singh and Werner Kaumanns (eds), *Macaque Societies: A Model for the Study of Social Organization*, Cambridge: Cambridge University Press, 2004, p. 209.

7. Polis, Gary, 'The evolution and dynamics of intraspecific predation', *Annual Review of Ecology and Systematics* 12:1 (1981), pp. 225–51.

8. Ibid.

9. Hobbes, op. cit., p. 88.

10. Sapolsky, Robert, *Behave: The Biology of Humans at Our Best and Worst*, London: Bodley Head, 2017, p. 121.

11. Daly, Martin and Margo Wilson, *Killing the Competition: Economic Inequality and Homicide*, New York, NY: Routledge, 1990, p. 9.

12. Eisner, Manuel, 'Long-term historical trends in violent crime', *Crime and Justice* 30 (2003), pp. 83–142.

13. Daly and Wilson, op. cit., pp. 2, 51, 53.

14. Ibid., p. 50.

15. Ibid., pp. 56–7.

16. Ibid., p. 14.
17. Ibid., pp. 119–20.
18. There is a vast debate on culture in the scholarly literature which would take several books to discuss.
19. Gastil, Raymond D., 'Homicide and a Regional Culture of Violence', *American Sociological Review* 36:3 (June 1971), pp. 412–27.
20. Kashima, Yoshihisa, 'How can you capture cultural dynamics?', *Frontiers in Psychology* 5 (2014).
21. See, for instance, Henrich, Joseph, 'Rice, psychology, and innovation', *Science* 344.6184 (2014), pp. 593–4.
22. Varner, Iris and Katrin Varner, 'The Relationship Between Culture and Legal Systems and the Impact on Intercultural Business Communication', *Global Advances in Business Communication* 3:1 (2014), p. 3.
23. Daly, Martin and Margo Wilson, *Homicide*, New York, NY: Aldine de Gruyter, 1988, pp. 286–7.
24. Daly and Wilson, *Homicide*, pp. 34–5; Pinker, Steven, *How the Mind Works*, London: Penguin, 1999, p. 428.
25. Wilson, Margo and Martin Daly, 'Competitiveness, Risk Taking, and Violence: The Young Male Syndrome', *Ethology and Sociobiology* 6:1 (1985), pp. 59–73.
26. Daly and Wilson, *Killing the Competition*, p. 54; Daly and Wilson, *Homicide*, pp. 125–6; Ressler, Robert, Ann Burgess and John Douglas, *Sexual Homicide: Patterns and Motives*, New York, NY: The Free Press, 1992, p. 8.
27. Eisner, op. cit.
28. Ibid.
29. Daly and Wilson, *Homicide*, p. 284.
30. Daly and Wilson, *Killing the Competition.*, pp. 54–5.
31. Daly and Wilson, *Homicide*, p. 201.
32. Payne, Kenneth, *The Psychology of Modern Conflict*, New York, NY: Palgrave Macmillan, 2015, p. 50.
33. Townsend, John and Gary Levy, 'Effects of potential partners'

costume and physical attractiveness on sexuality and partner selection', *The Journal of Psychology* 124:4 (1990), pp. 371–89.

34. Kenrick, Douglas et al., 'Evolution, Traits, and the Stages of Human Courtship: Qualifying the Parental Investment Model', *Journal of Personality* 58:1 (1990), pp. 97–116.

35. Puts, David, 'Beauty and the beast: Mechanisms of sexual selection in humans', *Evolution and Human Behavior* 31:3 (2010), pp. 157–75.

36. Ibid.

37. Clutton-Brock, Timothy, 'Size, sexual dimorphism, and polygyny in primates', in Jungers, William J. (ed.), *Size and Scaling in Primate Biology*, New York, NY: Springer US, pp. 51–60.

38. Strenze, Tarmo, 'Intelligence and socioeconomic success: A meta-analytic review of longitudinal research', *Intelligence* 35:5 (2007), pp. 401–26.

39. Daly and Wilson, *Homicide*, p. 143.

40. Clutton-Brock, Timothy and Paul H. Harvey, 'Primate ecology and social organization', *Journal of Zoology* 183:1 (1977), pp. 1–39.

41. Daly and Wilson, *Killing the Competition*, p. 55.

42. Daly and Wilson, *Homicide*, p. 137.

43. Clutton-Brock, op. cit., pp. 51–60.

44. Dupanloup, Isabelle et al., 'A recent shift from polygyny to monogamy in humans is suggested by the analysis of worldwide Y-chromosome diversity', *Journal of Molecular Evolution* 57:1 (2003), pp. 85–97.

45. Mark, Joshua J., 'Ramesses II', *Ancient History Encyclopaedia*, 2 September 2009, http://www.ancient.eu/Ramesses_II/, last accessed 31Aug 2017; Sapolsky, op. cit., p. 366.

46. Zerjal, Tatiana et al., 'The genetic legacy of the Mongols', *The American Journal of Human Genetics* 72:3 (2003), pp. 717–21.

47. Wilson and Daly, 'Competitiveness, Risk Taking', pp. 59–73.

48. Ridley, Matt, 'Polygamy Fuels Violence', *The Rational Optimist Blog*, 24 December 2014, http://www.rationaloptimist.com/blog/polygamy-fuels-violence, last accessed 31 Aug 2017; Otterbein, Keith, *Feuding and Warfare*, Longhorn, PA: Gordon & Breach, 1994, p. 103.

49. Henrich, Joseph, Robert Boyd, and Peter Richerson, 'The puzzle of monogamous marriage', *Phil. Trans. R. Soc. B* 367.1589 (2012), pp. 657–69. The authors of this excellent paper looked at how the one-child policy was implemented gradually, with different regions adopting it at different times—thus allowing the changing sex ratios to be studied alongside changing rates of violence.

50. Wilson and Daly, 'Competitiveness, Risk Taking', pp. 59–73.

51. Daly and Wilson, *Killing the Competition.*, p. 47; Pinker, op. cit., p. 478.

52. Daly and Wilson, *Homicide*, p. 168.

53. Daly and Wilson, *Killing the Competition*, p. 53.

54. Daly and Wilson, *Killing the Competition*, p. 100.

55. Daly and Wilson, *Homicide*, p. 132.

56. Gat, Azar, *The Causes of War & The Spread of Peace: But Will War Rebound?*, Oxford: Oxford University Press, 2017, p. 180.

57. Sapolsky, op. cit., p. 314.

58. Gat, *The Causes of War*, op. cit., pp. 47–9.

59. Anderson, Cameron and Gavin Kilduff, 'The pursuit of status in social groups', *Current Directions in Psychological Science* 18:5 (2009), pp. 295–8.

60. Miles, David, *The Tale of the Axe: How the Neolithic Revolution Transformed Britain*, London: Thames and Hudson, 2016, p. 183.

61. Kazun, A. D., '"Rally Around the Flag" Effect. How and Why Support of the Authorities Grows During International Conflicts and Tragedies?' *Polis. Political Studies* 1:1 (2017), pp. 136–46.

62. Richardson, L, *Statistics of Deadly Quarrels*, Pittsburgh, PA: Boxwood Press, 1960.

63. Pinker, Steven, *The Better Angels of Our Nature: The Decline of Violence in History and its Causes*, London: Allen Lane, 2011, pp. 215–6.
64. Ibid.
65. 'Is Bush's Iraq Stance Rooted in Revenge?', *ABC News*, 18 March 2003, http://abcnews.go.com/US/story?id=90764&page=1, last accessed 31 Aug 2017.
66. 'George W. Bush discusses his father, Jeb in 2016, and the Iraq War', *Face The Nation*, 9 November 2014, available at https://www.youtube.com/watch?v=tZXYvtJCPkg, accessed 31 Aug 2017.
67. Mason, Rowena, Anushka Asthana and Heather Stewart, 'Tony Blair: "I express more sorrow, regret and apology than you can ever believe', *The Guardian*, 6 July 2016, https://www.theguardian.com/uk-news/2016/jul/06/tony-blair-deliberately-exaggerated-threat-from-iraq-chilcot-report-war-inquiry, last accessed 31 Aug 2017.
68. Johnson, Samuel et al., 'Opponent uses of simplicity and complexity in causal explanation', *Proceedings of the 39th Annual Conference of the Cognitive Science Society* (2017), p. 606.
69. 'Concepts: Power Law', *New England Complex Systems Institute*, n.d., http://www.necsi.edu/guide/concepts/power-law.html, last accessed 31 Aug 2017.
70. Cederman, Lars-Erik, 'Modeling the size of wars: from billiard balls to sandpiles', *American Political Science Review* 97:1 (2003), pp. 135–50.
71. Pinker, *Better Angels*, p. 210.
72. Ibid., pp. 215–6.
73. 'The Mathematical Structure of Terrorism', *Phys.Org*, 22 May 2006, http://phys.org/news/2006-05-mathematical-terrorism.html, last accessed 31 Aug 2017.
74. Pinker, *Better Angels*, pp. 215–6.
75. Chatterjee, Arnab and Bikas Chakrabarti, 'Fat tailed distributions for deaths in conflicts and disasters', *Reports in Advances of Physical Sciences* 1:1 (2017).

76. Schneier, Bruce, *Liars and Outliers*, Indianapolis, IN: John Wiley & Sons, 2012, p. 155.

77. Pinker, Steven, *The Stuff of Thought*, London: Penguin, 2007, Preface.

78. Sapolsky, op. cit., p. 432.

79. See, for instance, Schneider, Rebecca, Robert Zulandt and Paul Moore, 'Individual and status recognition in the crayfish, Orconectes rusticus: the effects of urine release on fight dynamics', *Behaviour* 138:2 (2001), pp. 137–53.

80. Sapolsky, op. cit. p. 431.

81. Ibid., pp. 106–7.

82. Ibid.

83. Eisenegger, Christoph, Johannes Haushofer and Ernst Fehr, 'The role of testosterone in social interaction', *Trends in Cognitive Sciences* 15:6 (2011), pp. 263–71.

84. Fuster, Joaquín, 'Frontal lobe and cognitive development', *Journal of Neurocytology* 31:3–5 (2002), pp. 373–85.

85. Eisenegger, op. cit., pp. 263–71.

86. Sapolsky, op. cit., p. 105.

87. Schultheiss, Oliver, Kenneth Campbell and David McClelland, 'Implicit power motivation moderates men's testosterone responses to imagined and real dominance success', *Hormones and Behavior* 36:3 (1999), pp. 234–41.

88. Li, Cheng-Yu et al., 'Fighting experience alters brain androgen receptor expression dependent on testosterone status', *Proceedings of the Royal Society of London B: Biological Sciences* 281:1796 (2014).

89. Sapolsky, op. cit., pp. 102–3.

90. Ibid.

91. Whilst it has been the case for the vast majority of history that leaders are male, and hence have higher levels of testosterone, this is now changing, with potentially unknown effects on how human leaders play out status challenges. Interestingly, one study has shown that queens have been more likely to wage

war than kings, but the reasons for this are uncertain. The study authors found that unmarried queens were more likely than unmarried kings to be attacked, and that married queens were more likely to attack than married kings—but queens may also be motivated by other non-evolutionary factors like socialisation, or attempting to operate effectively in a 'man's world'. See 'Who gets into more wars, kings or queens?', *The Economist*, 1 June 2017, https://www.economist.com/news/europe/21722877-european-history-answer-queens-especially-married-ones-who-gets-more-wars-kings, last accessed 31 Aug 2017.

92. Mehta, Pranjal et al., 'Hormonal underpinnings of status conflict: Testosterone and cortisol are related to decisions and satisfaction in the hawk-dove game', *Hormones and Behavior* 92 (2017), pp. 114–54.

5. ESCAPING VIOLENCE THROUGH BELONGING

1. Ishiguro, Kazuo, *When We Were Orphans*, London: Faber and Faber, 2013.
2. Small, Meredith, 'The evolution of female sexuality and mate selection in humans', *Human Nature* 3:2 (1992), pp. 133–56.
3. Puts, David, 'Beauty and the beast: Mechanisms of sexual selection in humans', *Evolution and Human Behavior* 31:3 (2010), pp. 157–75.
4. Nettle, Daniel, 'Height and reproductive success in a cohort of British men', *Human Nature* 13:4 (2002), pp. 473–91.
5. Singh, Devendra, 'Female mate value at a glance: Relationship of waist-to-hip ratio to health, fecundity and attractiveness', *Neuroendocrinology Letters* 23:Suppl. 4 (2002), pp. 81–91.
6. Jones, Benedict et al., 'Facial symmetry and judgements of apparent health: support for a "good genes" explanation of the attractiveness–symmetry relationship', *Evolution and Human Behavior* 22:6 (2001), pp. 417–29.

7. Wedekind, Claus et al., 'MHC-dependent mate preferences in humans', *Proceedings of the Royal Society of London B: Biological Sciences* 260:1359 (1995), pp. 245–9.

8. Pinker, Steven, *How the Mind Works*, London: Penguin, 1999, p. 417.

9. Domínguez-Rodrigo, Manuel, 'Hunting and scavenging by early humans: the state of the debate', *Journal of World Prehistory* 16:1 (2002), pp. 1–54.

10. Gazda, Stefanie et al., 'A division of labour with role specialization in group–hunting bottlenose dolphins (Tursiops truncatus) off Cedar Key, Florida', *Proceedings of the Royal Society of London B: Biological Sciences* 272:1559 (2005), pp. 135–40.

11. Hamilton, M et al., 'Nonlinear scaling of space use in human hunter-gatherers', *Proceedings of the National Academy of Sciences*, 104:11 (2007), pp. 4765–9.

12. Ridley, Matt, *The Rational Optimist*, London: HarperCollins, 2011, p. 38.

13. North, Douglass, John Wallis and Barry Weingast, *Violence and Social Orders: A Conceptual Framework for Interpreting Recorded Human History*, Cambridge: Cambridge University Press, 2009, p. xvii.

14. I have borrowed the term groupishness from Jonathan Haidt's book *The Righteous Mind*, London: Penguin, 2012, p. 219.

15. Ibid., p. 221.

16. Moffett, Mark, 'Human identity and the evolution of societies', *Human Nature* 24:3 (2013), pp. 219–67.

17. Henrich, Joseph, *The Secret of Our Success*, Princeton, NJ: Princeton University Press, 2016, p. 188.

18. Dawkins, Richard, *The Blind Watchmaker: Why the Evidence of Evolution Reveals a Universe without Design*, London: W. W. Norton & Company, 2015.

19. Pedersen, Cort, 'Biological aspects of social bonding and the roots of human violence', *Annals of the New York Academy of Sciences* 1036:1 (2004), pp. 106–27.

20. Ibid.

21. Cobo, E, 'Uterine and milk-ejecting activities during human labor', *Journal of Applied Physiology* 24:3 (1968), pp. 317–23.

22. Loup, F. et al., 'Localization of high-affinity binding sites for oxytocin and vasopressin in the human brain. An autoradiographic study', *Brain Research* 555:2 (1991), pp. 220–32.

23. Gholipour, Bahar, '5 Ways Fatherhood Changes a Man's Brain', *Live Science*, 14 June 2014, http://www.livescience.com/46322-fatherhood-changes-brain.html, last accessed 01 Sep 2017.

24. MacDonald, Kai and Tina Marie MacDonald, 'The peptide that binds: a systematic review of oxytocin and its prosocial effects in humans', *Harvard Review of Psychiatry* 18:1 (2010), pp. 1–21.

25. Atran, Scott, *Talking to the Enemy*, London: Penguin, 2010, p. 303.

26. Bartels, Andreas and Semir Zeki, 'The neural correlates of maternal and romantic love', *Neuroimage* 21:3 (2004), pp. 1155–66.

27. Strathearn, Lane, 'Maternal neglect: oxytocin, dopamine and the neurobiology of attachment', *Journal of Neuroendocrinology* 23:11 (2011), pp. 1054–65.

28. Ibid.

29. Zak, Paul, Robert Kurzban and William Matzner, 'Oxytocin is associated with human trustworthiness', *Hormones and Behavior* 48:5 (2005), pp. 522–7.

30. Damasio, Antonio, 'Human behaviour: brain trust', *Nature* 435:7042 (2005), pp. 571–2.

31. Baumgartner, Thomas, et al., 'Oxytocin shapes the neural circuitry of trust and trust adaptation in humans', *Neuron* 58:4 (2008), pp. 639–50.

32. Zak, Paul, Angela Stanton and Sheila Ahmadi, 'Oxytocin increases generosity in humans', *PLoS One* 2:11 (2007).

33. Payne, Kenneth, *The Psychology of Modern Conflict*, New York: Palgrave Macmillan, 2015, p. 68.

34. De Dreu, Carsten and Mariska E. Kret, 'Oxytocin conditions intergroup relations through upregulated in-group empathy, cooperation, conformity, and defense', *Biological Psychiatry* 79:3 (2016), pp. 165–73.

35. Dölen, Gül et al., 'Social reward requires coordinated activity of accumbens oxytocin and 5HT', *Nature* 501:7466 (2013), p. 179.

36. For a fascinating paper that makes this and wider points about the crossover between status and maternal care, see Jaeggi, Adrian et al., 'Salivary oxytocin increases concurrently with testosterone and time away from home among returning Tsimane' hunters', *Biology Letters* 11.3 (2015).

37. Crespi, Bernard, 'Oxytocin, testosterone, and human social cognition', *Biological Reviews* 91:2 (2016), pp. 390–408.

38. Ma, Xiaole et al., 'Oxytocin increases liking for a country's people and national flag but not for other cultural symbols or consumer products', *Frontiers in Behavioral Neuroscience* 8:266 (2014).

39. Kreutz, Gunter, 'Does singing facilitate social bonding?', *Music Med* 6:2 (2014), pp. 51–60.

40. Holbrook, Colin, Jennifer Hahn-Holbrook and Julianne Holt-Lunstad, 'Self-reported spirituality correlates with endogenous oxytocin', *Psychology of Religion and Spirituality* 7:1 (2015), p. 46.

41. Pepping, Gert-Jan and Erik J. Timmermans, 'Oxytocin and the biopsychology of performance in team sports', *The Scientific World Journal* (2012).

42. De Dreu, Carsten et al., 'Oxytocin promotes human ethnocentrism', *Proceedings of the National Academy of Sciences* 108:4 (2011), pp. 1262–6.

43. De Dreu, Carsten et al., 'The neuropeptide oxytocin regulates parochial altruism in intergroup conflict among humans', *Science* 328:5984 (2010), pp. 1408–11.

44. Yong, Ed, 'Oxytocin Boosts Dishonesty', *The Scientist*, 31 March 2014, http://www.the-scientist.com/?articles.view/articleNo/39595/title/Oxytocin-Boosts-Dishonesty/, last accessed 01 Sep 2017.

45. Ne'eman, Ronnie et al., 'Intranasal administration of oxytocin increases human aggressive behaviour', *Hormones and Behavior* 80 (2016), pp. 125–31.

46. Atran, Scott, *In Gods We Trust: The Evolutionary Landscape of Religion*, Oxford: Oxford University Press, 2002, p. 145.

47. De Dreu, Carsten, 'Oxytocin modulates cooperation within and competition between groups: an integrative review and research agenda', *Hormones and Behavior* 61:3 (2012), pp. 419–28.

48. Ibid.

49. De Dreu et al., 'Oxytocin promotes human ethnocentrism', op. cit., pp. 1262–6.

50. Declerck, Carolyn, Christophe Boone and Toko Kiyonari, 'Oxytocin and cooperation under conditions of uncertainty: the modulating role of incentives and social information', *Hormones and Behavior* 57:3 (2010), pp. 368–74.

51. Atran, Scott, *Talking to the Enemy: Violent Extremism, Sacred Values, and What It Means to Be Human*, London: Penguin, 2010, p. 39.

52. Ibid.

53. De Dreu, Carsten et al., 'Oxytocin motivates non-cooperation in intergroup conflict to protect vulnerable in-group members', *PLoS One* 7·11 (2012).

54. De Dreu and Kret, op. cit., pp. 165–73.

55. Ibid.

56. Donaldson, Zoe and Larry J. Young, 'Oxytocin, vasopressin, and the neurogenetics of sociality', *Science* 322:5903 (2008), pp. 900–4.

57. Chen, Frances et al., 'Common oxytocin receptor gene (OXTR), polymorphism and social support interact to reduce

stress in humans', *Proceedings of the National Academy of Sciences* 108:50 (2011).

58. Cesarini, David et al., 'Heritability of cooperative behavior in the trust game', *Proceedings of the National Academy of Sciences* 105:10 (2008), pp. 3721–6.

59. Luo, Siyang et al., 'Oxytocin receptor gene and racial ingroup bias in empathy-related brain activity', *NeuroImage* 110 (2015), pp. 22–31.

60. Ebstein, Richard et al., 'The contributions of oxytocin and vasopressin pathway genes to human behavior', *Hormones and Behavior* 61:3 (2012), pp. 359–79.

61. Malik, Ayesha et al., 'The role of oxytocin and oxytocin receptor gene variants in childhood-onset aggression', *Genes, Brain and Behavior* 11:5 (2012), pp. 545–51.

62. '"This Is Belonging" British Army Recruitment "Sing" TV Advert', *YouTube*, https://www.youtube.com/watch?v=UeuaL0OgJZ0, last accessed 01 Sep 2017.

63. Burgoyne, Patrick, 'Karmarama highlights sense of belonging in new British Army recruitment campaign', *Creative Review*, 6 January 2017, https://www.creativereview.co.uk/karmarama-highlights-sense-belonging-new-british-army-recruitment-campaign/, last accessed 01 Sep 2017.

6. THE GROWTH OF HUMAN GROUPS

1. Sun Tzu, *The Art of War*, Minneapolis, MN: Filiquarian Publishing LLC, 2007, p. 27.

2. Hamilton, William, 'Geometry for the selfish herd', *Journal of Theoretical Biology* 31:2 (1971), pp. 295–311.

3. Werner, Gregory and Michael G. Dyer, 'Evolution of herding behavior in artificial animals', in *From Animals to Animats 2: Proceedings of the Second International Conference on Simulation of Adaptive Behavior*, vol. 2, Cambridge, MA: MIT Press, 1993.

4. Dimock, G. and M. Selig, 'The aerodynamic benefits of self-organization in bird flocks', *Urbana* 51 (2003), pp. 1–9.

5. Aunger, R and Valerie Curtis, *Gaining Control: How Human Behavior Evolved*, Oxford: Oxford University Press, 2015, p. 52.

6. Henrich, Joseph, *The Secret of Our Success*, Princeton, NJ: Princeton University Press, 2016, p. 213.

7. Ibid., p. 185.

8. Swann, Bill, 'People With "Fused" Identities Are Willing to Die for Their Social Group', *Association for Psychological Science*, 18 August 2010, http://www.psychologicalscience.org/news/releases/people-with-fused-identities-are-willing-to-die-for-their-social-group.html, last accessed 01 Sep 2017.

9. I am grateful to Michael Niconchuk of Beyond Conflict for highlighting this to me.

10. Haidt, Jonathan, *The Righteous Mind*, London: Penguin, 2012, p. 199.

11. Morris, Ian, *War: What Is It Good For?*, London: Profile Books, 2015, p. 80.

12. Haidt, op. cit., p. 245.

13. Morris, op. cit., p. 80.

14. Hamilton, Milne et al., 'Nonlinear scaling of space use in human hunter-gatherers', *Proceedings of the National Academy of Sciences*, 104:11 (2007), pp. 4765–9.

15. Taylor, Peter, 'Altruism in viscous populations—an inclusive fitness model', *Evolutionary Ecology* 6:4 (1992), pp. 352–6.

16. Smith, Martin, Bradley Kish and Charles Crawford, 'Inheritance of wealth as human kin investment', *Ethology and Sociobiology* 8:3 (1987), pp. 171–82.

17. Morris, op. cit., p. 80.

18. Ibid.

19. I developed this concept of the five group problems from Jonathan Haidt's work on the moral foundations. See Haidt, op. cit. See also Chapter 9.

20. Pinker, Steven, *How the Mind Works*, London: Penguin, 1999, p. 192.

21. Haidt, op. cit., p. 144.
22. See Chapter 5 for descriptions of the oxytocin mechanism, and the in-group out-group distinction.
23. Goodhart, David, *The Road to Somewhere: The Populist Revolt and the Future of Politics*, London: Hurst, 2017, p. 1.
24. Sapolsky, Robert, *Behave: The Biology of Humans at Our Best and Worst*, London: Bodley Head, 2017, p. 575.
25. Atran, Scott and Robert Axelrod, 'Reframing sacred values', *Negotiation Journal* 24:3 (2008), pp. 221–46.
26. Besançon, Marie, 'Relative resources: Inequality in ethnic wars, revolutions, and genocides', *Journal of Peace Research* 42:4 (2005), pp. 393–415.
27. Enamorado, Ted et al., 'Income inequality and violent crime: Evidence from Mexico's drug war', *Journal of Development Economics* 120 (2016), pp. 128–43.
28. Dunbar, Robin, 'Neocortex size as a constraint on group size in primates', *Journal of Human Evolution* 22:6 (1992), pp. 469–93.
29. Social Science Bites, 'Robin Dunbar on Dunbar Numbers', *Social Science Space*, 4 November 2013, http://www.socialsciencespace.com/2013/11/robin-dunbar-on-dunbar-numbers/, last accessed 02 Sep 2017.
30. Harari, Yuval, *Sapiens: A Brief History of Humankind*, London: Vintage, 2011, pp. 10–11.
31. Delaney, Kevin J., 'Something weird happens to companies when they hit 150 people', *Quartz*, 29 November 2016, https://qz.com/846530/something-weird-happens-to-companies-when-they-hit-150-people/, last accessed 02 Sep 2017.
32. On the decline of violence over macro history, see Morris, op. cit., pp. 7, 59, 103–5; Keeley, Lawrence, *War Before Civilization: The Myth of the Peaceful Savage*, New York, NY: Oxford University Press, 1996, pp. 195–7; Gat, Azar, *War in Human Civilization*, Oxford: Oxford University Press, 2006, pp. 402–6; Pinker, Steven, *The Better Angels of Our Nature:*

The Decline of Violence in History and Its Causes, London: Allen Lane, 2011, p. 53. This has occurred alongside an increasing world population arranged in ever-fewer political groupings (bands, tribes, city-states, empires, nation states, supranational structures, etc.).

33. Hobbes, Thomas, *Leviathan* (revised student edition, ed. R. Tuck), Cambridge: Cambridge University Press, 1997, p. 88.
34. Gat, Azar, *The Causes of War & The Spread of Peace: But Will War Rebound?*, Oxford: Oxford University Press, 2017, pp. 129–86.
35. Pinker, *The Better Angels*, op. cit., pp. 682, 690.
36. Ibid.
37. Morris, op. cit., p. 80.
38. Eisner, Manuel, 'Long-term historical trends in violent crime', *Crime and Justice* 30 (2003), pp. 83–142.
39. Ibid.
40. Pinker, *The Better Angels*, op. cit., p. 61.
41. Ibid., pp. 62–3.
42. Hobbes, op. cit., p. 104.
43. Wright, Quincy, *A Study of War*, Chicago, IL: University of Chicago Press, 1965, p. 215.
44. Damluji, Hassan, personal communication, May 2017.
45. Keeley, op. cit., p. 186, Table 2.3.
46. Pinker, *The Better Angels*, op. cit., pp. 229–30.
47. Gat, *Causes of War*, op. cit., p. 408.
48. Pinker, *The Better Angels*, op. cit., pp. 195 & 227 (fig 5–15); Gat, *Causes of War*, op. cit., p. 69.
49. It is likely that ancient hunter-gatherers in the Stone Age had even higher rates of violence. Some prehistoric archaeological sites from 10,000 BCE demonstrate rates of violent death of 1,030/100,000 per year, or more than 1 per cent per year (Keeley, op. cit., p. 196). One of the main differences between ancient and present-day hunter-gatherers is that today's hunter-

gatherers live in marginal spaces, like deserts, wastelands or forests—in short, where other people don't want to live. In comparison, Stone Age hunter-gatherer bands lived in the most fertile regions across the best latitudes—roughly an area from the Mediterranean basin through the Fertile Crescent and Persia, and the northern sub-continent, to China (Morris, Op. Cit., p. 75). These more productive ecologies supported higher population densities, which meant that these bands of humans were more likely to come into contact with each other. Contact, of course, leads to competition for resources, and fighting.

50. Overall, and particularly when we are talking about aggressive rather than defensive fighting, it is men who have fought. The biological underpinnings for this average rule—far higher levels of testosterone and the implications of this—are explored in Chapter 4. This is not to say that women never fight—most commonly, they do so when their group is about to be wiped out.

51. Keeley, op. cit., p. 195.

52. Ibid., p. 196.

53. Pinker, *The Better Angels*, op. cit., p. 52.

54. Battle deaths of 1,021 (icasualty.org) and spread across a population of 301.2 million.

55. Morris, op. cit., pp. 7–8.

56. Henrich, op. cit., p. 185.

57. Sapolsky, op. cit., p. 379.

58. Payne, Kenneth, *The Psychology of Modern Conflict*, New York, NY: Palgrave Macmillan, 2015, p. 33.

59. Pinker, *The Better Angels*, op. cit., p. 615.

60. Kogan, Aleksandr et al., 'Thin-slicing study of the oxytocin receptor (OXTR) gene and the evaluation and expression of the prosocial disposition', *Proceedings of the National Academy of Sciences* 108:48 (2011), pp. 19189–92.

61. Turchin, Peter, *Ultra Society: How 10,000 Years of War Made*

Humans the Greatest Cooperators on Earth, Chaplin, CT: Beresta Books, 2016, p. 88.
62. Pinker, *The Better Angels*, op. cit., pp. 617–8.

7. FRAMEWORKS

1. Martin, Mike, *An Intimate War*, London: Hurst, 2014.

8. THE CONSCIOUS AND REASONING BRAIN

1. Jung, Carl, *Psychology and Alchemy—Collected Works of C. G. Jung*, vol. 12, London: Routledge, 1968, p. 99.
2. There are literally thousands of definitions of consciousness. What I offer here is a slightly altered version of what appears on the *Wikipedia* entry for 'Consciousness', https://en.wikipedia.org/wiki/Consciousness, last accessed 02 Sep 2017.
3. Mercier, Hugo and Dan Sperber, *The Enigma of Reason: A New Theory of Human Understanding*, London: Allen Lane, 2017, p. 15.
4. Mercier and Sperber, op. cit., p. 112.
5. Flinn, Mark, David Geary and Carol Ward, 'Ecological dominance, social competition, and coalitionary arms races: Why humans evolved extraordinary intelligence', *Evolution and Human Behavior* 26:1 (2005), pp. 10–46.
6. Robinson, Zack, Corey Maley and Gualtiero Piccinini, 'Is Consciousness a Spandrel?', *Journal of the American Philosophical Association* 1:2 (2015), pp. 365–83.
7. Hadit, Jonathan, *The Righteous Mind*, London: Penguin, 2012, p. 61.
8. Mithen, Steven, *The Prehistory of the Mind: A Search for the Origins of Art, Religion and Science*, London: Phoenix, 1996, p. 38.
9. Mithen, op. cit., pp. 76, 223.
10. Gat, Azar, 'Social organization, group conflict and the demise of Neanderthals', *Mankind Quarterly* 39:4 (1999), p. 437.

11. Carruthers, Peter and Andrew Chamberlain (eds), *Evolution and the Human Mind: Modularity, Language and Meta-Cognition*, Cambridge: Cambridge University Press, 2000, p. 210.

12. Mithen, Steven, *The Singing Neanderthals*, London: Orion Books, 2005, p. 134.

13. Mithen, *Prehistory*, op. cit., pp. 161, 214.

14. Graziano, Michael, 'A New Theory Explains How Consciousness Evolved', *The Atlantic*, 6 June 2016, http://www.theatlantic.com/science/archive/2016/06/how-consciousness-evolved/485558/, last accessed 02 Sep 2017.

15. Carruthers and Chamberlain, op. cit., p. 276.

16. Tekleab, Amanuel et al., 'Are we on the same page? Effects of self-awareness of empowering and transformational leadership', *Journal of Leadership & Organizational Studies* 14:3 (2008), pp. 185–201.

17. Charlton, B, 'Evolution and the cognitive neuroscience of awareness, consciousness and language', *Cognition* 50 (2000), pp. 7–15.

18. Griffin, Donald, *Animal Minds: Beyond Cognition to Consciousness*, Chicago, IL: University of Chicago Press, 2013, p. 3.

19. Gallup, Gordon, 'Chimpanzees: self-recognition', *Science* 167:3914 (1970), pp. 86–7.

20. Anderson, James and Gordon Gallup, 'Mirror self-recognition: a review and critique of attempts to promote and engineer self-recognition in primates', *Primates* 56:4 (2015), pp. 317–26.

21. Mercier and Sperber, op. cit., p. 4.

22. Ibid., p. 180.

23. Ibid., p. 23.

24. Cook, Chad, 'Mode of administration bias', *Journal of Manual and Manipulative Therapy* 18:2 (2010), pp. 61–3.

25. Kahneman, Daniel, *Thinking, Fast and Slow*, London: Penguin, 2012.

26. Such as Jonathan Haidt.
27. Kahneman, op. cit., p. 13.
28. Ibid., p. 43.
29. Haidt, op. cit., p. 63.
30. Mercier and Sperber, op. cit., p. 186.
31. Ibid., p. 127.
32. Ibid., pp. 104, 182.
33. Ibid., pp. 183–6.
34. Ibid., p. 143.
35. Ibid., p. 315.
36. This is a very long-running argument in philosophy. For a view rooted in the cognitive sciences, see Bear, Adam, 'What Neuroscience Says about Free Will', *Scientific American*, 28 April 2016, https://blogs.scientificamerican.com/mind-guest-blog/what-neuroscience-says-about-free-will/, last accessed 02 Sep 2017.
37. Zyga, Lisa, 'Free will is an illusion, biologist says', *Phys.org*, 3 March 2010, https://phys.org/news/2010-03-free-illusion-biologist.html, last accessed 02 Sep 2017.
38. Ibid.
39. Mercier and Sperber, op. cit., pp. 266–7.
40. Gat, Azar, *War in Human Civilization*, Oxford: Oxford University Press, 2006, p. 55.

9. MORAL CODES

1. George, Alison, 'Is the Tea Party Fair-Minded? Psychologist Jonathan Haidt on morality and politics', *Slate*, http://www.slate.com/articles/health_and_science/new_scientist/2012/03/jonathan_haidt_on_morality_and_american_politics_.html, last accessed 03 Sept 2017.
2. Interviews with UK military and civilian personnel directly involved in the Libyan campaign, 2011.
3. Mulholland, Hélène, 'Libya: military action necessary, legal and

right, says David Cameron', *The Guardian*, 21 March 2011, https://www.theguardian.com/politics/2011/mar/21/libya-military-action-necessary-david-cameron, last accessed 03 Sep 2017.

4. House of Commons Foreign Affairs Committee, 'Libya: Examination of intervention and collapse and the UK's future policy options', Third Report of Session 2016–17, 6 September 2016, https://publications.parliament.uk/pa/cm201617/cmselect/cmfaff/119/119.pdf, last accessed 03 Sept 2017.

5. See Chapter 5 for a description of the oxytocin mechanism.

6. Haidt, Jonathan, *The Righteous Mind*, London: Penguin, 2012, p. xiv.

7. Harman, Gilbert, 'Moral relativism defended', *The Philosophical Review* 84:1 (1975), pp. 3–22.

8. Shermer, Michael and Dennis McFarland, *The Science of Good and Evil: Why People Cheat, Gossip, Care, Share, and Follow the Golden Rule*, London: Macmillan, 2004, pp. 19–20.

9. Atran, Scott, *In Gods We Trust: The Evolutionary Landscape of Religion*, Oxford: Oxford University Press, 2002, p. 136.

10. These are Jonathan Haidt's moral foundations.

11. Haidt, op. cit., p. 55.

12. Pinker, Steven, *The Stuff of Thought*, London: Penguin, 2007, p. 241.

13. Friedman, Daniel and Nirvikar Singh, 'Equilibrium vengeance', *Games and Economic Behavior* 66:2 (2009), pp. 813–29.

14. Esfahani Smith, Emily, 'Is Human Morality a Product of Evolution?', *The Atlantic*, 2 December 2015, https://www.theatlantic.com/health/archive/2015/12/evolution-of-morality-social-humans-and-apes/418371/, last accessed 03 Sep 2017.

15. There is likely to be variation in the genetic codes for the various different brain modules, or in the neurones that make them up, but evidence for this is sparse. Population-level studies show that there is much greater variation between individuals than between groups of individuals (such as ethnic groups or countries).

16. Burkeman, Oliver, 'Jared Diamond: Humans, 150,000 years ago, wouldn't figure on a list of the five most interesting species on Earth', *The Guardian*, https://www.theguardian.com/books/2014/oct/24/jared-diamond-bestselling-biogeographer-answers-critics, last accessed 03 Sep 2017.

17. Ibid.

18. Sapolsky, Robert, 'The influence of social hierarchy on primate health', *Science* 308:5722 (2005), pp. 648–52.

19. Sapolsky, Robert, *Behave: The Biology of Humans at Our Best and Worst*, London: Bodley Head, 2017, pp. 486–7.

20. Ibid., p. 407.

21. Steward, Julian Haynes, 'The concept and method of cultural ecology', in Haenn, Nora and Richard Wilk (eds), *The Environment in Anthropology: A Reader in Ecology, Culture and Sustainable Living*, New York, NY: NYU Press, 2005, pp. 5–9.

22. Triandis, Harry et al., 'Individualism and collectivism: Cross-cultural perspectives on self-ingroup relationships', *Journal of Personality and Social Psychology* 54:2 (1988), p. 323.

23. Talhelm, Thomas et al., 'Large-scale psychological differences within China explained by rice versus wheat agriculture', *Science* 344:6184 (2014), pp. 603–8.

24. Ibid.

25. Ibid.

26. Fincher, Corey L et al., 'Pathogen prevalence predicts human cross-cultural variability in individualism/collectivism', *Proceedings of the Royal Society of London B: Biological Sciences* 275:1640 (2008), pp. 1279–85.

27. Van de Vliert, Evert et al., 'Climato-economic imprints on Chinese collectivism', *Journal of Cross-Cultural Psychology* 44:4 (2013), pp. 589–605.

28. Murray, Damian, 'Cultural adaptations to the differential threats posed by hot versus cold climates', *Behavioral and Brain Sciences* 36:5 (2013), pp. 497–8.

29. Ibid.

30. Uskul, Ayse, Shinobu Kitayama and Richard Nisbett, 'Ecocultural basis of cognition: Farmers and fishermen are more holistic than herders', *Proceedings of the National Academy of Sciences* 105:25 (2008), pp. 8552–6.

31. This entire section is a synthesis of Jonathan Haidt's work on moral foundations. Originally Haidt proposed six moral foundations, but I have slimmed them down to five. I also developed my idea of the five group problems on the foundations elucidated in Haidt's work. See Haidt, op. cit.

32. Haidt, op. cit., p. 168.

33. Curtis, Valerie, *Don't Look, Don't Touch: The Science Behind Revulsion*, Oxford: Oxford University Press, 2013, pp. 23–5.

34. Ibid., p. 56.

35. Lewis-Williams, David and David Pearce, *Inside the Neolithic Mind*, London: Thames and Hudson, 2009, p. 284.

36. Curtis, op. cit., p. 56.

37. Ibid., p. 85.

38. Haidt, op. cit., p. 145.

39. See Chapter 9.

10. BELIEF IN THE SUPERNATURAL

1. Martin, Mike, *An Intimate War*, London: Hurst, 2014, p. 77.

2. I am particularly grateful to Hassan Damluji for his comments on earlier drafts of this chapter.

3. Dunbar, Robin, 'The origin of religion as a small scale phenomenon', in Clarke, Steve, Russell Powell and Julian Savulescu (eds), *Religion, Intolerance, and Conflict: A Scientific and Conceptual Investigation*, Oxford: Oxford University Press, 2013, pp. 48–66.

4. Sapolsky, Robert, *Behave: The Biology of Humans at Our Best and Worst*, London: Bodley Head, 2017, p. 304.

5. Martin, op. cit.

6. Edwards, David, *Caravan of Martyrs: Sacrifice and Suicide Bombing in Afghanistan*, Oakland, CA: University of California Press, 2017, pp. 26–9.

7. Atran, Scott, *In Gods We Trust: The Evolutionary Landscape of Religion*, Oxford: Oxford University Press, 2002, pp. 144–5.

8. Dunbar, op. cit., pp. 48–66.

9. For example, warring city-states in Ancient Greece that shared the same pantheon of Hellenistic gods.

10. Sapolsky, op. cit., p. 623.

11. Ibid., p. 304.

12. Atran, op. cit., p. 84.

13. Atran, Scott, 'Folk biology and the anthropology of science: Cognitive universals and cultural particulars', *Behavioral and Brain Sciences* 21:4 (1998), pp. 547–69.

14. Atran, *In Gods We Trust*, op. cit., p. 6.

15. Ibid., p. 7

16. Ibid., pp. 207–10.

17. Henrich, Joseph, 'The evolution of costly displays, cooperation and religion: Credibility enhancing displays and their implications for cultural evolution', *Evolution and Human Behavior* 30:4 (2009), pp. 244–60.

18. Byrne, Richard and Andrew Whiten (eds), *Machiavellian Intelligence: Social Expertise and the Evolution of Intellect in Monkeys, Apes, and Humans*, Oxford: Oxford University Press, 1989.

19. Atran, *In Gods We Trust*, op. cit., p. 11.

20. Ibid., p. 71.

21. Wunn, Ina, 'Beginning of religion', *Numen* 47:4 (2000), pp. 434–5.

22. Mithen, Steven, *The Prehistory of the Mind: A Search for the Origins of Art, Religion and Science*, London: Phoenix, 1996, pp. 200–2.

23. Lewis-Williams, David and David Pearce, *Inside the Neolithic Mind*, London: Thames and Hudson, 2009, pp. 193–7.

24. Kapogiannis, Dimitrios et al., 'Cognitive and neural foundations of religious belief', *Proceedings of the National Academy of Sciences* 106:12 (2009), pp. 4876–81; Schjoedt, Uffe et al., 'Highly religious participants recruit areas of social cognition in personal prayer', *Social Cognitive and Affective Neuroscience* 4:2 (2009), pp. 199–207.

25. Atran, *In Gods We Trust*, op cit., p. 15.

26. Dunbar, Robin, 'Theory of mind and the evolution of language', in Hurford, James R., Michael Studdert-Kennedy and Chris Knight (eds), *Approaches to the Evolution of Language: Social and Cognitive Bases*, Cambridge: Cambridge University Press, 1998, p. 102.

27. Lewis-Williams and Pearce, op. cit., p. 27.

28. Ibid.

29. Ibid., p. 91.

30. Pinker, Steven, 'The evolutionary psychology of religion', presentation to the annual meeting of the Freedom From Religion Foundation, 29 October 2004.

31. McKay, Ryan and Harvey Whitehouse, 'Religion and morality', *Psychological Bulletin* 141:2 (2015), p. 447.

32. Seul, Jeffrey, '"Ours is the way of god": Religion, identity, and intergroup conflict', *Journal of Peace Research* 36:5 (1999), pp. 553–69.

33. Sosis, Richard, 'Religious behaviors, badges, and bans: Signaling theory and the evolution of religion', in McNamara, Patrick (ed.), *Where God and Science Meet: How Brain and Evolutionary Studies Alter Our Understanding of Religion* vol. 1, Westport, CT: Praeger Perspectives, 2006, pp. 61–86.

34. Atran, *In Gods We Trust*, op. cit., pp. 144–5.

35. Ibid., p. 206.

36. Atran, Scott, *Talking to the Enemy: Violent Extremism, Sacred Values, and What it Means to be Human*, London: Penguin, 2010, p. 449.

37. Ibid., p. 35.

11. SHARED IDEOLOGIES

1. Anderson, Benedict, *Imagined Communities*, London: Verso, 1983, p. 141.
2. Lewis-Williams, David and David Pearce, *Inside the Neolithic Mind*, London: Thames and Hudson, 2009, pp. 283–4; Richards, Michael, Rick Schulting and Robert Hedges, 'Archaeology: sharp shift in diet at onset of Neolithic', *Nature* 425:6956 (2003), p. 366; Miles, David, *The Tale of the Axe: How the Neolithic Revolution Transformed Britain*, London: Thames and Hudson, 2016, p. 244.
3. Jaspers, Karl, 'The Axial Age of Human History', *Commentary* 6 (1948), p. 430.
4. Miles, op. cit., p. 213.
5. Thomas, Julian, 'Current debates on the Mesolithic-Neolithic transition in Britain and Ireland', *Documenta Praehistorica* 31 (2004), pp. 113–130.
6. Pinker, Steven, *How the Mind Works*, London: Penguin, 1999, pp. 383–5.
7. Miles, op. cit., p. 87.
8. Curry, Andrew, 'Gobekli Tepe: The World's First Temple?', *Smithsonian Magazine*, November 2008, http://www.smithsonianmag.com/history/gobekli-tepe-the-worlds-first-temple-83613665/?page=2, last accessed 03 Sep 2017.
9. Gat, Azar, 'Social organization, group conflict and the demise of Neanderthals', *Mankind Quarterly* 39:4 (1999), p. 437.
10. Curry, op. cit.
11. Ibid.
12. 'History of Stonehenge', *English Heritage*, http://www.english-heritage.org.uk/visit/places/stonehenge/history/, last accessed 03 Sep 2017.
13. Gerring, John, 'Ideology: A definitional analysis', *Political Research Quarterly* 50:4 (1997), pp. 957–94.
14. Developed from the *Shorter Oxford English Dictionary*'s defi-

nition: 'a system of ideas or way of thinking pertaining to a class or individual, esp. as a basis of some economic or political theory or system'. 6ᵗʰ edn, Oxford: Oxford University Press, 2007.

15. Social science scholars do not use these exact terms but talk of ideologies satisfying questions about identity, justice and rules or institutions—all of which address the five problems. See Mock, Steven and Thomas Homer-Dixon, *The Ideological Conflict Project: Theoretical and Methodological Foundations*, Waterloo, ON: Centre for International Governance Innovation, 2015, p. 3.

16. Hobbes, Thomas, *Leviathan* (revised student edition, ed. R. Tuck), Cambridge: Cambridge University Press, 1997.

17. Ridley, Matt, *The Rational Optimist*, London: Fourth Estate, 2010, pp. 91, 118.

18. Anderson, op. cit., p. 71.

19. Atran, Scott, *Talking to the Enemy: Violent Extremism, Sacred Values, and What It Means to Be Human*, London: Penguin, 2010, p. 452.

20. In that in Ancient Egypt, where the first known laws were developed, law was seen as a method of administering the state, the head of which was divine in origin. See *Law in Ancient Egypt*, n.d., http://www.ucl.ac.uk/museums-static/digitale-gypt/administration/law.html, last accessed 03 Sep 2017.

21. Kramer, Samuel, 'Ur-Nammu law code', *Orientalia* 23:1 (1954), pp. 40–51.

22. Ibid.

23. Graham, Jesse et al., 'Moral foundations theory: The pragmatic validity of moral pluralism', *Advances in Experimental Social Psychology* (2012).

24. Elliot, Andrew and Patricia Devine, 'On the motivational nature of cognitive dissonance: Dissonance as psychological discomfort', *Journal of Personality and Social Psychology* 67:3 (1994), p. 382.

25. Mock and Homer-Dixon, op. cit., p. 21.

26. Ibid.

27. Ibid.

28. Ibid., p. 10.

29. Ibid., p. 21.

30. Ibid.

31. Ibid., p. 18.

32. Barabási, Albert-László, *Linked: How Everything is Connected to Everything Else and What It Means for Business, Science, and Everyday Life*, New York, NY: Basic Books, 2014, p. 129.

33. Ibid., p. 80.

34. Ibid., p. 68.

35. Wolfram, Stephen, 'Data Science of Facebook World', *Stephen Wolfram Blog*, 24 April 2013, http://blog.stephenwolfram.com/2013/04/data-science-of-the-facebook-world/, last accessed 03 Sep 2017.

36. Barabási, op. cit., pp. 135–6.

37. Certo, Trevis, 'Influencing initial public offering investors with prestige: Signaling with board structures', *Academy of Management Review* 28:3 (2003), pp. 432–46.

38. Fowler, James, Christopher Dawes and Nicholas Christakis, 'Model of genetic variation in human social networks', *Proceedings of the National Academy of Sciences* 106:6 (2009), pp. 1720–4.

39. Judge, Timothy, Amy Colbert and Remus Ilies, 'Intelligence and leadership: a quantitative review and test of theoretical propositions', *Journal of Applied Psychology* 89:3 (2004), p. 542.

40. Judge, Timothy et al., 'Personality and leadership: a qualitative and quantitative review', *Journal of Applied Psychology* 87:4 (2002), p. 765.

41. 'Minority Rules: Scientists Discover Tipping Point for the Spread of Ideas', *Phys.Org*, 25 July 2011, https://phys.org/news/2011-07-minority-scientists-ideas.html, last accessed 03 Sep 2017.

42. Christakis, Nicholas and James Fowler, *Connected: The Amazing Power of Social Networks and How They Shape Our Lives*, London: HarperPress, 2011, pp. 206–8.

43. Mullen, Brian, Rupert Brown and Colleen Smith, 'Ingroup bias as a function of salience, relevance, and status: An integration', *European Journal of Social Psychology* 22:2 (1992), pp. 103–22.

44. Atran, Scott, *In Gods We Trust: The Evolutionary Landscape of Religion*, Oxford: Oxford University Press, 2002, p. 249.

45. Mock and Homer-Dixon, op. cit., p. 21.

46. Hibbing, John, Kevin Smith and John Alford, *Predisposed: Liberals, Conservatives, and the Biology of Political Differences*, Abingdon: Routledge, 2013, p. 51.

47. Mock and Homer-Dixon, op. cit., p. 25.

48. De Dreu, Carsten et al., 'Oxytocin motivates non-cooperation in intergroup conflict to protect vulnerable in-group members', *PLoS One* 7:11 (2012).

49. Gaddis, Michael, *There Is No Crime for Those Who Have Christ: Religious Violence in the Christian Roman Empire*, Berkeley, CA: University of California Press, 2005, pp. 24–5.

50. Hoffer, Eric, *The True Believer*, New York, NY: Harper and Row, 1951, p. 43.

51. Ahmed, Leila, 'Veil of Ignorance: Have we Gotten the Headscarf all Wrong?', *Foreign Policy*, 25 April 2011, http://foreignpolicy.com/2011/04/25/veil-of-ignorance-2/, last accessed 03 Sep 2017.

12. *REFLECTIONS*

1. At that time, the UK infantry was male-only.

2. Nordland, Rob, '7 U.S. Soldiers Wounded in Insider Attack in Afghanistan', *The New York Times*, 17 June 2017, https://www.nytimes.com/2017/06/17/world/asia/afghanistan-us-soldiers-insider-attack.html?_r=0, last accessed 18 Dec 2017.

3. Martin, Mike, *An Intimate War*, London: Hurst, 2014, pp. 4–5.
4. Ibid., p. 245.
5. Ibid., p. 238.
6. Martin, Mike, 'Kto Kovo? Tribes and Jihad in Pushtun Lands', in Collombier, Virginie and Olivier Roy (eds), *Tribes and Global Jihadism*, London: Hurst, 2017, pp. 33–56.

CONCLUSIONS

1. Chesterton, G.K., *Collected Works*, vols 27–37 (*Illustrated London News* columns, 1905–36), San Francisco, CA: Ignatius Press, 1990.
2. Clausewitz, Carl von, *On War*, Princeton, NJ: Princeton University Press, 1989, p. xix.
3. Atran, Scott, *Talking to the Enemy: Violent Extremism, Sacred Values, and What It Means to Be Human*, London: Penguin, 2010, p. 325.
4. Samuni, Liran et al., 'Oxytocin reactivity during intergroup conflict in wild chimpanzees', *Proceedings of the National Academy of Sciences* 114:2 (2016), pp. 268–73.
5. Pratto, Felicia, Lisa Stallworth and Jim Sidanius, 'The gender gap: Differences in political attitudes and social dominance orientation', *British Journal of Social Psychology* 36:1 (1997), pp. 49–68.
6. Gat, Azar, *The Causes of War and the Spread of Peace: But Will War Rebound?*, Oxford: Oxford University Press, 2017, p. 243.
7. Piketty, Thomas, *Capital in the Twenty-First Century*, Cambridge, MA: Harvard University Press, 2017, pp. 26, 165.
8. Kalyvas, Stathis, *The Logic of Violence in Civil War*, Cambridge: Cambridge University Press, 2006, p. 2.
9. Atran, op. cit., p. 52.
10. Mock, Steven and Thomas Homer-Dixon, *The Ideological Conflict Project: Theoretical and Methodological Foundations*, Waterloo, ON: Centre for International Governance Innovation, 2015, pp. 22–5.

11. Sambanis, Nicholas, 'A review of recent advances and future directions in the quantitative literature on civil war', *Defence and Peace Economics* 13:3 (2002), pp. 215–43.

12. Sambanis, Nicholas, 'Using case studies to refine and expand the theory of civil war', Social development papers, *Conflict Prevention and Reconstruction* series, no. CPR 5, Washington, DC: World Bank, 2005, pp. 303–34.

13. Ruby, Charles, 'The definition of terrorism', *Analyses of Social Issues and Public Policy* 2:1 (2002), pp. 9–14.

14. Young, Joseph and Michael Findley, 'Promise and pitfalls of terrorism research', *International Studies Review* 13:3 (2011), pp. 411–31.

15. I accept that the prevalence of suicide bombers is so small as to be statistically insignificant, especially against the grand averages we have been highlighting as evidence throughout the book. This means that suicide bombers sit on the extreme end of certain behavioural characteristics/spectrums. Even so, the question of why people kill themselves is fascinating from an evolutionary point of view.

16. Roy, Olivier, *Jihad and Death: The Global Appeal of Islamic State*, London: Hurst, 2017, pp. 33–5.

17. Atran, Scott, 'Genesis of Suicide Terrorism', *Science* 299:5612 (2003), pp. 1534–9.

18. Roy, *Jihad and Death*, op. cit., p. 24.

19. Roy, Olivier, 'What is the driving force behind Jihadist terrorism?', *Inside Story*, 18 December 2015, http://insidestory.org. au/what-is-the-driving-force-behind-jihadist-terrorism, last accessed 04 Sep 2017; Cottee, Simon, 'Reborn into Terrorism', *The Atlantic*, 25 January 2016, http://www.theatlantic.com/international/archive/2016/01/isis-criminals-converts/426822/, last accessed 04 Sep 2017.

20. Roy, *Jihad and Death*, op. cit., pp. 21–2.

21. Horgan, John, 'Psychology of terrorism: Introduction to the special issue', *American Psychologist* 72:3 (2017), p. 201.

22. McCauley, Clark and Sophia Moskalenko, 'Understanding political radicalization: The two-pyramids model', *American Psychologist* 72:3 (2017), p. 205.

23. Atran, *Talking to the Enemy*, op. cit., p. 108; Roy, *Jihad and Death*, op. cit., p. 24.

24. Atran, Scott, 'The moral logic and growth of suicide terrorism', *Washington Quarterly* 29:2 (2006), pp. 127–47.

25. Lyons-Padilla, Sarah et al., 'Belonging nowhere: Marginalization & radicalization risk among Muslim immigrants', *Behavioral Science & Policy* 1:2 (2015), pp. 1–12.

26. Atran, *Talking to the Enemy*, op. cit., p. 166.

27. Atran, Scott, 'ISIS is a revolution', *Aeon*, 15 December 2015, https://aeon.co/essays/why-isis-has-the-potential-to-be-a-world-altering-revolution, last accessed 04 Sep 2017.

28. Chotiner, Isaac, 'The Islamization of Radicalism: Olivier Roy on the misunderstood connection between terror and religion', *Slate*, 22 June 2016, http://www.slate.com/articles/news_and_politics/interrogation/2016/06/olivier_roy_on_isis_brexit_orlando_and_the_islamization_of_radicalism.html, last accessed 04 Sep 2017.

29. Valasik, Matthew and Matthew Phillips, 'Understanding modern terror and insurgency through the lens of street gangs: ISIS as a case study', *Journal of Criminological Research, Policy and Practice* 3:3 (2017), pp. 192–207.

30. Hegghammer, Thomas (ed.), *Jihadi Culture: The Art and Social Practices of Militant Islamists*, Cambridge: Cambridge University Press, 2017, pp. 14–5, 195–6.

31. Ibid., p. 15.

32. Ibid., p. 43.

33. Ibid., pp. 39–41.

34. Atran, Scott, *In Gods We Trust: The Evolutionary Landscape of Religion*, Oxford: Oxford University Press, 2002, pp. 133, 145.

35. McCauley, Clark, 'Toward a psychology of humiliation in

asymmetric conflict', *American Psychologist* 72:3 (2017), p. 255.

36. Edwards, David, *Caravan of Martyrs: Sacrifice and Suicide Bombing in Afghanistan*, Oakland, CA: University of California Press, 2017, pp. 168–9, 171.

37. Ibid., p. 123.

38. Ibid., p. 160.

39. Ibid., p. 212.

40. Atran, *Talking to the Enemy*, op. cit., p. 358.

41. Ibid., p. 327.

42. Williams, Ray, 'The Psychology of Terrorism', *Psychology Today*, 21 November 2015, https://www.psychologytoday. com/blog/wired-success/201511/the-psychology-terrorism, last accessed 04 Sep 2017.

43. Atran, 'The moral logic', op. cit.

44. Mercier, Hugo and Dan Sperber, *The Enigma of Reason: A New Theory of Human Understanding*, London: Allen Lane, 2017, pp. 257–9.

45. Atran, *Talking to the Enemy*, op. cit., pp. 377–93.

46. Skerry, Peter, 'Problems of the Second Generation: To be Young, Muslim, and American', *Brookings Institute*, 28 June 2013, https://www.brookings.edu/articles/problems-of-the-second-generation-to-be-young-muslim-and-american/ (last accessed 29 Dec 2017).

47. Sen, Amartya, *Identity and Violence: The Illusion and Destiny*, London: Penguin, 2006, p. 15.

48. *'Prevent* Strategy', HM Government, presented to Parliament by the Secretary of State for the Home Department by Command of Her Majesty, June 2011, https://www.gov.uk/ government/uploads/system/uploads/attachment_data/ file/97976/prevent-strategy-review.pdf, last accessed 04 Sep 2017.

49. 'Protecting children from the risk of radicalization should be seen as part of schools' and childcare providers' wider safe-

guarding duties, and is similar in nature to protecting children from other harms (e.g. drugs, gangs, neglect, sexual exploitation)'. See 'The Prevent Duty: Departmental Advice for Schools and Childcare Providers', HM Government Department for Education, June 2015, https://www.gov.uk/government/uploads/system/uploads/attachment_data/file/439598/prevent-duty-departmental-advice-v6.pdf, last accessed 04 Sep 2017. For the 2003 origins of the programme, see 'Project CONTEST: The Government's Counter-Terrorism Strategy', House of Commons Home Affairs Committee, Ninth Report of Session 2008–09, 29 June 2009, https://publications.parliament.uk/pa/cm200809/cmselect/cmhaff/212/212.pdf, last accessed 20 Dec 2017.

50. *'Prevent* Strategy', op. cit.
51. Borum, Randy, 'Radicalization into violent extremism I: A review of social science theories', *Journal of Strategic Security* 4:4 (2011), p. 7.
52. Faure Walker, Rob, 'Preventing Education', *Rob Faure Walker Blog*, 14 July 2016, http://robfaurewalker.blogspot.co.uk/2016_07_01_archive.html, last accessed 05 Sep 2017.
53. Dodd, Vikram, 'School questioned Muslim pupil about ISIS after discussion on eco-activism', *The Guardian*, 22 September 2015, https://www.theguardian.com/education/2015/sep/22/school-questioned-muslim-pupil-about-isis-after-discussion-on-eco-activism, last accessed 05 Sep 2017.
54. 'The Cucumber Case', *Prevent Watch*, January 2016, http://www.preventwatch.org/the-cucumber-case/, last accessed 05 Sep 2017.
55. Faure Walker, op. cit.
56. Atran, *Talking to the Enemy*, op. cit., p. 219.
57. Ellis, Heidi and Saida Abdi, 'Building community resilience to violent extremism through genuine partnerships', *American Psychologist* 72:3 (2017), p. 289; Bhui, Kamaldeep et al., 'Pathways to sympathies for violent protest and terrorism', *The British Journal of Psychiatry* 209:6 (2016), pp. 483–90.

58. Stern, Jessica and J. M. Berger, *ISIS: The State of Terror*, London: William Collins, 2015, p. 243.

59. Atran, *Talking to the Enemy*, op. cit., pp. 267–70.

60. Ibid., p. 41.

61. Atran, 'The moral logic', op cit.

62. Ibid.

POSTSCRIPT: A GLOBAL GROUP

1. Morris, Ian, *Why the West Rules for Now*, London: Profile, 2011, pp. 190–1.

2. Ibid., pp. 46–8.

3. Anderson, Benedict, *Imagined Communities*, London: Verso, 1983, p. 86.

4. Ibid., p. 53.

5. Ibid., p. 77.

6. Turchin, Peter, *Ultra Society: How 10,000 Years of War Made Humans the Greatest Cooperators on Earth*, Chaplin, CT: Beresta Books, 2016, p. 213.

7. 'Double Irish with a Dutch Sandwich', *Investopedia*, n.d., http://www.investopedia.com/terms/d/double-irish-with-a-dutch-sandwich.asp, last accessed 05 Sep 2017.

8. Lewis, Helen, 'Online Vitriol and death threats—a way of life for MPs', *The Financial Times*, 17 July 2017, https://www.ft.com/content/3c5a16b4-6ac8-11e7-b9c7-15af748b60d0, last accessed 05 Sep 2017.

9. Atran, Scott, *Talking to the Enemy: Violent Extremism, Sacred Values, and What It Means to Be Human*, London: Penguin, 2010, p. 471.

10. In June 2017, 51.7 per cent of the world's population was using the Internet. See 'World Internet Usage and Population Statistics, June 30, 2017—Update', *Internet World Stats*, http://www.internetworldstats.com/stats.htm, last accessed 29 Dec 2017.

11. Aboujaoude, Elias, 'Online Personality Breakdown and the end of Democracy', *The Financial Times*, 29 December 2016, http://on.ft.com/2ivmrvv, last accessed 05 Sep 2017.

12. See Olio website: https://olioex.com/, last accessed 05 Sep 2017.

13. Urban, Tim, 'The AI Revolution: The Road to Super-intelligence', *Wait But Why*, 22 January 2015, http://waitbut-why.com/2015/01/artificial-intelligence-revolution-1.html, last accessed 05 Sep 2017.

14. Urban, Tim, 'Neuralink and the Brain's Magical Future', *Wait But Why*, 20 April 2017, http://waitbutwhy.com/2017/04/neuralink.html, last accessed 05 Sep 2017.

15. Grau, Carles et al., 'Conscious brain-to-brain communication in humans using non-invasive technologies', *PLoS One* 9:8 (2014).

BIBLIOGRAPHY

Books and chapters in edited volumes

Anderson, Benedict, *Imagined Communities*, London: Verso, 1983.

Atran, Scott, *Cognitive Foundations of Natural History: Towards an Anthropology of Science*. Cambridge: Cambridge University Press, 1993.

——, *In Gods We Trust: The Evolutionary Landscape of Religion*, Oxford: Oxford University Press, 2002.

——, *Talking to the Enemy: Violent Extremism, Sacred Values, and What It Means to Be Human*, London: Penguin, 2010.

Aunger, R and Valerie Curtis, *Gaining Control: How Human Behavior Evolved*, Oxford: Oxford University Press, 2015.

Barabási, Albert-László, *Linked: How Everything is Connected to Everything Else and What It Means for Business, Science, and Everyday Life*, New York, NY: Basic Books, 2014.

Brown, Donald, *Human Universals*, New York, NY: McGraw Hill Inc., 1991.

Buss, David, *The Evolution of Desire: Strategies of Human Mating*, 4th edn, New York, NY: Basic Books, 2016.

Byrne, Richard and Andrew Whiten, *Machiavellian Intelligence: Social Expertise and the Evolution of Intellect in Monkeys, Apes, and Humans*, Oxford: Oxford University Press, 1989.

Carey, Susan and Elizabeth Spelke, 'Domain-Specific Knowledge and Conceptual Change', in Hirschfeld, Lawrence A. and Susan A. Gelman (eds), *Mapping the Mind: Domain Specificity in*

Cognition and Culture, Cambridge: Cambridge University Press, 1994.

Carruthers, Peter and Andrew Chamberlain (eds), *Evolution and the Human Mind: Modularity, Language and Meta-Cognition*, Cambridge: Cambridge University Press, 2000.

Chesterton, Gilbert, *Collected Works—ILN*, (1911).

Chomsky, Noam, *Aspects of the Theory of Syntax*, Cambridge, MA: MIT Press, 2014.

Christakis, Nicholas and James Fowler, *Connected: The Amazing Power of Social Networks and How They Shape Our Lives*, London: HarperPress, 2011.

Clausewitz, Carl von, *On War*, Princeton, NJ: Princeton University Press, (1989).

Curtis, Valerie, *Don't Look, Don't Touch: The Science Behind Revulsion*, Oxford: Oxford University Press, 2013.

Daly, Martin and Margo Wilson, *Homicide*, New York, NY: Aldine de Gruyter, 1988.

———, *Killing the Competition: Economic Inequality and Homicide*, New York, NY: Routledge, 1990.

Dawkins, Richard, *The Blind Watchmaker: Why the Evidence of Evolution Reveals a Universe without Design*, London: W. W. Norton & Company, 2015.

Dunbar, Robin, 'The origin of religion as a small scale phenomenon', in Clarke, Steve, Russell Powell and Julian Savulescu (eds), *Religion, Intolerance, and Conflict: A Scientific and Conceptual Investigation*, Oxford: Oxford University Press, 2013.

———, 'Theory of Mind and the Evolution of Language', in Hurford, James R., Michael Studdert-Kennedy and Chris Knight (eds), *Approaches to the Evolution of Language*, Cambridge: Cambridge University Press, 1998.

Eagleman, David, *The Brain: The Story of You*, Edinburgh: Canongate Books, 2015.

Edwards, David, *Caravan of Martyrs: Sacrifice and Suicide Bombing in Afghanistan*, Oakland, CA: University of California Press, 2017.

BIBLIOGRAPHY

Ellis, Bruce, 'The Evolution of Sexual Attraction: Evaluative Mechanisms in Women', in Barkow, Jerome H., Leda Cosmides and John Tooby (eds), *The Adapted Mind: Evolutionary Psychology and the Generation of Culture*, New York, NY: Oxford University Press, 1992, pp. 267–88.

Fodor, Jerry, *Modularity of Mind: An Essay on Faculty Psychology*, Cambridge, MA: MIT Press, 1983.

Gaddis, Michael, *There Is No Crime for Those Who Have Christ: Religious Violence in the Christian Roman Empire*, Berkeley, CA: University of California Press, 2005.

Gat, Azar, *War in Human Civilization*, Oxford: Oxford University Press, 2006.

——, *The Causes of War and the Spread of Peace: But Will War Rebound?*, Oxford: Oxford University Press, 2017.

Griffin, Donald, *Animal Minds: Beyond Cognition to Consciousness*, Chicago, IL: University of Chicago Press, 2013.

Gurr, Ted, *Why Men Rebel*, Abingdon: Routledge, 2012.

Haidt, Jonathan, *The Righteous Mind*, London: Penguin, 2012.

Harari, Yuval, *Sapiens: A Brief History of Humankind*, London: Vintage, 2014.

Hegghammer, Thomas (ed.), *Jihadi Culture: The Art and Social Practices of Militant Islamists*, Cambridge: Cambridge University Press, 2017.

Henrich, Joseph, *The Secret of Our Success*, Princeton, NJ: Princeton University Press, 2016.

Hibbing, John, Kevin Smith and John Alford, *Predisposed: Liberals, Conservatives, and the Biology of Political Differences*, Abingdon: Routledge, 2013.

Hobbes, Thomas, *Leviathan* (revised student edition, ed. R. Tuck), Cambridge: Cambridge University Press, 1997.

Hoffer, Eric, *The True Believer*, New York, NY: Harper and Row, 1951.

Ishiguro, Kazuo, *When We Were Orphans*, London: Faber and Faber, 2013.

BIBLIOGRAPHY

Johnston, Victor S., *Why We Feel: The Science of Human Emotions*, New York, NY: Perseus Publishing, 1999.

Jung, Carl, *Psychology and Alchemy—Collected Works of C. G. Jung*, vol. 12, London: Routledge, 1968.

Kahneman, Daniel, *Thinking, Fast and Slow*, London: Penguin, 2012.

Kalyvas, Stathis, *The Logic of Violence in Civil War*, Cambridge: Cambridge University Press, 2006.

Lang, Peter et al. (eds), *Attention and Orienting: Sensory and Motivational Processes*, New York, NY: Routledge, 2013.

Lewis, Michael, Jeannette Haviland-Jones and Lisa Feldman Barrett (eds), *Handbook of Emotions*, 3rd edn, New York, NY: Guildford Press, 2008.

Lewis-Williams, David and David Pearce, *Inside the Neolithic Mind*, London: Thames and Hudson, 2009.

Malešević, Siniša, *The Rise of Organised Brutality: A Historical Sociology of Violence*, Cambridge: Cambridge University Press, 2017.

Martin, Mike, *A Brief History of Helmand*, Warminster: Afghan COIN Centre, 2011.

———, *An Intimate War: An Oral History of the Helmand Conflict*, London: Hurst, 2014.

———, 'Kto Kovo? Tribes and Jihad in Pushtun Lands', in Collombier, Virginie and Olivier Roy (eds), *Tribes and Global Jihadism*, London: Hurst, 2017.

Mercier, Hugo and Dan Sperber, *The Enigma of Reason: A New Theory of Human Understanding*, London: Allen Lane, 2017.

Miles, David, *The Tale of the Axe: How the Neolithic Revolution Transformed Britain*, London: Thames and Hudson, 2016.

Mithen, Steven, *The Prehistory of the Mind: A Search for the Origins of Art, Religion and Science*, London: Phoenix, 1996.

———, *The Singing Neanderthals*, London: Orion Books, 2005.

Morris, Ian, *Why the West Rules for Now*, London: Profile, 2011.

———, *War: What Is It Good For?*, London: Profile, 2015.

North, Douglass, John Wallis and Barry Weingast, *Violence and*

BIBLIOGRAPHY

Social Orders: A Conceptual Framework for Interpreting Recorded Human History, Cambridge: Cambridge University Press, 2009.

Otterbein, Keith, *Feuding and Warfare*, Longhorn, PA: Gordon & Breach, 1994.

Payne, Kenneth, *The Psychology of Modern Conflict*, New York, NY: Palgrave Macmillan, 2015.

Piketty, Thomas, *Capital in the Twenty-First Century*, Cambridge, MA: Harvard University Press, 2017.

Pinker, Steven, *How the Mind Works*, London: Penguin, 1999.

———, *The Blank Slate: The Modern Denial of Human Nature*, London: Penguin, 2003.

———, *The Stuff of Thought*, London: Penguin, 2007.

———, *The Better Angels of Our Nature: The Decline of Violence in History and Its Causes*, London: Allen Lane, 2011.

Ressler, Robert, Ann Burgess and John Douglas, *Sexual Homicide: Patterns and Motives*, New York, NY: The Free Press, 1992.

Richardson, L, *Statistics of Deadly Quarrels*, Pittsburgh, PA: Boxwood Press, 1960.

Ridley, Matt, *The Rational Optimist*, London: Fourth Estate, 2011.

Roy, Olivier, *Jihad and Death: The Global Appeal of Islamic State*, London: Hurst, 2017.

Samuels, Richard, 'Massively modular minds: evolutionary psychology and cognitive architecture', in Carruthers, Peter and Andrew Chamberlain (eds), *Evolution and the Human Mind: Modularity, Language and Meta-Cognition*, Cambridge: Cambridge University Press, 2000.

Sapolsky, Robert, *Behave: The Biology of Humans at Our Best and Worst*, London: Bodley Head, 2017.

Schneier, Bruce, *Liars and Outliers*, Indianapolis, IN: John Wiley & Sons, 2012.

Sen, Amartya, *Identity and Violence: The Illusion and Destiny*, London: Penguin, 2006.

BIBLIOGRAPHY

Shermer, Michael and Dennis McFarland, *The Science of Good and Evil: Why People Cheat, Gossip, Care, Share, and Follow the Golden Rule*, London: Macmillan, 2004.

Sosis, Richard, 'Religious Behaviors, Badges, and Bans: Signalling Theory and the Evolution of Religion', in McNamara, Patrick (ed.), *Where God and Science Meet: How Brain and Evolutionary Studies Alter Our Understanding of Religion* vol. 1, Westport, CT: Praeger Perspectives, 2006.

Stern, Jessica and J. M. Berger, *ISIS: The State of Terror*, London: William Collins, 2015.

Steward, Julian Haynes, 'The Concept and Method of Cultural Ecology', in Haenn, Nora and Richard Wilk (eds), *The Environment in Anthropology: A Reader in Ecology, Culture and Sustainable Living*, New York, NY: NYU Press, 2006.

Sun Tzu, *The Art of War*, CreateSpace Independent Publishing platform, 2014.

Thierry, Bernard, Mewa Singh and Werner Kaumanns (eds), *Macaque Societies: A Model for the Study of Social Organization*, Cambridge: Cambridge University Press, (2004).

Thucydides, *History of the Peloponnesian War*, CreateSpace Independent Publishing Platform, 2017.

Tropp, Linda (ed.), *The Oxford Handbook of Intergroup Conflict*, Oxford: Oxford University Press, 2012.

Turchin, Peter, *Ultra Society: How 10,000 Years of War Made Humans the Greatest Cooperators on Earth*, Chaplin, CT: Beresta Books, 2016.

Wallin, Nils Lennart, Björn Merker and Steven Brown (eds), *The Origins of Music*, Cambridge, MA: MIT Press, 2001.

Journal articles and academic papers

Abbot, Patrick, et al., 'Inclusive fitness theory and eusociality', *Nature* 471:7339 (2011).

Adolphs, Ralph, 'Social cognition and the human brain', *Trends in Cognitive Sciences* 3:12 (1999).

Ainslie, George, 'Cold climates demand more intertemporal self-control than warm climates', *Behavioral and Brain Sciences* 36:5 (2013).

Alford, John, Carolyn Funk and John Hibbing, 'Are political orientations genetically transmitted?', *American Political Science Review* 99:2 (2005).

Anderson, Cameron and Gavin Kilduff, 'The pursuit of status in social groups', *Current Directions in Psychological Science* 18:5 (2009).

Anderson, James and Gordon Gallup, 'Mirror self-recognition: a review and critique of attempts to promote and engineer self-recognition in primates', *Primates* 56:4 (2015).

Anderson, Peter and Walter Schwab, 'The organization and structure of nerve and muscle in the jellyfish Cyanea capillata (Coelenterata; Scyphozoa)', *Journal of Morphology* 170:3 (1981).

Aron, Arthur, et al., 'Reward, motivation, and emotion systems associated with early-stage intense romantic love', *Journal of Neurophysiology* 94:1 (2005).

Aureli, Filippo, 'Post-conflict anxiety in nonhuman primates: The mediating role of emotion in conflict resolution', *Aggressive Behavior* 23:5 (1997).

Atran, Scott, 'Folk biology and the anthropology of science: Cognitive universals and cultural particulars', *Behavioral and Brain Sciences* 21:4 (1998).

———, 'Genesis of Suicide Terrorism', *Science* 299:5612, (2003).

———, 'The moral logic and growth of suicide terrorism', *Washington Quarterly* 29:2 (2006).

Ayling, Ron and Kimberly Kelly, 'Dealing with conflict: natural resources and dispute resolution', *The Commonwealth Forestry Review* 76:3 (1997).

Bartels, Andreas and Semir Zeki, 'The neural correlates of maternal and romantic love', *Neuroimage* 21:3 (2004).

Baumgartner, Thomas, et al., 'Oxytocin shapes the neural circuitry of trust and trust adaptation in humans', *Neuron* 58:4 (2008).

BIBLIOGRAPHY

Benard, Stephen, 'Intergroup Conflict And Intragroup Dynamics: How Conflict Creates Norms And Hierarchies', PhD thesis, Cornell University (2008).

Bhui, Kamaldeep et al., 'Pathways to sympathies for violent protest and terrorism', *The British Journal of Psychiatry* 209:6 (2016).

Bick, Johanna et al., 'Foster mother–infant bonding: associations between foster mothers' oxytocin production, electrophysiological brain activity, feelings of commitment, and caregiving quality', *Child Development* 84:3 (2013).

Borum, Randy, 'Radicalization into violent extremism: a review of social science theories', *Journal of Strategic Security* 4:4 (2011).

Bowles, Samuel and Herbert Gintis, 'The evolution of strong reciprocity: cooperation in heterogeneous populations', *Theoretical Population Biology* 65:1 (2004).

Braithwaite, Alex, Niheer Dasandi and David Hudson, 'Does poverty cause conflict? Isolating the causal origins of the conflict trap', *Conflict Management and Peace Science* 33:1 (2016).

Buss, David et al., 'Sex differences in jealousy: Evolution, physiology, and psychology', *Psychological Science* 3:4 (1992).

Cederman, Lars-Erik, 'Modeling the size of wars: from billiard balls to sandpiles', *American Political Science Review* 97:1 (2003).

Certo, Trevis, 'Influencing initial public offering investors with prestige: signalling with board structures', *Academy of Management Review* 28:3 (2003), pp. 432–46.

Cesarini, David et al., 'Heritability of cooperative behavior in the trust game', *Proceedings of the National Academy of Sciences* 105:10 (2008).

Chagnon, Napoleon, 'Life histories, blood revenge, and warfare in a tribal population', *Science* 239:4843 (1988).

Chapman, Hanah et al., 'In bad taste: Evidence for the oral origins of moral disgust', *Science* 323:5918 (2009).

Charlton, B, 'Evolution and the cognitive neuroscience of awareness, consciousness and language', *Cognition* 50 (2000).

Chatterjee, Arnab and Bikas Chakrabarti, 'Fat tailed distributions for deaths in conflicts and disasters', *Reports in Advances of Physical Sciences* 1:1 (2017).

Chen, Frances et al., 'Common oxytocin receptor gene (OXTR) polymorphism and social support interact to reduce stress in humans', *Proceedings of the National Academy of Sciences* 108:50 (2011).

Christie, Daniel and Noraini Noor, 'Humanising and Dehumanising the Other: Ethnic Conflict in Malaysia', in Seedat, Mohamed, Shahnaaz Suffla, Daniel J. Christie (eds), *Enlarging the Scope of Peace Psychology*, Berlin: Springer International Publishing, 2017.

Clutton-Brock, Timothy, 'Size, sexual dimorphism, and polygyny in primates', in Jungers, William J. (ed.), *Size and Scaling in Primate Biology*, New York, NY: Springer US, 1985.

———— and Paul H. Harvey, 'Primate ecology and social organization', *Journal of Zoology* 183:1 (1977).

Cobo, E, 'Uterine and milk-ejecting activities during human labor', *Journal of Applied Physiology* 24:3 (1968).

Collier, Paul and Anke Hoeffler, 'Greed and grievance in civil war', *Oxford Economic Papers* 56 (2004).

Cook, Chad, 'Mode of administration bias', *Journal of Manual and Manipulative Therapy* 18:2 (2010).

Crespi, Bernard, 'Oxytocin, testosterone, and human social cognition', *Biological Reviews* 91:2 (2016).

Damasio, Antonio, 'Human behaviour: brain trust', *Nature* 435.7042 (2005).

Dasgupta, Aditya, Kishore Gawande and Devesh Kapur, '(When) Do Antipoverty Programs Reduce Violence? India's Rural Employment Guarantee and Maoist Conflict', *International Organization* (2017).

De Cruz, Helen, 'Why are some numerical concepts more successful than others? An evolutionary perspective on the history of number concepts', *Evolution and Human Behavior* 27:4 (2006).

BIBLIOGRAPHY

De Dreu, Carsten, 'Oxytocin modulates cooperation within and competition between groups: an integrative review and research agenda', *Hormones and Behavior* 61:3 (2012).

—— and Mariska E. Kret, 'Oxytocin conditions intergroup relations through upregulated in-group empathy, cooperation, conformity, and defense', *Biological Psychiatry* 79:3 (2016).

—— et al., 'The neuropeptide oxytocin regulates parochial altruism in intergroup conflict among humans', *Science* 328:5984 (2010).

—— et al., 'Oxytocin promotes human ethnocentrism', *Proceedings of the National Academy of Sciences* 108:4 (2011).

—— et al., 'Oxytocin motivates non-cooperation in intergroup conflict to protect vulnerable in-group members', *PLoS One* 7:11 (2012).

De Quervain, Dominique et al., 'The neural basis of altruistic punishment', *Science* 305:5688 (2004).

Declerck, Carolyn, Christophe Boone and Toko Kiyonari, 'Oxytocin and cooperation under conditions of uncertainty: the modulating role of incentives and social information', *Hormones and Behavior* 57:3 (2010).

Dimock, G. and M. Selig, 'The aerodynamic benefits of self-organization in bird flocks', *Urbana* 51 (2003).

Dölen, Gül et al., 'Social reward requires coordinated activity of accumbens oxytocin and 5HT', *Nature* 501:7466 (2013).

Domínguez-Rodrigo, Manuel, 'Hunting and scavenging by early humans: the state of the debate', *Journal of World Prehistory* 16:1 (2002).

Donaldson, Zoe and Larry J. Young, 'Oxytocin, vasopressin, and the neurogenetics of sociality', *Science* 322:5903 (2008).

Driscoll, Catherine, 'The evolutionary culture concepts', *Philosophy of Science* 84:1 (2017).

Dupanloup, Isabelle et al., 'A recent shift from polygyny to monogamy in humans is suggested by the analysis of worldwide Y-chromosome diversity', *Journal of Molecular Evolution* 57:1 (2003).

Ebstein, Richard et al., 'The contributions of oxytocin and vaso-pressin pathway genes to human behavior', *Hormones and Behavior* 61:3 (2012).

Eisenegger, Christoph, Johannes Haushofer and Ernst Fehr, 'The role of testosterone in social interaction', *Trends in Cognitive Sciences* 15:6 (2011).

Eisner, Manuel, 'Long-term historical trends in violent crime', *Crime and Justice* 30 (2003).

Elliot, Andrew and Patricia Devine, 'On the motivational nature of cognitive dissonance: Dissonance as psychological discomfort', *Journal of Personality and Social Psychology* 67:3 (1994).

Ellis, Heidi and Saida Abdi, 'Building community resilience to violent extremism through genuine partnerships', *American Psychologist* 72:3 (2017).

Fearon, James and David Laitin, 'Ethnicity, Insurgency, and Civil War', *American Political Science Review* 97:1 (2003).

Fincher, Corey L et al., 'Pathogen prevalence predicts human cross-cultural variability in individualism/ collectivism', *Proceedings of the Royal Society of London B: Biological Sciences* 275:1640 (2008).

Flinn, Mark, David Geary and Carol Ward, 'Ecological dominance, social competition, and coalitionary arms races: Why humans evolved extraordinary intelligence', *Evolution and Human Behavior* 26:1 (2005).

Fowler, James, Laura Baker and Christopher Dawes, 'Genetic variation in political participation', *American Political Science Review* 102:2 (2008).

Fowler, James, Christopher Dawes and Nicholas Christakis, 'Model of genetic variation in human social networks', *Proceedings of the National Academy of Sciences* 106:6 (2009).

Friedman, Daniel and Nirvikar Singh, 'Equilibrium vengeance', *Games and Economic Behavior* 66:2 (2009).

Fuster, Joaquín, 'Frontal lobe and cognitive development', *Journal of Neurocytology* 31:3–5 (2002).

Gallup, Gordon, 'Chimpanzees: self-recognition', *Science* 167:3914 (1970).

Gat, Azar, 'Social organization, group conflict and the demise of Neanderthals', *Mankind Quarterly* 39:4 (1999).

Gazda, Stefanie et al., 'A division of labour with role specialization in group-hunting bottlenose dolphins (Tursiops truncatus) off Cedar Key, Florida', *Proceedings of the Royal Society of London B: Biological Sciences* 272:1559 (2005).

Gerring, John, 'Ideology: A definitional analysis', *Political Research Quarterly* 50:4 (1997).

Graham, Jesse et al., 'Moral foundations theory: The pragmatic validity of moral pluralism', *Advances in Experimental Social Psychology* (2012).

Grau, Carles et al., 'Conscious brain-to-brain communication in humans using non-invasive technologies', *PLoS One* 9:8 (2014).

Haidt, Jonathan, Clark McCauley and Paul Rozin, 'Individual differences in sensitivity to disgust: A scale sampling seven domains of disgust elicitors', *Personality and Individual Differences* 16:5 (1994).

Hamilton, M et al., 'Nonlinear scaling of space use in human hunter-gatherers', *Proceedings of the National Academy of Sciences*, 104:11 (2007).

Hamilton, William, 'Geometry for the selfish herd', *Journal of Theoretical Biology* 31:2 (1971).

Harman, Gilbert, 'Moral relativism defended', *The Philosophical Review* 84:1 (1975).

Harris, Marvin, 'Animal Capture and Yanomamo Warfare: Retrospect and New Evidence', *Journal of Anthropological Research* 40:1 (1984).

Henrich, Joseph, 'The evolution of costly displays, cooperation and religion: Credibility enhancing displays and their implications for cultural evolution', *Evolution and Human Behavior* 30.4, (2009).

———, 'Rice, psychology, and innovation', *Science* 344:6184 (2014).

———, Robert Boyd, and Peter Richerson, 'The puzzle of monogamous marriage' *Phil. Trans. R. Soc. B* 367:1589 (2012).

Heutink, Peter, Frank Verhuls, and Dorret Boomsma, 'A longitudinal twin study on IQ, executive functioning, and attention problems during childhood and early adolescence', *Acta Neurol. Belg* 106 (2006).

Hogg, Michael and Sarah Hains, 'Friendship and Group Identification: A New Look at the Role of Cohesiveness in Groupthink', *European Journal of Social Psychology* 28:3 (1998).

Holbrook, Colin, Jennifer Hahn-Holbrook and Julianne Holt-Lunstad, 'Self-reported spirituality correlates with endogenous oxytocin', *Psychology of Religion and Spirituality* 7:1 (2015).

Horgan, John, 'Psychology of terrorism: Introduction to the special issue', *American Psychologist* 72:3 (2017).

Jaeggi, Adrian, et al., 'Salivary oxytocin increases concurrently with testosterone and time away from home among returning Tsimane' hunters', *Biology Letters* 11:3 (2015).

Jaspers, Karl, 'The Axial Age of Human History', *Commentary* 6 (1948).

Johnson, Samuel et al., 'Opponent uses of simplicity and complexity in causal explanation', *Proceedings of the 39th Annual Conference of the Cognitive Science Society* (2017).

Jones, Benedict et al., 'Facial symmetry and judgements of apparent health: support for a "good genes" explanation of the attractiveness–symmetry relationship', *Evolution and Human Behavior* 22:6 (2001).

Judge, Timothy, Amy Colbert and Remus Ilies, 'Intelligence and leadership: a quantitative review and test of theoretical propositions', *Journal of Applied Psychology* 89:3 (2004).

Judge, Timothy et al., 'Personality and leadership: a qualitative and quantitative review', *Journal of Applied Psychology* 87:4 (2002).

Kalin, Ned and Steven Sheltona, 'Nonhuman primate models to study anxiety, emotion regulation, and psychopathology', *Annals of the New York Academy of Sciences* 1008:1 (2003).

Kapogiannis, Dimitrios et al., 'Cognitive and neural foundations of religious belief', *Proceedings of the National Academy of Sciences* 106:12 (2009).

Kandler, Christian, Wiebke Bleidorn and Rainer Riemann, 'Left or right? Sources of political orientation: The roles of genetic factors, cultural transmission, assortative mating, and personality', *Journal of Personality and Social Psychology* 102:3 (2012).

Kashima, Yoshihisa, 'How can you capture cultural dynamics?', *Frontiers in Psychology* 5 (2014).

Kazun, A. D, '"Rally Around the Flag" Effect. How and Why Support of the Authorities Grows During International Conflicts and Tragedies', *Polis. Political Studies* 1:1 (2017).

Keltner, Dacher and Brenda Buswell, 'Embarrassment: its distinct form and appeasement functions', *Psychological Bulletin* 122:3 (1997).

Kenrick, Douglas et al., 'Evolution, Traits, and the Stages of Human Courtship: Qualifying the Parental Investment Model', *Journal of Personality* 58:1 (1990).

Kogan, Aleksandr et al., 'Thin-slicing study of the oxytocin receptor (OXTR) gene and the evaluation and expression of the prosocial disposition', *Proceedings of the National Academy of Sciences* 108:48 (2011).

Konner, Melvin and S. Boyd Eaton, 'Palaeolithic nutrition: twenty-five years later', *Nutrition in Clinical Practice* 25:6 (2010).

Kramer, Samuel, 'Ur-Nammu law code', *Orientalia* 23:1 (1954).

Kreutz, Gunter, 'Does singing facilitate social bonding?', *Music Med* 6:2 (2014).

Kunovich, Robert and Randy Hodson, 'Conflict, religious identity, and ethnic intolerance in Croatia', *Social Forces* 78:2 (1999).

Lewis, Gary and Timothy Bates, 'Common genetic influences underpin religiosity, community integration, and existential uncertainty', *Journal of Research in Personality* 47:4 (2013).

Li, Cheng-Yu et al., 'Fighting experience alters brain androgen receptor expression dependent on testosterone status', *Proceedings of the Royal Society of London B: Biological Sciences* 281:1796 (2014).

Loup, F. et al., 'Localization of high-affinity binding sites for oxytocin and vasopressin in the human brain. An autoradiographic study', *Brain Research* 555:2 (1991).

Luo, Siyang et al., 'Oxytocin receptor gene and racial ingroup bias in empathy-related brain activity', *NeuroImage* 110 (2015).

Lyons-Padilla, Sarah et al., 'Belonging nowhere: Marginalization & radicalization risk among Muslim immigrants', *Behavioral Science & Policy* 1:2 (2015).

Ma, Xiaole et al., 'Oxytocin increases liking for a country's people and national flag but not for other cultural symbols or consumer products', *Frontiers in Behavioral Neuroscience* 8 (2014).

MacDonald, Kai and Tina Marie MacDonald, 'The peptide that binds: a systematic review of oxytocin and its prosocial effects in humans', *Harvard Review of Psychiatry* 18:1 (2010).

Mace, Ruth and Antonio Silva, 'The role of cultural group selection in explaining human cooperation is a hard case to prove', *Behavioral and Brain Sciences* 39 (2016).

Malik, Ayesha et al., 'The role of oxytocin and oxytocin receptor gene variants in childhood-onset aggression', *Genes, Brain and Behavior* 11:5 (2012).

Marlowe, Frank, 'A critical period for provisioning by Hadza men: Implications for pair bonding', *Evolution and Human Behavior* 24:3 (2003).

McCauley, Clark, 'Toward a psychology of humiliation in asymmetric conflict', *American Psychologist* 72:3 (2017).

———, and Sophia Moskalenko, 'Understanding political radicalization: The two-pyramids model', *American Psychologist* 72:3 (2017).

McKay, Ryan and Harvey Whitehouse, 'Religion and morality', *Psychological Bulletin* 141:2 (2015).

Mehta, Pranjal et al., 'Hormonal underpinnings of status conflict: Testosterone and cortisol are related to decisions and satisfaction in the hawk-dove game', *Hormones and Behavior* 92 (2017).

Mesulam, Marsel, 'Large-scale neurocognitive networks and distributed processing for attention, language, and memory', *Annals of Neurology* 28:5 (1990).

Mock, Steven and Thomas Homer-Dixon, *The Ideological Conflict Project: Theoretical and Methodological Foundations*, Waterloo, ON: Centre for International Governance Innovation, 2015.

Moffett, Mark, 'Human identity and the evolution of societies', *Human Nature* 24:3 (2013).

Mullen, Brian, Rupert Brown and Colleen Smith, 'Ingroup bias as a function of salience, relevance, and status: An integration', *European Journal of Social Psychology* 22:2 (1992).

Murray, Damian, 'Cultural adaptations to the differential threats posed by hot versus cold climates', *Behavioral and Brain Sciences* 36:5 (2013).

Ne'eman, Ronnie et al., 'Intranasal administration of oxytocin increases human aggressive behaviour', *Hormones and Behavior* 80 (2016).

Nesse, Randolph and Phoebe Ellsworth, 'Evolution, emotions, and emotional disorders', *American Psychologist* 64:2 (2009).

Nettle, Daniel, 'Height and reproductive success in a cohort of British men', *Human Nature* 13:4 (2002).

Orey, Byron D'Andra and Hyung Park, 'Nature, nurture, and ethnocentrism in the Minnesota Twin Study', *Twin Research and Human Genetics* 15:1 (2012).

Pedersen, Cort, 'Biological aspects of social bonding and the roots of human violence', *Annals of the New York Academy of Sciences* 1036:1 (2004).

Pepping, Gert-Jan and Erik J. Timmermans, 'Oxytocin and the biopsychology of performance in team sports', *The Scientific World Journal* (2012).

Pison, Gilles, '1914–2014: A century of change in the French population pyramid', *Population & Societies* 509 (2014).

Polis, Gary, 'The evolution and dynamics of intraspecific predation', *Annual Review of Ecology and Systematics* 12:1 (1981).

Pratto, Felicia, Lisa Stallworth and Jim Sidanius, 'The gender gap: Differences in political attitudes and social dominance orientation', *British Journal of Social Psychology* 36:1 (1997).

Puts, David, 'Beauty and the beast: Mechanisms of sexual selection in humans', *Evolution and Human Behavior* 31:3 (2010).

Richards, Michael, Rick Schulting and Robert Hedges, 'Archaeology: sharp shift in diet at onset of Neolithic', *Nature* 425:6956 (2003).

Robinson, Zack, Corey Maley and Gualtiero Piccinini, 'Is Consciousness a Spandrel?', *Journal of the American Philosophical Association* 1:2 (2015).

Ross, Michael, 'What do we know about Natural Resources and Civil War?', *Journal of Peace Research* 41:3 (2004).

Ruby, Charles, 'The definition of terrorism', *Analyses of Social Issues and Public Policy* 2:1 (2002).

Saddington, Denis, 'Under the centurion's boot: corruption and its containment in the Roman army', *Acta Classica: Proceedings of the Classical Association of South Africa*, Supplement 4 (2012).

Sambanis, Nicholas, 'A review of recent advances and future directions in the quantitative literature on civil war', *Defence and Peace Economics* 13:3 (2002).

———, 'Using case studies to refine and expand the theory of civil war', Social development papers, *Conflict Prevention and Reconstruction* series, no. CPR 5, Washington, DC: World Bank, 2005.

Samuni, Liran et al., 'Oxytocin reactivity during intergroup conflict in wild chimpanzees', *Proceedings of the National Academy of Sciences* 114:2 (2016).

Schjoedt, Uffe et al., 'Highly religious participants recruit areas of social cognition in personal prayer', *Social Cognitive and Affective Neuroscience* 4:2 (2009).

Schneider, Rebecca, Robert Zulandt and Paul Moore, 'Individual and status recognition in the crayfish, Orconectes rusticus: the effects of urine release on fight dynamics', *Behaviour* 138:2 (2001).

Schultheiss, Oliver, Kenneth Campbell and David McClelland, 'Implicit power motivation moderates men's testosterone responses to imagined and real dominance success', *Hormones and Behavior* 36:3 (1999).

Seul, Jeffrey, '"Ours is the way of god": Religion, identity, and intergroup conflict', *Journal of Peace Research* 36:5 (1999).

Singh, Devendra, 'Female mate value at a glance: Relationship of waist-to-hip ratio to health, fecundity and attractiveness', *Neuroendocrinology Letters* 23:Suppl. 4 (2002).

Small, Meredith, 'The evolution of female sexuality and mate selection in humans', *Human Nature* 3:2 (1992).

Smith, James, 'Socioeconomic status and health', *The American Economic Review* 88:2 (1998).

Sperber, Dan and Lawrence Hirschfeld, 'The cognitive foundations of cultural stability and diversity', *Trends in Cognitive Sciences* 8:1 (2004).

Strathearn, Lane, 'Maternal neglect: oxytocin, dopamine and the neurobiology of attachment', *Journal of Neuroendocrinology* 23:11 (2011).

Strenze, Tarmo, 'Intelligence and socioeconomic success: A meta-analytic review of longitudinal research,' *Intelligence* 35:5 (2007).

Talhelm, Thomas et al., 'Large-scale psychological differences within China explained by rice versus wheat agriculture', *Science* 344:6184 (2014).

Tekleab, Amanuel et al., 'Are we on the same page? Effects of self-awareness of empowering and transformational leadership', *Journal of Leadership & Organizational Studies* 14:3 (2008).

Thomas, Julian, 'Current debates on the Mesolithic-Neolithic transition in Britain and Ireland', *Documenta Praehistorica* 31 (2004).

Townsend, John and Gary Levy, 'Effects of potential partners' costume and physical attractiveness on sexuality and partner selection', *The Journal of Psychology* 124:4 (1990).

Traulsen, Arne and Martin Nowak, 'Evolution of cooperation by multilevel selection', *Proceedings of the National Academy of Sciences* 103:29 (2006).

Triandis, Harry et al., 'Individualism and collectivism: Cross-cultural perspectives on self-ingroup relationships', *Journal of Personality and Social Psychology* 54:2 (1988).

Urquiza-Haas, Esmeralda and Kurt Kotrschal, 'The mind behind anthropomorphic thinking: attribution of mental states to other species, *Animal Behaviour* 109 (2015).

Uskul, Ayse, Shinobu Kitayama and Richard Nisbett, 'Ecocultural basis of cognition: Farmers and fishermen are more holistic than herders', *Proceedings of the National Academy of Sciences* 105:25 (2008).

Valasik, Matthew and Matthew Phillips, 'Understanding modern terror and insurgency through the lens of street gangs: ISIS as a case study', *Journal of Criminological Research, Policy and Practice* 3:3 (2017).

Van de Vliert, Evert et al., 'Climato-economic imprints on Chinese collectivism', *Journal of Cross-Cultural Psychology* 44:4 (2013).

Van Kleef, Gerben, 'How emotions regulate social life: The emotions as social information (EASI) model', *Current Directions in Psychological Science* 18:3 (2009).

Varner, Iris and Katrin Varner, 'The Relationship Between Culture and Legal Systems and the Impact on Intercultural Business Communication', *Global Advances in Business Communication* 3:1 (2014).

Walt, Stephen, 'International Relations: One World, Many Theories', *Foreign Policy* 110 (1998).

Wedekind, Claus et al., 'MHC-dependent mate preferences in

humans', *Proceedings of the Royal Society of London B: Biological Sciences* 260:1359 (1995).

Werner, Gregory and Michael G. Dyer, 'Evolution of herding behavior in artificial animals', in *From Animals to Animats 2: Proceedings of the Second International Conference on Simulation of Adaptive Behavior*, vol. 2, Cambridge, MA: MIT Press, 1993.

Williams, Lawrence and John Bargh, 'Experiencing physical warmth promotes interpersonal warmth', *Science* 322:5901 (2008).

Wilson, David Sloan, 'A theory of group selection', *Proceedings of the National Academy of Sciences* 72:1 (1975).

Wilson, Margo and Martin Daly, 'Competitiveness, Risk Taking, and Violence: The Young Male Syndrome', *Ethology and Sociobiology* 6:1 (1985).

Wunn, Ina, 'Beginning of religion', *Numen* 47:4 (2000).

Young, Joseph and Michael Findley, 'Promise and pitfalls of terrorism research', *International Studies Review* 13:3 (2011).

Zak, Paul, Robert Kurzban and William Matzner, 'Oxytocin is associated with human trustworthiness', *Hormones and Behavior* 48:5 (2005).

———, Angela Stanton and Sheila Ahmadi, 'Oxytocin increases generosity in humans', *PLoS One* 2:11 (2007).

Zerjal, Tatiana et al., 'The genetic legacy of the Mongols', *The American Journal of Human Genetics* 72:3 (2003).

Online documents and articles

"'A Crusader-Zionist-Hindu War Against Muslims": Edited translation of an audiotape attributed to al-Qaeda leader Osama bin Laden', *Outlook*, 23 April 2006, https://www.outlookindia.com/website/story/a-crusader-zionist-hindu-war-against-muslims/231048, last accessed 30 Aug 2017.

Aboujaoude, Elias, 'Online Personality Breakdown and the end of Democracy', *The Financial Times*, 29 December 2016, http://on.ft.com/2ivmrvv, last accessed 05 Sep 2017.

BIBLIOGRAPHY

Ahmed, Leila, 'Veil of Ignorance: Have We Gotten the Headscarf All Wrong?', *Foreign Policy*, 25 April 2011, http://foreignpolicy.com/2011/04/25/veil-of-ignorance-2/, last accessed 03 Sep 2017.

Atran, Scott, 'ISIS is a revolution', *Aeon*, 15 December 2015, https://aeon.co/essays/why-isis-has-the-potential-to-be-a-world-altering-revolution, last accessed 04 Sep 2017.

Bear, Adam, 'What Neuroscience Says about Free Will', *Scientific American*, 28 April 2016, https://blogs.scientificamerican.com/mind-guest-blog/what-neuroscience-says-about-free-will/, last accessed 02 Sep 2017.

Burkeman, Oliver, 'Jared Diamond: Humans, 150,000 years ago, wouldn't figure on a list of the five most interesting species on Earth', *The Guardian*, https://www.theguardian.com/books/2014/oct/24/jared-diamond-bestselling-biogeographer-answers-critics, last accessed 03 Sep 2017.

Burgoyne, Patrick, 'Karmarama highlights sense of belonging in new British Army recruitment campaign', *Creative Review*, 6 January 2017, https://www.creativereview.co.uk/karmarama-highlights-sense-belonging-new-british-army-recruitment-campaign/, last accessed 01 Sep 2017.

Chotiner, Isaac, 'The Islamization of Radicalism: Olivier Roy on the misunderstood connection between terror and religion', *Slate*, 22 June 2016, http://www.slate.com/articles/news_and_politics/interrogation/2016/06/olivier_roy_on_isis_brexit_orlando_and_the_islamization_of_radicalism.html, last accessed 04 Sep 2017.

Churchill, Winston: 'Never ... was so much owed by so many to so few', *Hansard* HC Deb., vol. 364, col. 1159 (20 August 1940), https://www.parliament.uk/about/living-heritage/transformingsociety/private-lives/yourcountry/collections/churchillexhibition/churchill-the-orator/human-conflict/, last accessed 19 Dec 2017.

'Competition', *Untamed Science*, n.d., http://www.untamedscience.com/biology/ecology/interactions-among-organisms/competition/, last accessed 30 Aug 2017.

'Concepts: Power Law', *New England Complex Systems Institute*, n.d., http://www.necsi.edu/guide/concepts/powerlaw.html, last accessed 31 Aug 2017.

Cottee, Simon, 'Reborn into Terrorism', *The Atlantic*, 25 January 2016, http://www.theatlantic.com/international/archive/2016/01/isis-criminals-converts/426822/, last accessed 04 Sep 2017.

Curry, Andrew, 'Gobekli Tepe: The World's First Temple?', *Smithsonian Magazine*, November 2008, http://www.smithsonianmag.com/history/gobekli-tepe-the-worlds-first-temple-83613665/?page=2, last accessed 03 Sep 2017.

Dodd, Vikram, 'School questioned Muslim pupil about ISIS after discussion on eco-activism', *The Guardian*, 22 September 2015, https://www.theguardian.com/education/2015/sep/22/school-questioned-muslim-pupil-about-isis-after-discussion-on-eco-activism, last accessed 05 Sep 2017.

'Double Irish with a Dutch Sandwich', *Investopedia*, n.d., http://www.investopedia.com/terms/d/double-irish-with-a-dutch-sandwich.asp, last accessed 05 Sep 2017.

Esfahani Smith, Emily, 'Is Human Morality a Product of Evolution?', *The Atlantic*, 2 December 2015, https://www.theatlantic.com/health/archive/2015/12/evolution-of-morality-social-humans-and-apes/418371/, last accessed 03 Sep 2017.

'Evolutionary Psychology', *Internet Encyclopaedia of Philosophy*, n.d., http://www.iep.utm.edu/evol-psy/, last accessed 29 Aug 2017.

Faure Walker, Rob, 'Preventing Education', *Rob Faure Walker Blog*, 14 July 2016, http://robfaurewalker.blogspot.co.uk/2016_07_01_archive.html, last accessed 05 Sep 2017.

George, Alison, 'Is the Tea Party Fair-Minded? Psychologist Jonathan Haidt on morality and politics', *Slate*, http://www.slate.com/articles/health_and_science/new_scientist/2012/

03/jonathan_haidt_on_morality_and_american_politics_. html, last accessed 03 Sept 2017.

'George W. Bush discusses his father, Jeb in 2016, and the Iraq War', *Face The Nation*, 9 November 2014, available at https:// www.youtube.com/watch?v=tZXYvtJCPkg, accessed 31 Aug 2017.

Gholipour, Bahar, '5 Ways Fatherhood Changes a Man's Brain', *Live Science*, 14 June 2014, http://www.livescience.com/ 46322-fatherhood-changes-brain.html, last accessed 01 Sep 2017.

Graziano, Michael, 'A New Theory Explains How Consciousness Evolved', *The Atlantic*, 6 June 2016, http://www.theatlantic. com/science/archive/2016/06/how-consciousness-evolved/ 485558/, last accessed 02 Sep 2017.

'History of Stonehenge', *English Heritage*, http://www.english-heritage.org.uk/visit/places/stonehenge/history/, last accessed 03 Sep 2017.

Hollande, François, 'Speech by the President of the Republic before a joint session of Parliament, Versailles', 16 November 2015, transcript available from *France Diplomatie*, http://www. diplomatie.gouv.fr/en/french-foreign-policy/defence-security/ parisattacks-paris-terror-attacks-november-2015/article/ speech-by-the-president-of-the-republic-before-a-joint-session-of-parliament, last accessed 29 Aug 2017.

House of Commons Foreign Affairs Committee, 'Libya: Examination of intervention and collapse and the UK's future policy options', *Third Report of Session 2016–17*, 6 September 2016, https://publications.parliament.uk/pa/cm201617/ cmselect/cmfaff/119/119.pdf, last accessed 03 Sept 2017.

'Is Bush's Iraq Stance Rooted in Revenge?', *ABC News*, 18 March 2003, http://abcnews.go.com/US/story?id=90764&page=1, last accessed 31 Aug 2017.

Law in Ancient Egypt, n.d., *UCL website*, http://www.ucl.ac.uk/ museums-static/digitalegypt/administration/law.html, last accessed 03 Sep 2017.

Lewis, Helen, 'Online Vitriol and death threats—a way of life for MPs', *The Financial Times*, 17 July 2017, https://www.ft.com/content/3c5a16b4-6ac8-11e7-b9c7-15af748b60d0, last accessed 05 Sep 2017.

Mark, Joshua J., 'Ramesses II', *Ancient History Encyclopaedia*, 2 September 2009, http://www.ancient.eu/Ramesses_II/, last accessed 31Aug 2017.

Mason, Rowena, Anushka Asthana and Heather Stewart, 'Tony Blair: "I express more sorrow, regret and apology than you can ever believe', *The Guardian*, 6 July 2016, https://www.theguardian.com/uk-news/2016/jul/06/tony-blair-deliberately-exaggerated-threat-from-iraq-chilcot-report-war-inquiry, last accessed 31 Aug 2017.

'Minority Rules: Scientists Discover Tipping Point for the Spread of Ideas', *Phys.Org*, 25 July 2011, https://phys.org/news/2011-07-minority-scientists-ideas.html, last accessed 03 Sep 2017.

Mulholland, Hélène, 'Libya: military action necessary, legal and right, says David Cameron', *The Guardian*, 21 March 2011, https://www.theguardian.com/politics/2011/mar/21/libya-military-action-necessary-david-cameron, last accessed 03 Sep 2017.

Nordland, Rob, '7 U.S. Soldiers Wounded in Insider Attack in Afghanistan', *The New York Times*, 17 June 2017, https://www.nytimes.com/2017/06/17/world/asia/afghanistan-us-soldiers-insider-attack.html?_r=0, last accessed 18 Dec 2017.

Pinker, Steven, 'The evolutionary psychology of religion', presentation to the annual meeting of the Freedom From Religion Foundation, 29 October 2004.

'*Prevent* Strategy', HM Government, presented to Parliament by the Secretary of State for the Home Department by Command of Her Majesty, June 2011, https://www.gov.uk/government/uploads/system/uploads/attachment_data/file/97976/prevent-strategy-review.pdf, last accessed 29 Aug 2017.

'*Prevent* Strategy 2011', HM Government, collection of papers available at https://www.gov.uk/government/publications/ prevent-strategy-2011, last accessed 04 Sep 2017.

Ridley, Matt, 'Polygamy Fuels Violence', *The Rational Optimist Blog*, 24 December 2014, http://www.rationaloptimist.com/ blog/polygamy-fuels-violence, last accessed 31 Aug 2017;

Rose, Damon, 'The Hidden Burden of War Injuries and other Stories', *BBC News Ouch Blog*, 3 January 2014, http://www. bbc.co.uk/news/blogs-ouch-25581022, last accessed 30 Aug 2017.

Roy, Olivier, 'What is the driving force behind Jihadist terrorism?', *Inside Story*, 18 December 2015, http://insidestory.org.au/ what-is-the-driving-force-behind-jihadist-terrorism, last accessed 04 Sep 2017; '

Rubin, Gretchen, 'Feeling Lonely? Consider Trying These 7 Strategies', *Gretchen Rubin Blog*, 6 November 2013, http:// gretchenrubin.com/happiness_project/2013/11/feeling-lonely-consider-trying-these-7-strategies/, last accessed 30 Aug 2017.

Saad, Lydia, 'Conservatives Hang On to Ideology Lead by a Thread', *Gallup*, http://www.gallup.com/poll/188129/con-servatives-hang-ideology-lead-thread.aspx, last accessed 30 Aug 2017.

Storrs, Carina, 'In the Swiss Army Knife of the brain, the ability to recognize faces may be a specialised tool', *Scientific American*, 7 January 2010, https://blogs.scientificamerican.com/observa-tions/in-the-swiss-army-knife-of-the-brain-the-ability-to-rec-ognize-faces-may-be-a-specialized-tool/, last accessed 29 Aug 2017.

Swann, Bill, 'People With "Fused" Identities Are Willing to Die for Their Social Group', *Association for Psychological Science*, 18 August 2010, http://www.psychologicalscience.org/news/ releases/people-with-fused-identities-are-willing-to-die-for-their-social-group.html, last accessed 01 Sep 2017.

'The Cucumber Case', *Prevent Watch*, January 2016, http://www.

preventwatch.org/the-cucumber-case/, last accessed 05 Sep 2017.

'The Mathematical Structure of Terrorism', *Phys.Org*, 22 May 2006, http://phys.org/news/2006-05-mathematical-terrorism.html, last accessed 31 Aug 2017.

'The Prevent Duty: Departmental Advice for Schools and Childcare Providers', HM Government Department for Education, June 2015, https://www.gov.uk/government/uploads/system/uploads/attachment_data/file/439598/prevent-duty-departmental-advice-v6.pdf, last accessed 04 Sep 2017.

'"This Is Belonging" British Army Recruitment "Sing" TV Advert', *YouTube*, https://www.youtube.com/watch?v=Ueua L0OgJZ0, last accessed 01 Sep 2017.

Townsend, Colin R., Michael Begon and John L. Harper, 'Glossary', in *Essentials of Ecology* (3rd ed), Oxford: Blackwell Publishing, available online at http://www.blackwellpublishing.com/Townsend/Glossary/GlossaryS.asp, last accessed 30 Aug 2017.

'Transcript: President Bush's Speech on the War on Terrorism', 30 November 2005, *The Washington Post*, http://www.washingtonpost.com/wp-dyn/content/article/2005/11/30/AR2005113000667.html, last accessed 30 Aug 2017.

Urban, Tim, 'Neuralink and the Brain's Magical Future', *Wait But Why*, 20 April 2017, http://waitbutwhy.com/2017/04/neuralink.html, last accessed 05 Sep 2017.

———, 'The AI Revolution: The Road to Superintelligence', *Wait But Why*, 22 January 2015, http://waitbutwhy.com/2015/01/artificial-intelligence-revolution-1.html, last accessed 05 Sep 2017.

'Who gets into more wars, kings or queens?', *The Economist*, 1 June 2017, https://www.economist.com/news/europe/21722877-european-history-answer-queens-especially-married-ones-who-gets-more-wars-kings, last accessed 31 Aug 2017.

BIBLIOGRAPHY

Williams, Ray, 'The Psychology of Terrorism', *Psychology Today*, 21 November 2015, https://www.psychologytoday.com/blog/wired-success/201511/the-psychology-terrorism, last accessed 04 Sep 2017.

Wolfram, Stephen, 'Data Science of Facebook World', *Stephen Wolfram Blog*, 24 April 2013, http://blog.stephenwolfram.com/2013/04/data-science-of-the-facebook-world/, last accessed 03 Sep 2017.

Yong, Ed, 'Oxytocin Boosts Dishonesty', *The Scientist*, 31 March 2014, http://www.the-scientist.com/?articles.view/articleNo/39595/title/Oxytocin-Boosts-Dishonesty/, last accessed 01 Sep 2017.

Zyga, Lisa, 'Free will is an illusion, biologist says', *Phys.org*, 3 March 2010, https://phys.org/news/2010-03-free-illusion-biologist.html, last accessed 02 Sep 2017.

INDEX

Afghanistan: 41, 43, 123–4, 162, 191, 200, 210; Operation Herrick, 4, 125; Saur Revolution (1978), 124; Soviet Invasion of (1979–89), 124–5, 192–3

African Union (AU): 220

alt-right (ideology): 212

altruism: 26; reciprocal, 50

Amazon.com: 222

anarchism: 176

anger (emotion): 48, 146, 152; evolution of, 51

anthropology: 15, 25, 91; analysis of war, 5–6

anxiety (emotion): 48–9; social, 48

Aristotle: 30

Association of South East Asian Nations (ASEAN): 220

Axial Age: 222

belonging/group membership: 52–3, 84, 86–90, 98–9, 101–2, 107–9, 140–1, 173, 195, 197–9, 210–11, 221; as heuristic brain mechanisms, 45; as motivation for fighting, 1–2, 89–90; cognitive mecha-

nisms for, 102–3; collective enforcement, 111–12; disease, 111; evolutionary security environment, 95–6; group growth, 103–5; hierarchy, 110–13; membership costs, 108–9; neurological basis of, 90–1; resources, 86–7; risk of violence, 115–18; security of, 87–8; sexual partners, 84–5, 88; trade, 111

Bereman, Geoffrey: murder of (1278), 65

Blair, Tony: foreign policy of, 75

Buddhism: 176, 219

Bush, George W.: family of, 75; foreign policy of, 75

Cameron, David: Libyan policy of, 144–5, 160

capital: accumulation of, 203

capitalism: 184; democratic, 176; liberal, 204

Catholicism: 202

Chagnon, Napoleon: 6

China, People's Republic of: one-child policy in, 70

Christianity: 162, 171, 176, 189, 219; Bible, 202; fundamental-

INDEX

INDEX